The gentleman's guide in his tour through Italy. With a correct map, and directions for travelling in that country.

Thomas Martyn

The gentleman's guide in his tour through Italy. With a correct map, and directions for travelling in that country.
Martyn, Thomas
ESTCID: T081070
Reproduction from British Library
Anonymous. By Thomas Martyn. With an index of place names. Vertical chain lines.
London : printed for, and sold by, G. Kearsley. It may also be had of Mr. Ledger of Dover, the booksellers at Margate, Brighthelmstone, and all the other bathing towns, upon the coast., 1787.
xlviii,398,x p., plate : map ; 12°

Eighteenth Century
Collections Online
Print Editions

Gale ECCO Print Editions

Relive history with *Eighteenth Century Collections Online*, now available in print for the independent historian and collector. This series includes the most significant English-language and foreign-language works printed in Great Britain during the eighteenth century, and is organized in seven different subject areas including literature and language; medicine, science, and technology; and religion and philosophy. The collection also includes thousands of important works from the Americas.

The eighteenth century has been called "The Age of Enlightenment." It was a period of rapid advance in print culture and publishing, in world exploration, and in the rapid growth of science and technology – all of which had a profound impact on the political and cultural landscape. At the end of the century the American Revolution, French Revolution and Industrial Revolution, perhaps three of the most significant events in modern history, set in motion developments that eventually dominated world political, economic, and social life.

In a groundbreaking effort, Gale initiated a revolution of its own: digitization of epic proportions to preserve these invaluable works in the largest online archive of its kind. Contributions from major world libraries constitute over 175,000 original printed works. Scanned images of the actual pages, rather than transcriptions, recreate the works *as they first appeared.*

Now for the first time, these high-quality digital scans of original works are available via print-on-demand, making them readily accessible to libraries, students, independent scholars, and readers of all ages.

For our initial release we have created seven robust collections to form one the world's most comprehensive catalogs of 18th century works.

Initial Gale ECCO Print Editions collections include:

> ### *History and Geography*
> Rich in titles on English life and social history, this collection spans the world as it was known to eighteenth-century historians and explorers. Titles include a wealth of travel accounts and diaries, histories of nations from throughout the world, and maps and charts of a world that was still being discovered. Students of the War of American Independence will find fascinating accounts from the British side of conflict.

Social Science
Delve into what it was like to live during the eighteenth century by reading the first-hand accounts of everyday people, including city dwellers and farmers, businessmen and bankers, artisans and merchants, artists and their patrons, politicians and their constituents. Original texts make the American, French, and Industrial revolutions vividly contemporary.

Medicine, Science and Technology
Medical theory and practice of the 1700s developed rapidly, as is evidenced by the extensive collection, which includes descriptions of diseases, their conditions, and treatments. Books on science and technology, agriculture, military technology, natural philosophy, even cookbooks, are all contained here.

Literature and Language
Western literary study flows out of eighteenth-century works by Alexander Pope, Daniel Defoe, Henry Fielding, Frances Burney, Denis Diderot, Johann Gottfried Herder, Johann Wolfgang von Goethe, and others. Experience the birth of the modern novel, or compare the development of language using dictionaries and grammar discourses.

Religion and Philosophy
The Age of Enlightenment profoundly enriched religious and philosophical understanding and continues to influence present-day thinking. Works collected here include masterpieces by David Hume, Immanuel Kant, and Jean-Jacques Rousseau, as well as religious sermons and moral debates on the issues of the day, such as the slave trade. The Age of Reason saw conflict between Protestantism and Catholicism transformed into one between faith and logic -- a debate that continues in the twenty-first century.

Law and Reference
This collection reveals the history of English common law and Empire law in a vastly changing world of British expansion. Dominating the legal field is the *Commentaries of the Law of England* by Sir William Blackstone, which first appeared in 1765. Reference works such as almanacs and catalogues continue to educate us by revealing the day-to-day workings of society.

Fine Arts
The eighteenth-century fascination with Greek and Roman antiquity followed the systematic excavation of the ruins at Pompeii and Herculaneum in southern Italy; and after 1750 a neoclassical style dominated all artistic fields. The titles here trace developments in mostly English-language works on painting, sculpture, architecture, music, theater, and other disciplines. Instructional works on musical instruments, catalogs of art objects, comic operas, and more are also included.

The BiblioLife Network

This project was made possible in part by the BiblioLife Network (BLN), a project aimed at addressing some of the huge challenges facing book preservationists around the world. The BLN includes libraries, library networks, archives, subject matter experts, online communities and library service providers. We believe every book ever published should be available as a high-quality print reproduction; printed on-demand anywhere in the world. This insures the ongoing accessibility of the content and helps generate sustainable revenue for the libraries and organizations that work to preserve these important materials.

The following book is in the "public domain" and represents an authentic reproduction of the text as printed by the original publisher. While we have attempted to accurately maintain the integrity of the original work, there are sometimes problems with the original work or the micro-film from which the books were digitized. This can result in minor errors in reproduction. Possible imperfections include missing and blurred pages, poor pictures, markings and other reproduction issues beyond our control. Because this work is culturally important, we have made it available as part of our commitment to protecting, preserving, and promoting the world's literature.

GUIDE TO FOLD-OUTS MAPS and OVERSIZED IMAGES

The book you are reading was digitized from microfilm captured over the past thirty to forty years. Years after the creation of the original microfilm, the book was converted to digital files and made available in an online database.

In an online database, page images do not need to conform to the size restrictions found in a printed book. When converting these images back into a printed bound book, the page sizes are standardized in ways that maintain the detail of the original. For large images, such as fold-out maps, the original page image is split into two or more pages

Guidelines used to determine how to split the page image follows:

- Some images are split vertically; large images require vertical and horizontal splits.
- For horizontal splits, the content is split left to right.
- For vertical splits, the content is split from top to bottom.
- For both vertical and horizontal splits, the image is processed from top left to bottom right.

THE GENTLEMAN's GUIDE

IN HIS TOUR THROUGH

ITALY.

WITH

A CORRECT MAP,

AND

DIRECTIONS FOR TRAVELLING

IN THAT COUNTRY.

LONDON:

Printed for, and sold by, G. KEARSLEY, No 46, Fleet Street. It may also be had of Mr Ledger of Dover, the booksellers at Margate, Brighthelmstone, and all the other Bathing Towns, upon the Coast

M,DCC,LXXXVII.

[Price *Four Shillings* and *Six Pence*, half bound.]

ENTERED AT STATIONERS' HALL

☞ An improved Edition of the TOUR through FRANCE and SWITZERLAND, printed in the same size, may likewise be had as above, and at the principal Inns at CALAIS and BOULOGNE. Also in another volume, the TOUR of HOLLAND, Dutch, Brabant, and the Austrian Netherlands.

THE PREFACE.

IT will naturally be asked, why we have more travels into Italy, when we have had too many already? The answer I shall make to the question is this: Most of our travelling books have been evidently written with a view to be read by the fire side at home, rather than to accompany a man abroad; to amuse the indolent, rather than to instruct the active. And of those few whose aim it has been to inform the traveller on the spot, their works have been either very partial and defective, or else too voluminous to be carried about with tolerable convenience.

Every prudent traveller endeavours to bring his baggage within as narrow a compass as possible: he will therefore scarcely be persuaded to encumber himself with a multitude of incomplete works, each of which is to supply the defects of the rest; or with a book in many volumes, however its reputation may be established but if he can meet with one volume of a portable size, which in general seems likely to yield him the information he wants; he may perhaps be induced to give it a place in his portmanteau.

The author of the work now offered to the public has endeavoured to answer this purpose. He has not the vanity to flatter himself, that this performance will supersede all others, but if the generality of travellers, with the assistance of those local works, which every considerable town of Italy will furnish, find what they look for, clearly and correctly set down, he shall have accomplished the principal end he aimed at.

The method which the author took to form his book was this: He first extracted from his own journal whatever appeared to deserve the attention of the public, he then looked over the most esteemed writers of travels*; he next consulted some friends, both

---

* Mr Sandys set out for Italy in 1610. Mr. Raymond in 1646. Mr. Lassels was five times there,

both countrymen and Italians, in whose knowledge and judgement he most confided; and lastly, he digested his materials thus collected into as small a compass as he could, and arranged them so as to meet the eye as readily as possible. He had not visited every part of Italy; in many places his stay had

there, he was at Rome in 1650 Mr Ray was in Italy in 1663. Bishop Burnet in 1685 and 6 Mr. Misson in 1687 and 8 Mr Addison from 1700 to 1703. Mr. Richardson in 1720 Mr. Wright from 1720 to 1722. Mr. Keysler from 1729 to 1731. Mr Gray with Horace Walpole, Esq in 1739, 40, and 41. Mr Russell from 1739 to 1749. M. Cochin in 1749 or 50. Mr. Northall in 1752. The Chevalier de la Condamine in 1754. John Earl of Corke and Orrery in 1754 and 55. Mr Grosley in 1758. Abbé Richard in 1761 and 62. Dr. Smollet in 1763, 64, and 65. Mr Sharp in 1765 and 66. M. De La Lande, the same years. Dr. Burney left London in June 1770. Lady Miller travelled in 1770 and 71. Mr Ferber in 1771 and 1772 William Young, Esq. in 1772. Only ten copies of his journal were printed at a private press. Mr. Sherlock in 1777. The authors of Voyage pittoresque de Naples et de Sicile, were there the same year. Mr. Swinburne, from 1777 to 1780. Dr. Moore, I suppose, about the same time

not been long: but even where he had ſtaid the longeſt, he had not the folly to ſet up his own judgement and obſervation againſt thoſe, whoſe opportunities and abilities were ſuperior to his. he has availed himſelf therefore of every light which he could derive from men as well as books. He is happy in acknowledging the aſſiſtance of one gentleman, who has opened ſeveral freſh ſources of uſeful information, in the beaten track of Italy*, and from whoſe ſuperior knowledge and judgement the public may hope for much intelligence on hiſtorical, political, and œconomical ſubjects: of a ſecond, whoſe taſte in the fine arts, and acquaintance with the great Italian maſters in painting, would enable him to give an account of their works, and a critique on their ſeveral excellencies and defects, far ſuperior to any thing that has yet been done, did not his love of retirement induce him to ſhun the public eye †: of a third, who,

* See diſſertations on the water, ſoil, climate, and general face of Italy, in Young's Annals of Agriculture, vol. I. p. 405. II. 195 and 254. III. 137. and V. 317.

† See the notes ſigned K. particularly in page 12. where the connection, which the ſtudy of painting has, with hiſtory and antiquities, is hinted at.

not

not to mention his consummate skill in the sciences, is well acquainted with almost every part of Italy, and being a native of that country, has enabled me to correct those errors which every foreigner unavoidably falls into, from his partial knowledge of language, manners, and customs.

With such assistance, the author hopes, that whatever faults there may be in the style and arrangement of the following work, the facts at least will be found tolerably correct.

Some information relative to the money, measures, method of travelling, &c. in Italy.

MONEY.

The most current money, or that on which there is the least loss, is the Sequin of Rome, Florence, or Venice. French Louis d'ors are also very negotiable. The money of Genoa will not be taken in any other state; and in general it is adviseable not to have more of the current coin of any state, than you are likely to dispose of before you quit it, except the Sequins above mentioned.

NICE.

Doppia di Savoia: gold: 24 Piedmontese livres.

Mezzo-doppia: gold: 12 livres.

Scudo and mezzo-scudo: silver: 6 and 3 livres.

Pezza di 30 soldi; or quarter of a scudo.

Pieces of 7½ sols, and 2½: copper silvered.

Pieces of 1 sol; and ⅛ of a sol, called a *piccalon*.

Louis d'ors; 6 and 3 livre pieces of France, are common.

The Piedmontese Livre is 20 sols, and nearly the same value as an English shilling.

TURIN.

A pound sterling is worth 20 livres, but the exchange being generally against London, you will get only 19 livres 10, 7, or 5 sols for a pound.

Pistole of Piedmont: gold: 24 livres.

Pieces of 6 livres, 3 liv. and 1 liv. 10 sols: silver.

GENOA.

Genoa.

A pound sterling is worth 28 livres.
A Sequin of Florence   13l. 10s.
A Louis d'or   -   -   29l. 4s.
A piastre, or Spanish dollar, 6l. 10s.

The value varying according to the course of exchange.

Milan.

30 livres bank worth 32 livres current.
Sequin of Florence or Venice worth 14l. 10s. bank, or 17l. 10s. current.
Sequin of Rome, 14l. 4s. bank; and 20l. 10s or 21l. current.
Pistole of Piedmont, 45 Milanese livres current.

Parma.

Livre worth 5 baiocchi or soldi.
Paolo rather less than 6d. English, or 12 sols French.
Sequin of Florence, 20 paoli, or 44 livres of Parma.
Louis d'or, 97 livres of Parma.

Modena.

Livre worth 6 baiocchi or soldi.
Paolo   -   10 baiocchi of Rome.

[x]

Roman crown, 10 paoli.
Roman sequin, 19½ ditto.
Florence ditto, 20 ditto.

BOLOGNA.

Livre worth 2 paoli.
Sequin of Rome worth 20½ paoli.
——— Florence ——— 20 paoli.

ROME.

Sequin, 20½ paoli. Scudo, 10 paoli. Paolo, 10 baiocchi.

Sequin of Florence, 20½ paoli but current only for 20½.

Sequin of Venice, 20 paoli.

Onza of Naples, 24 paoli.

Louis d'or, 44 or 45 paoli. Guinea, 42 or 43. In drawing upon London, the pound sterling about 42 paoli.

No exchange but with Paris and Amsterdam. They reckon by Scudi and Baiocchi. Cash being very scarce at Rome, money transactions are mostly carried on in bills of the mount of piety, and hospital of S. Spirito, call'd Cedules. The current coin is to the paper as about 1 to 16: and if ye present a bill of 100 crowns to the
bank

bank for exchange, you will have 8 or 10 crowns in cash, and the rest in other paper.

NAPLES.

1 Oncia or onza, 3 ducats. 1 ducat, 10 carlini. 1 carlino, 10 grana. 1 grano, 12 calli.

An oncia is worth about 25 Roman paoli; 5 oncie make 6 sequins, and 7 oncie make about 4 pounds sterling.

A Roman crown is worth $12\frac{1}{2}$ carlini. A Sequin $25\frac{1}{2}$ carlini.

A pound sterling is worth 52 carlini, or 2 seq. 2 carl.

A Neapolitan ducat is worth 45d. English, and the carlino, $4\frac{1}{2}$d. at par: but the exchange is continually varying, and makes a difference of 10 or 15 per cent.

Besides the coins already mentioned, they have in gold, pieces of 6, 4, and 2 ducats. In silver, no less than fifteen coins, from 13 carl. 2 gr. down to 5 grana; of which those of 6, 4, and 3 carlini, are common; the ducat is very scarce; the *Patacca*, of 5 carlini, is also scarce; the piece of 2 carlini is called *Tari* and the carlino of Naples is the Tari of Sicily. In brass they have six coins, from 1 grano 6 calli, called the *Publica*, down to 3 calli, or less than half a farthing; the piece of 6 calli is called the *Tornese*.

Accounts are kept in ducats, carlini and grana; but merchants keep theirs only in ducats and grana.

FLORENCE.

Livre, 1½ paolo.
Sequin, 20 paol.
Sequin of Rome, 19½ paoli.

VENICE.

Sequin, 22 livres worth about nine shillings and six pence english.
Filippo, 11 livres.
Ducat of silver, 8 livres.
Ducat current, 6 livres, 4 soldi.
Lirazza, 1 liv. and half, or 30 soldi.
Lira, or livre, 20 soldi nominal, like the French livre, and English pound.
Da quindeze, 15 soldi.
Da dieze, 10 soldi.
Traero, 5 soldi.
The Soldo is about a farthing english.
The Sequin of Rome passes for 21 livres; and that of Florence for 21½.

MEASURES.

PIEDMONT.

The mile is 800 trabucchi. The trabucco is 6 Piedmontese feet, or 20 1/10 inches English.

A Piedmontese mile therefore is 2688 yards and 10 inches English; or 4 y. 10 i. more than an English mile and half.

GENOA.

The mile of Genoa is nearly the same with that of Piedmont.

PARMA.

When you enter the states of Parma, you will find that they reckon by Italian miles, which are 61 yards and 1 foot shorter than an English mile.

BOLOGNA and FLORENCE.

The mile of Tuscany is supposed to be 1000 geometrical paces, or 5000 french feet. M. Dutens reckons it to be 5150 french feet, or 4835 f. 3 i. 4 l. english, or 148 yards, 8 inches, 8 lines short of an english mile.

ROME.

ROME.

The Roman mile is nearly the same with this; and probably with the ancient Roman mile.

NAPLES.

The mile is 7000 palmi; and the palmo being nearly 10½ i. english, the neapolitan mile is longer than the english by about 249 yards *.

Weights and measures at Naples.

1 Cantaro contains 100 Rotoli. 1 Rotolo, 33½ ounces.

1 Pound, 12 ounces.

The Cantaro is equal to 196 english pounds averdupois, and the Rotolo to 2 english pounds. The pound is a trifling fraction above 11 ounces english.

Long measure.

1 Canna contains 8 palmi; and 2⅓ yards english; a palmo is 10½ i. english †.

Land

---

* This article is chiefly from M. Dutens.

† Or more accurately, according to M Dutens, 10 i. ,31. The *palmo* of Genoa, for silk is 9 i. ,60.

for

Land measure.

The *Moggia* contains 900 *passi*; each *passo* containing 7⅓ *palmi*.

Dry measure.

Wheat is measured by the *tomolo*, of which 5⅓ make an English quarter of 8 bushels.

Wine measure

Wine is measured by the barrel, containing 66 caraffi, equal 9½ English gallons. In the city of Naples, the barrel contains only 60 caraffi.

for cloth 9 i ,80. At Rome, in architecture it is 8 i ,78. in other things 9 i ,79 —The *braccio*, at Venice is 25 i ,30 for silk, and 27 inches for linen or woollen cloth. At Florence, it is 22 i ,80 for silk, and 22 i ,61 for cloth. At Rome it is 34 i ,27. At Milan, for architecture 23 i. ,60. for silk 20 i ,70 for cloth 26 i ,20. At Bologna 24 i ,50 At Parma and Piacenza 26 i. ,90 —The *Canna*, at Genoa is 67 i. ,60. At Rome, 78 inches. At Naples 82 i. ,90. The *foot* at Turin is 20 i ,17. at Venice 14 inches. at Bologna 15 inches.———
These are english measures, in inches and decimal parts, and are taken from M. Datens.

Oil

Oil measure.

1 *Salma* contains 16 *Stars*; 1 *Star* 10½ rotoli; 1 Rotolo 33½ ounces; which is 2 pounds English.

A Salma is about 40 English gallons*.

If you travel post, you must pay according to the rates here set down.

PIEDMONT†.

For a four-wheeled carriage with three horses - - - - 6 livres.
For the same with four horses 8 livres.
For a pair of horses - - 4 liv. 10 sols.
For a saddle-horse - - 2 livres.
A coach carrying four persons, should have four horses, for which you pay - - - - 9 livres.

* This article is from Mr. Swinburne.

† The *cambiatura* is abolished in Piedmont. It is retained in the Milanese, and in the Venetian states, where it is called the *bolletino*. It is a permission granted to travellers, to take the post at a less price than it is fixed at by government, with conditions however not to make the horses gallop, nor to travel after sun-set.

And

And so in proportion for 6 horses, &c.

It is customary to give about 30 sols to each postillion*.

The posts of Piedmont are about five miles of the country, or seven and an half miles English.

GENOA.

For a pair of horses, 9 livres of Genoa per post.

For a saddle horse, 3 livres per post.

THE MILANESE.

For a pair of horses, 8 liv. 12½ sols, or half a sequin.

For a saddle horse, 4 livres, each post.

There is now no *cambiatura*.

PARMA and PIACENZA.

For a pair of horses, 15 paoli per post.
For a saddle horse, 5 ditto ditto.
After the first stage, 5 paoli for each horse.

---

* The *Ostauiere* will also put in his claim, and another fellow who throws water on your wheels, but there is no necessity to comply with their importunities.

MODENA.

Modena.

For each horse, 5 paoli.

Tuscany, and Ecclesiastical State.

For a pair of horses to a carriage, 8 paoli.
For a saddle horse - - - 3 ditto.

Kingdom of Naples.

For a pair of horses to a carriage, 11 carlini.
For a saddle horse - - - 5½ carlini.
At a post-royal, an addition of 5½ carlini.
Three carlini are due to each postillion.

State of Venice.

For each horse, whether for the
carriage or saddle - - - 5½ livres.
If you have the *bolletino*.

In case you do not choose to be at the expence of travelling by the post, there are *Vetturini* or carriers in almost every part of Italy, who furnish carriages and horses, or mules, from one place to another, at a certain price. This is an usual mode of travelling among the natives, even of good condition. It is necessary for a stranger to make an agreement with them in writing for the price, the time they are to be on the road, the places he is to stop at, &c. The price varies according to circumstances; they will abate you at least a third of the price they ask; and you may sometimes meet with return carriages very cheap. They are not very easy or elegant, and are mostly open before. The *Vetturini* will engage to find you provisions on the road, if you desire it. These men pay in general three pauls a head for a dinner, and four for supper, including the chamber. In cities they generally charge a stranger six pauls a head for each meal, and the apartment besides, according to the number of rooms. They usually ask much more than they will take; and seldom make any conscience of getting what they can, especially of an Englishman. Italian inns are generally represented as detestable; some of them are certainly bad enough, but there are many very good ones, especially in large towns, and on those roads which are much frequented by foreigners.

As soon as you are arrived in any town, and have made the agreement for your board and lodging, send out for a map of the country, a plan of the town, and the guide-book; there is scarcely a town in Italy, which has not

not one of these, tolerably executed, where every thing that is to be seen in the place, good, bad, and indifferent, is described most minutely. This, with the map and plan, M. Dutens's excellent *Itineraire*, and the following little work, will probably answer all the necessary demands of the traveller.

A prudent person, who is not ambitious of passing for an English man of fashion, may certainly live very reasonably in Italy. I have been assured by officers and other gentlemen, that they have kept the best company at Florence, Siena, and other capital towns; and have enjoyed every convenience of life except a carriage, at an expence of no more than a hundred pounds sterling a year, including dress, pocket expences, &c.

At Venice, which however is not the cheapest place in Italy to live in, a stranger may hire a good room for one or two livres * a day; and for four livres he may dine well; or he may provide himself with a genteel apartment and dinner for from eight to eleven livres a day. Wood for fuel will cost him about one livre. The wages of a man servant is sixteen livres a month, if he

* A livre is about five pence English.

boards him: or from sixty to eighty livres, if he is at board wages. The hire of a gondola is four livres a day; but if he keeps one constantly, he pays twenty-two livres a month for the gondola, and seventy-six or eighty for the gondolier.

A single man therefore may live at Venice, and keep a servant for seventy pounds a year: or he may live, and keep his gondola, which is equivalent to a carriage in any other place, for eighty pounds a year[*]. If he lives in a genteel style, keeping his servant and gondola, his expences will be about one hundred and twenty pounds. To these he must add clothes, theatres, coffee house, &c., which are not however expensive at Venice.

If he eats at home, which he will scarcely do, unless he is with a family, a cook will have eleven livres a month, if she eats in the house, or from forty to fifty livres, if she is at board wages.

This may serve to give a faint idea how a traveller may live in Italy, who does not profess to make a useless parade, but will take

[*] In this case, I suppose him to make use of the gondolier as a servant. A man servant, board wages included, is about eighteen pounds a year.

the trouble of inquiring into the real value of things, and not suffer himself to be imposed upon.

I do not wish, by this information, to incite my countrymen to live in Italy; though they may pay a little dearer for it, they will not upon the whole live any where with so much comfort as in England: my design is only, to prevent them from being grossly imposed upon, when they are there.

THE ITINERARY*.

From Lyon to Chambery.

From Lyon to	Posts.	Miles.
Bron	1	6
S. Laurent des Mures	1	5
La Verpillière	1½	7
Bourgoin	1½	7½
La Tour-du-Pin (a)	2	9
Gas	1	5¼
Pont-Beauvoisin (b)	1	6¼
Echelles	1½	9½
S. Jean-des-Coups	1	8
CHAMBERY	1	6
	12½	69½
To Turin		123¾
		193¼

(a) Palais Royal; a wretched inn
(b) Trois Couronnes.

N. B. *Considerable towns are printed in capitals, and such as the traveller may stop at, are in italics.*

* Post-books are to be met with at Bologna, Venice, &c. At Rome there is one in italian and french,

[xxiv]

From Geneva to Turin.

From Geneva to	Posts	Miles	Time. h. '	
Frangy	2½	15	4	30
Remilly	2	14	3	45
Aix-les-bains	1½	11	3	
CHAMBERY	1	6	1	45
Montmelian	1½	9	2	
Mal-Taverne	1	14½	1	50
Aiguebelle	1		1	10
Erpiere	1	7	1	20
La Chambre	1	7½	1	45
S. Jean de Maurienne	1	7	1	30
S. Michel	1½	8	2	
S. André	1½	8	2	30
Modane	1	3½	2	15
Villarodin	1	2½	1	30
Bramens	1	3½	1	55
Lannebourg	1½	8	2	30
Across Mont-Cenis to La Novaleze	2½	14	5	10
Suze	1	5½	1	15
La Zaconiere	1½	9½	2	
S. Ambroise	1	6¾	1	15
Rivoli	1¼	8½	2	30
TURIN	1¼	8	1	30
	29½	177¼	48	55

french, containing not only the posts, but maps of all the routes, short notes of what is to be seen in the cities and towns, &c.—It is entitled, *La vera guida per chi viaggia in Italia.*

Inns

Inn are, at Frangy, Palais: at Remilly, Trois Rois: at Aix, la Ville de Geneve: at Chambery, S. Jean Baptiste, Quatre Nations: at S. Jean de Maurienne, S. George, good: at Novaleze, Ecu de France: at the rest, the Post.—At Turin, Auberge Royale, Hotel d'Angleterre, Hotel de France ci-devant les bonnes femmes, Trois Boeufs, Deux Boeufs. The gates of Turin are shut at half past six; but on proper application they will open them till ten.

From Turin to Genoa.

From Turin to	Posts.	Time.
Trufarello	1	1 40
Poirino (a)	1	1 45
S. Michele	1	1 30
Cabagniole	1	1 15
Asti (b)	1	1 30
Annone	1	1 25
Felissano	1	1 34
Alessandria (c)	1	1 50
Novi (d)	2	3
Voltaggio	2	2 45
Campo Marone (e)	2	3 15
Genoa (f)	1½	1 30
	15½	22 59

(a) After great rains the roads impassable, it is then best to go by Carile to Alessandria, though there are several rivers to cross, and the posts are ill ____.—(b) La Rosa rossa, not good.—(c) Il Re, good.—(d) Ponte di fuori, tolerable but dear.—(e) La Post.—(f) Santa Marta

The gates are shut an hour after twenty-four o'clock, or night-fall.

The times are not given as any certain direction, because they vary according to the state of the roads, the weight of the carriage, the humour of the drivers, &c.; but by comparing many observations, a tolerable medium may be struck out that will be very useful to the traveller.

From Genoa to Florence.

To Lerici by land is 67 miles, and can be gone only on horseback.

Hire a Felucca either to Lerici or Leghorn.

From *Lerici* (a) to	Posts	Miles.	Time.
Lesano	1	4	4	2 10
Lavenza	1	6	6	1 40
Massa (b)	1	5	4	1 10
Pietra Santa	1	7	7	1 50
Viareggia	1	6	6	1 30
Torretta	1	8	2	1 50
Pisa (c)	1	5	6	1 10
Livorno or Leghorn (d)	2	14	2	2 30
Pisa				
Lucca (e)	2	14	6	2 40
Borgoborgiano	1½	12	7	2 40
Pistoia	1½	10	7	2 45
Prato	1½	9	2	1 55
Firenze or Florence	1½	9	4	2 10

(a) La Posta, bad.—(b) La Posta, not bad.—(c) Tre Donzelle, Hussaro.—(d) Croce d'oro, Croce di Malta.—(e) La Panthera.

Gates shut at Pisa two hours after ventiquattro or night-fall, but are opened at any time. In going out of Florence or Lucca, you pay poste royale. On leaving Florence, it is necessary to have your baggage plumbed, to avoid being detained at the gate, and at Siena write also to Rome for a lascia-passare, to avoid being carried to the dogana there.

From Genoa to Milan.

Back to Novi, and from thence to

	Posts.	Miles.
TORTONA (a)	2	1
VOGHERA (b)	1½	9
PAVIA (c)	2	19 3
Bisnago	1	
MILAN (d)	1	

(a) The post.—*A mile from Tortona pass the Scrivia. Six miles from Tortona and four from Voghera pass the Coiron.*

(b) The Moor.—(c) The post.—(d) Albergo reale, excellent, I tre Re, bad.

From Milan to Bologna.

From Milan to	Posts.	Miles.
Marignano	1	10 2
Lodi (a)	1	10
Zurlesco	1	9 2
PIACENZA (b)	1	

(a) The Sun.—(b) San Marco.

[xxviii]

The direct road from Genoa to Bologna, is from

Voghera to	Posts	Miles		Time	
Bro...	2¼	14		2	30
Città S. Giovanni	1	9¾		1	10
PIACENZA, &c.	2	13½		2	20
Fiorenzola (a)	2	14		2	10
Borgo S. Donino	1	8	2	1	10
Castel-Guelfo	1	7	6	1	5
PARMA (b)	1	7	2	1	50
S. Ilario	1	6	4		58
Reggio (c)	1	10		1	30
Rubiera	1	8	4	1	30
MODENA (d)	1	8		2	10
Samoggia	1½	12	4	2	10
BOLOGNA (e)	1½	10	6	2	

(a) The post, good (b) The post, and the Peacock (c) The post, and the Lion (d) Allergo Ducale, a superb inn (e) Locanda reale, and Pelegrino

From Bologna to Rome.

From Bologna to	Posts	Miles		Time	
S. Nicolo	1¼	9	2	2	15
Imola	1¼	11		2	10
Faenza	1	9	4	2	0
Forli	1	9	4	1	35
		39	2	8	0

Cesena

[xxix]

			4½	39	2	8	0
Cesena	.	.	1½	11	6	2	15
Savignano	.	.	1	8	2	1	30
Rimini	.	.	1	9	6	2	0
Cattolica	.	.	1½	11	6	2	30
Pesaro	.	.	1	10		2	15
Fano	.	.	1	7		1	40
La Marotta	.	.	1	7	4	1	20
Sinigaglia	.	.	1	6		1	5
Case-brugiate	.	.	1	7	4	1	20
Ancona	.	.	1	9		2	30
Camerano	.	.	1	9	4	2	15
Loretto	.	.	1	8		2	
Sambuchetto	.	.	1	10	2	3	10
Macerata	.	.	1	6	2	1	10
Tolentino	.	.	1½	11		2	30
Valcimarra	.	.	1	8		1	50
Trave	.	.	1	7	4	1	45
Serravalle	.	.	1	7		1	30
Case nuove	.	.	1	9	4	2	35
Foligno	.	.	1	9		1	40
Le Vene	.	.	1	9		1	45
Spoleto	.	.	1	7	4	1	25
Strettura	.	.	1	9	2	2	30
Terni	.	.	1	8		1	55
Narni	.	.	1	8	2	1	40
Otricoli	.	.	1	8	6	2	30
Borghetto	.	.	¾	6	2	1	30
Civita Castellana	.	.	¾	6		1	
Rignano	.	.	1	7	4	2	
Castel nuovo	.	.	1	6		1	15
Malborghetto	.	.	¾	5		1	15
Prima porta	.	.	¾	4	4		50
Rome	.	.	1	6		1	25
			38	305	6	67	50

b 3 The

[xxx]

The inns upon this road are generally the post-houses; the best of these are at Macerata, Foligno, Spoleto, Narni: the locanda di Parma at Pesaro, excellent. The roads are in general good, and the horses excellent.

There are many good lodging-houses at Rome, especially near Piazza di Spagna: as at Dupres, Benedetto's, Meno's, Pio's, Margarita's, Damon's, Mad. Steuart's, Mad. Smith via croce, &c.

From Rome to Naples.

From Rome to	Posts	Miles		Time to Naples		Time to Rome	
Torre Mezzavia	1	8	2	1	20	1	
Marino	¾	6	2	1			50
Faiola	¾	4	6	1		1	10
Veletri	1	5	2	1	10	1	10
Case fondate	1	9	6	1	15	1	40
Sermoneta	1	5	6		45	1	15
Case nuove	1	8	6	1	25	1	25
Piperno	1	5		1		1	
Maruti	1	7	6	1	35	1	35
Terracina	1	7	4	1	22	2	
Fond.	1½	11	6	2	30	2	
Itri	1	7	4	1	45	1	45
M. a di Gaeta	1	4	2	1		1	
Crigliano	1	8			50		50
S. Aga	1	9	2	1	18	1	18
Sparanisi	1	10		1	23	1	2
Capua	1	8	6	1	12	1	5
Aversa	1	12	4	1	20	1	25
Naples	1	11	4	1	45	1	35
	19	152	4	24	55	25	3

Th

The inns upon this road are very bad; the only way to lodge comfortably, is to procure letters for the Ginetti palace at Veletri, and the convent of S. Erafmo, near Mola di Gaeta.

At Naples, very good hotels, delightfully fituated — Albergo Reale, Crocelli, Emanuele, Cafa ifolata, Stefano di Rofa.

From Rome to Florence.

From Rome to	Pofts	Miles		Time from Rome		Time from Florence	
Storta . .	1	9	1	1	15	1	30
Baccano . .	1	8	4	1	45	1	28
Monte Rofi	1	6	3	1	20	1	4
Ronciglione	1	9	0	1	45	1	40
La Montagna	1	6	6	3	45	1	
VITERBO	3/4	5	1	1	20	1	15
Montefiafcone	1	10		2	5	1	10
Bolfena . .	1	8	3	1	43	1	50
San Lorenzo nuovo . .	1	4	7	1	20		41
Acquapendente	3/4	6	1	2		1	3
Ponte Centino	1	5		1			40
Radicofani .	1½	8	5	2	35	1	34
Ricorfi . .	1	5	6	1	20	1	41
Scala . .	1	4	4	1	35	1	5
	14	98	1	24	48	18	1

Torrinieri

	14	98	1	24	48	18	1
Torrineri	1	9		1	50	2	
Buonconvento	1	5	5	1	2		55
Monterone	1	7	3	1	20	1	15
Siena	1	8	6	1	55	1	23
Castiglioncello	1	10	1	1	30	2	10
Poggibonzi	1	6	4	1	18	1	25
Tavernelle	1	7	3	2	2	1	40
S. Cassiano	1	8	2	2	4	1	55
FLORENCE	1½	9	7	2	28	2	15
	23½	171	0	40	17	32	59

From Radiofani to Ponte Centino you pay only one post.

Inns.— At Viterbo, Albergo Reale, pretty good, and I broke at the Post. At Siena, I tre Re, tolerable. At the rest, the Post, bad enough, except at San Lorenzo nuovo. At Florence, the finest hotel, by Meggit, called Locanda di Carlo, consisting of three palaces. Vanin's a very good hotel; and the inns of the black eagle and S. Louis.

From Florence to Rome by Perugia.

From Florence to	Posts	Miles	Time	
Pian della Fonte .	2	14	2	
Levane . . .	2	15	2	10
AREZZO	2	15	2	
Camoccia . . .	2	14	2	20
Torricella . . .	2	13 4	2	30
PERUGIA . . .	2	13	2	
Madonna degli Angeli	1	11	1	50
Foligno	1	9 4	1	
&c. as in the route from Bologna to Rome.				

Inns are—At Arezzo and Camoccia the post, at Perugia, with Luigi Ercolani.

This road is better than that by Siena; the country finer; and the inns better. It is 25 miles farther, but may be gone in less time.

From Florence to Bologna.

From Florence to	Posts	Miles	
Fontebuona . .	1	8	2
Caffigiolo . . .	1	7	4
Alle Maschere . .		3	
Monte Careli . .	1	4	
Cubillario . . .	1	7	6
Feligara . . .	1	5	2
Lorino	1	7	4
Pianoro . . .	1½	9	4
BOLOGNA . .	1½	10	2
	9	63	

As there are no tolerable inns on this road, except at le Mafchere, and that is not a poft, you muft pay the expences of the horfes and poftilions for ftopping there; and this will amount to a fequin or thereabouts for fix horfes and two poftilions. You may ftop at Loiano, but the inn is very bad; or at the *dogana* at Pietra Mala, between Cubillario and Feligara, on the fame condition as expreffed above, or at a convent of Benedictines near Loiano, at a place called Scarica l'afino,

From Bologna to Venice.

From Bologna to	Pofts	Miles	Time	
San Giorgio . . .	1½	9	1	45
Cento . . .	1	8	1	30
San Carlo . . .	1	7 4	1	10
FERRARA (b) . .	1½	9	1	50
Rovigo (a) . .	2	18	4	20
Monfelice . .	2	15	2	20
PADOUA (c) . .	1½	12	2	
Dolo . .	1½	10	1	45
Fufina . . .	1½	9	1	20
VENEZIA (d) . .		5	1	15
	13¼	102	4 19	15

(a) Poft. (b) Tre Mauri.—You may go by water to Venice, embarking on the Po, five miles from Ferrara.—(c) Aquila d'oro, good—Or down the Brenta from Padua.— Acrofs the Lagunes from Fufina.—(d) Buns Dart, near the Rialto, Petrillo at the white Lion, The R.

From

From Venice to Verona, Brescia, Bergamo, &c.

From Venice to	Posts	Miles		Time	
Fusina		5		1	
Dolo	1½	11		1	30
PADOUA*	1½	11	4	1	40
Slesiga	1	9	6	1	40
VICENZA (a)	1	10	6	2	
Montebello	1	10	6	1	30
Caldiero	1½	12		1	45
VERONA (b)	1	8	6	1	30
Castel nuovo	1½	11	6	1	45
Desenzano	1½	11	4	2	15
Ponte di San Marco	1	6	4	1	45
BRESCIA (c)	1½	9	4	1	30
Ospitaletto	1	8		1	30
Palazzuolo	1½	10		1	30
Cavernago	1	6		1	5
BERGAMO (d)	1	8	2	1	20
	18½	151	0	25	15

(a) Cappell rosso, Scudo di Francia (b) Due Torri, very good. (c) Torre. (d) Venice, Albergo Reale.

* *It will take about ten hours to go up the Brenta, from Venice to Padua.*

From Bergamo to Milan it is four posts, thirty-two miles; and will take four hours and an half.

From M[ilan] to Turin it is ten posts and an half, ninety-three miles, and the time about fifteen hours. The road lies through Novara and Vercelli; the inns at both, and also at Chivasco, are the three kings; that at Vercelli is the best. There are several rivers to pass, which are dangerous in a rainy season. this part of Lombardy is very rich and fertile.

From Verona through the Tyrol, Germany, &c.

From Verona to	Posts	Miles		Time	
		M.	F.	H.	′.
Volarni (a) . .	1	12	7	2	25
Pery . .	1	9	1	2	
Ala (b) . .	1	11		2	30
Roveredo (c) .	1	10	3	2	20
Trent (d) . .	2	14	7	3	
S. Michel (e) .	1¼	11	4	1	53
Nurmuch . .	1¼	11	7	2	45
Branzol (f) . .	1	7	2	1	30

(a) Country flat and well cultivated. Vines, mulberry trees, &c.

(b) Here Tyrol begins.

(c) The Post will go no farther with two-wheel'd carriages.

(d) Europe. Begin here to talk German.

(e) Covered wooden bridge.

(f) Porphyry mountains.

Bolzano

[xxxvii]

	Posts	Miles		Time	
Bolzano (a)	1	8		1	45
Teutschen	1	7	6	2	
Colman (b)	1	6	3	1	40
Brixen (c)	1	11	1	2	45
Mittewald	1	7	7	1	45
Stertzingen (d)	1	9	7	2	15
Brenner (e)	1	9	5	2	15
Steinach (f)	1	6	5	1	15
Schonberg	1	8	1	2	
Instruck (g)	1	7	2	1	40
Dorstenbach (h)	1	10	2	2	15
Obermiemingen	1			3	
Nazareit (i)	1			2	30
Lermes	1	10	7	3	8
Reita (k)	1			3	30

(a) The Sun, clean and very good. Situation charming.—*Narrow vallies by the torrent, covered bridges, black porphyry mountains.*

(b) *Fine views. Schist mountain.*

(c) Elephant—*Fine situation, a post and half is paid from Colman to Brixen.*

(d) Post!—*A glacier and silver mines*

(e) *A long ascent to Brenner, but the road excellent.*

(f) *Descent to Steinach. The mountain wholly of Schist.*

(g) Golden Eagle!

(h) *Fir and larch woods.*

(i) Post—*A steep ascent and descent to Nazareit, and another steep ascent from it*

(k) Post, clean and good—*Mountains calcareous and visibly lower.*

Fuessen

	Posts	Miles	Time
Fuessen (a)	¾		2
Saurnaester	1		2 30
Bruth (b)	1		2 45
Dissen	1		2 40
Hurlach	1		2 50
Augsbourg (c)	1		3 10
Susmarshausen	1½	16 3	3
Gunzburg (d)	1½	14 3	3 30
Ulm (e)	1½	15	2 40
Westersetten	1	10 4	2 15
Geisslingen	1	12 5	2 20
Goeppingen	1	12 1	2
Blockingen (f)	1	12 2	1 50
Stutgard (g)	1	14	3
Entzweingen	1½		3
Knittlengen	1¼		3 20
Bruchsal (h)	1½		2
Waghausel	1		1 50

(a) *Quit the Alps, and enter Suabia*

(b) *The roads made and kept up by toll-bars, through the Tyrol and Germany.*

(c) Three Moors, very good. Hence to Munich 4¼ posts, 42 miles, and the time 8 hours; the road is good. Munich is a fine large city on the Iser; the Elector's palace, and theatre are magnificent—*Country flat, soil sandy, road good.*

(d) *Roads and horses good.*

(e) Baumstarck, or arbre forte, very good.

(f) *A curious wooden bridge.*

(g) S. George, or the Cavalier, very good.

(h) Post, bad.

Schwetzingen

	Posts	Miles	Time
Schwetzingen (a)			
MANHEIM (b)	1½		3 50
Worms . .	1	13 4	2 45
Oppenheim . .	1¼	15 4	2 55
MENTZ (c) . .	1	12	2 45
Coblentz (d) . .			15
BONN (e) . .	3½		11 15
COLOGNE (f) . .	1½		5 14
Berchem . .	1½	15	3
Juliers . .	1	10	2 45
AIX-LA (g)			
CHAPELLE . .	1½	15	3 45
SPA (h) . .	3	33	10 15
LIEGE (i) . .	3	28	6

(a) *A country house of the Elector Palatine. Gardens worth seeing.*

(b) Felderſhoff or Cour de Manheim, good, but very dear. Ville de Frankfort and the Ram.

(c) The three Crowns—*Embark on the Rhine.*

(d) The three crowns, bad, the Poſt.

(e) Hofe van Engelland, or Cour d'Angleterre, good.

(f) Saint Eſprit, good—*Hence to Duſſeldorf only two poſts, 23 miles Gallery of pictures!*

(g) La Cour d'Angleterre, good. Dubich.

(h) Good lodging houſes in abundance—*By Forges and Chaufontaine.*

(i) Aigle noire! No poſt at Spa, hire horſes at Liege—*Between Horel and S. Frond enter the Low-Countries.*

Horel

	Posts	Miles	Time	
Horel (a)	1⅔		2	30
S. Frond	1⅔	20	1	50
Tirlemont (b)	2	9	2	
LOUVAIN (c)	2	11	2	15
Cortemberg	1½		1	20
BRUSSELLS (d)	1⅔	17	1	30
Aloft	3	17	2	45
Quadregt	1½	9	2	
GHENT (e)	1	6	1	
BRUGES (f)	By the Canal		8	15
OSTEND (g)	By the Canal		3	40

(a) *A Douane of the Emperors.*

(b) Grand cerf.

(c) Poft, Hotel de Cologne—*From Louvain it is 2 pofts to Mechlin, and 2 more to Antwerp, in all 25 miles. Here you may make the tour of Holland, and embark at Helvoetfluys for Harwich.*

(d) Hotel de la belle vue, de l'Imperatrice, d'Angleterre, d'Hollande—*From Bruffells to Paris by Mons, Valenciennes, Cambray, and Peronne, 34½ pofts, and 187 miles.*

(e) S. Sebaftian.

(f) Ville de commerce, or poft—*Boats fpacious and commodious. Carriage goes by land from Bruges, and the great boat does not come up to Oftend.*

(g) Hotel d'Angleterre, Baylis's.

Corrections at page 16.

The road has lately been opened for carriages, from Nice to Turin and Genoa, over the Col du Tende.

EURO-

[xli]

EUROPEAN TRAVELLERS

Are very materially accommodated by the following

PLAN

OF THE

Exchange Notes and Letters of Credit,

OF

Messrs. Ransom, Morland, and Hammersley,

BANKERS,

No 57, in PALL-MALL, LONDON.

A Correspondence is settled at most of the principal places on the Continent of Europe, in order to accommodate travellers with money, at any place, which best suits their conveniency; and to supply those with bills upon any particular place, who desire to make remittances from hence.

French being the most general language, is used for this plan.

Circular Exchange Notes,

Are given for any sum, from twenty pounds upwards, and answer the purpose abroad, of BANK-POST BILLS in England. They are

are payable to the order of the traveller, without any *commiſſion or charges*, at any one of the various places mentioned in a letter of order given along with them*: and although drawn at ſeven days ſight, in order to have a little time to ſtop payment at the adjacent places, ſhould they be loſt, and in that caſe, for the value to be re-paid in London; yet they are always paid at *ſight*, when preſented by the traveller himſelf. They are reduced into foreign money, at the current uſance courſe of exchange in London;—*in other words, the price of Engliſh money*—at the time and place of payment. The traveller, for his own ſecurity, will not indorſe any of the notes till he receives payment of them; at which time the agents are inſtructed to take two receipts, ſerving one purpoſe — one on the back of the notes; the other ſeparately, to prove the payment, in caſe any of the notes ſhould be loſt, in ſending them back diſcharged.

Letter of Order

Is always given with the circular notes, and contains a general addreſs to all the cor-

---

* See the names of thoſe places in page xlv.

respondents of the house, whose names are annexed to an alphabetical list of places: at the same time it recommends the traveller to their civilities. For safety, the traveller writes his own name in this letter of order, which the agents are instructed to compare with his signature, on paying the notes, so that it answers the purpose of a general letter of advice.

Transferable Exchange Notes

Are addressed to one place only, being reduced into the money of that place, at the last quoted exchange from thence, and may be transferred from one person to another, by simple indorsement. They are chiefly intended to remit particular sums abroad, or for the use of those persons who are constantly resident at one place, because they may be paid away to tradesmen and others, in the same manner as bank or banker's notes are passed from hand to hand in London.

Those, as well as the circular notes, are free of all charges.

Letters of Credit.

Although the use of them, on the former footing, cannot be recommended, nor can they

they be of such extended utility as the notes; nevertheless the house will, when required and satisfied of the security, give them, on such places as have a direct exchange upon London. They are subject to a single commission and postage at the place of payment, and to another to the house, when they are re-imbursed at home; but the money will be paid at the just course, without the exaction of any accumulated charges whatsoever.

Recovering Money from Abroad.

To render their extensive correspondence as useful as possible, the house will take bills, of drawers or endorsers of undoubted credit, upon most of the places, mentioned in their list, in order to recover money, which cannot be done in the common course of business.

[xlv]

Places where the Circular Notes may be received.

Aix la Chapelle	Lausanne
Aix in Provence	Leghorn
Alicante	Leipzig
Amsterdam	Liege
Amiens	Lille
Angers	Lisbon
Antwerp	Lyons
Augsburg	Madrid
Avignon	Malaga
Barcelona	Manheim
Bayonne	Marseilles
Basle	Middleburg
Berlin	Milan
Berne	Montpellier
Bruges	Moscow
Besançon	Munich
Bilboa	Nancy
Blois	Nantz
Bourdeaux	Naples
Bologna	Nice
Boulogne	L'Orient
Breslaw	Orleans
Brussels	Ostend
Brunswick	St. Omers
Cadiz	Paris

Caen

Caen	Parma
Calais	Petersburg
Carthagena	Prague
Cologne	Rheims
Copenhagen	Riga
Dantzig	Rochelle
Dijon	Rome
Dresden	Rotterdam
Dover	Rouen
Dunkirk	Seville
Florence	Spa
Francfort on the Mayn	Stockholm
Geneva	Strasburg
Genoa	Toulouse
Ghendt	Tours
Gibraltar	Trieste
Gothenburgh	Turin
The Hague	Valencia
Hamburgh	Venice
Hanover	Vienna
K'onigsberg	Warsaw

[xlvii]

BOOKS

Lately published and sold by

G. KEARSLEY, at Johnson's Head, No. 46, Fleet Street, London.

The three following articles will be found exceedingly useful to those who make excursions into the countries they describe, and are the only portable accounts that can be depended upon. The Maps are accurate, and the new regulations relative to travellers by post or otherwise, are all carefully corrected.

The GENTLEMAN's GUIDE in his TOUR through FRANCE. With a correct MAP of all the POST ROADS, the Expence of travelling in a Post Chaise, Stage Coach, or inland Water Carriage; Also, the Distances of the Towns, and the best Houses of Accommodation. The ninth edition, with considerable additions. Price 3s. 6d. half bound.

A SKETCH of a TOUR through SWISSERLAND. With an accurate MAP. Price 2s. half bound.

The TOUR of HOLLAND, DUTCH BRABANT, the AUSTRIAN NETHERLANDS, and Part of FRANCE, in which is included a Description of Paris and its environs. A new edition, corrected and improved, with a Map of Holland and the

the Netherlands, from the last surveys. Price 3s. 6d. half bound.

An ABRIDGEMENT of all Capt COOK's VOYAGES ROUND the WORD. Containing a faithful relation of the interesting transactions in each voyage, particularly those relative to the death of Capt. Cook, with a sketch of his life. Also Capt. Furneaux's Narrative of his proceedings during the separation of the ships. The head of Capt Cook, neatly engraved from the Royal Society's medal, with a chart of the new discoveries and the tracts of the ships, are also to given with this abridgement.—Those who superintend the education of youth cannot put a more acceptable work in their hands, than these late Voyages of Discovery, which abound with interesting descriptions and entertaining narrative.— The first volume contains the first and second voyages, and the second volume the third and last voyage. Each may be had separate. Price 3s. 6d. sewed, or 5s. together.

In the press, and shortly will be published in four volumes, price 12s, The BEAUTIES of the SPECTATOR, TATLER, GUARDIAN, RAMBLER, ADVENTURER, CONNOISSEUR, WORLD, and IDLER. To accommodate the purchasers of these entertaining volumes, they will be sold together, or in the following manner.—The selections from the Spectator, Tatler, and Guardian, in the two first volumes, will be sold separate for 6s. The third and fourth volumes will comprise those from the Rambler, Connoisseur, Adventurer, World, and Idler, and will be sold separate for 6s, or the four volumes bound together for 12s.

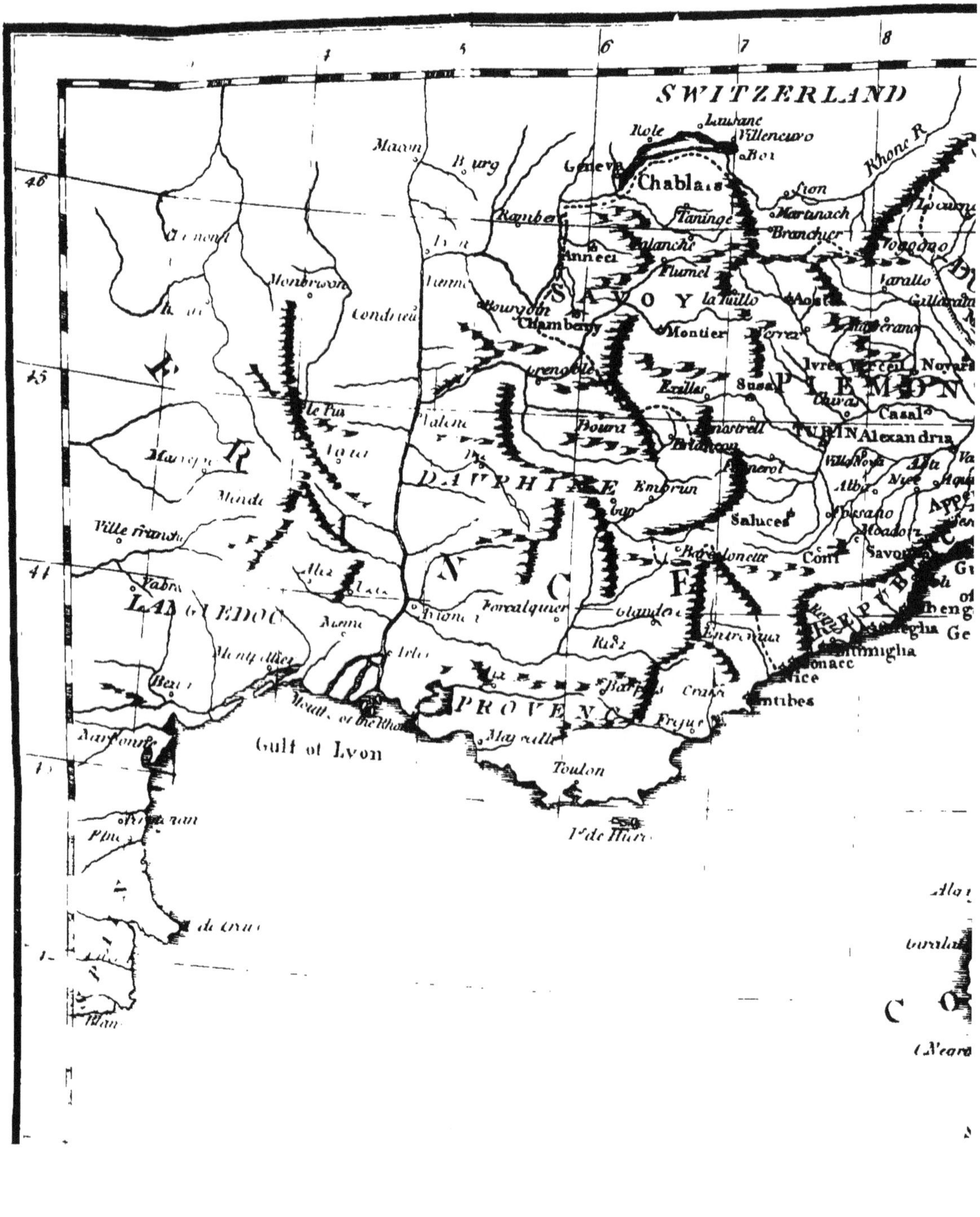

9
10
11
12
13
14
15
16
GERMANY
GRISONS
Val Tellina
Meran
Brixen
Belluno
Pontaba
Venzone
Udine
Goritia
Laybach
Gurfeld
Triest
Como
STATE OF VENICE
VENICE
Padoua
Rovigo
ISTRIA
Pola
Fiume
Segna
Cremona
Pavia
DUTCHY OF PARMA
Parma
Ferrara
Comachio
Bologna
BOLOGNESE
Ravenna
GULF OF VENICE OR ADR
Gulf of Quarnaro
Pago
Zara
Imola
GENOA
Porto Venere
Sarzana
Lucca
Pisa
Prato
FLORENCE
FLORENTIA
Livorno or Leghorn
TUSCANY
Volterra
Sienna
Urbino
Ancona
Loretto
Macerata
Fermo
Camerino
Piombino
Elba
Perugia
Chiusi
UMBRIA
Spoleto
Terni
Narni
Nocera
Teramo
Orbitello
Corte
Civita Vecchia
ROME
Tivoli
Albano
Aquila
Chieti
ABRUZZO
Gaeta
Tremiti
la Madalena

ITALY,
divided into
ITS SEVERAL DOMINIONS
and
THE ISLANDS OF
SICILY SARDINIA
and
CORSICA
from
MR D ANVILLE

MEDITE

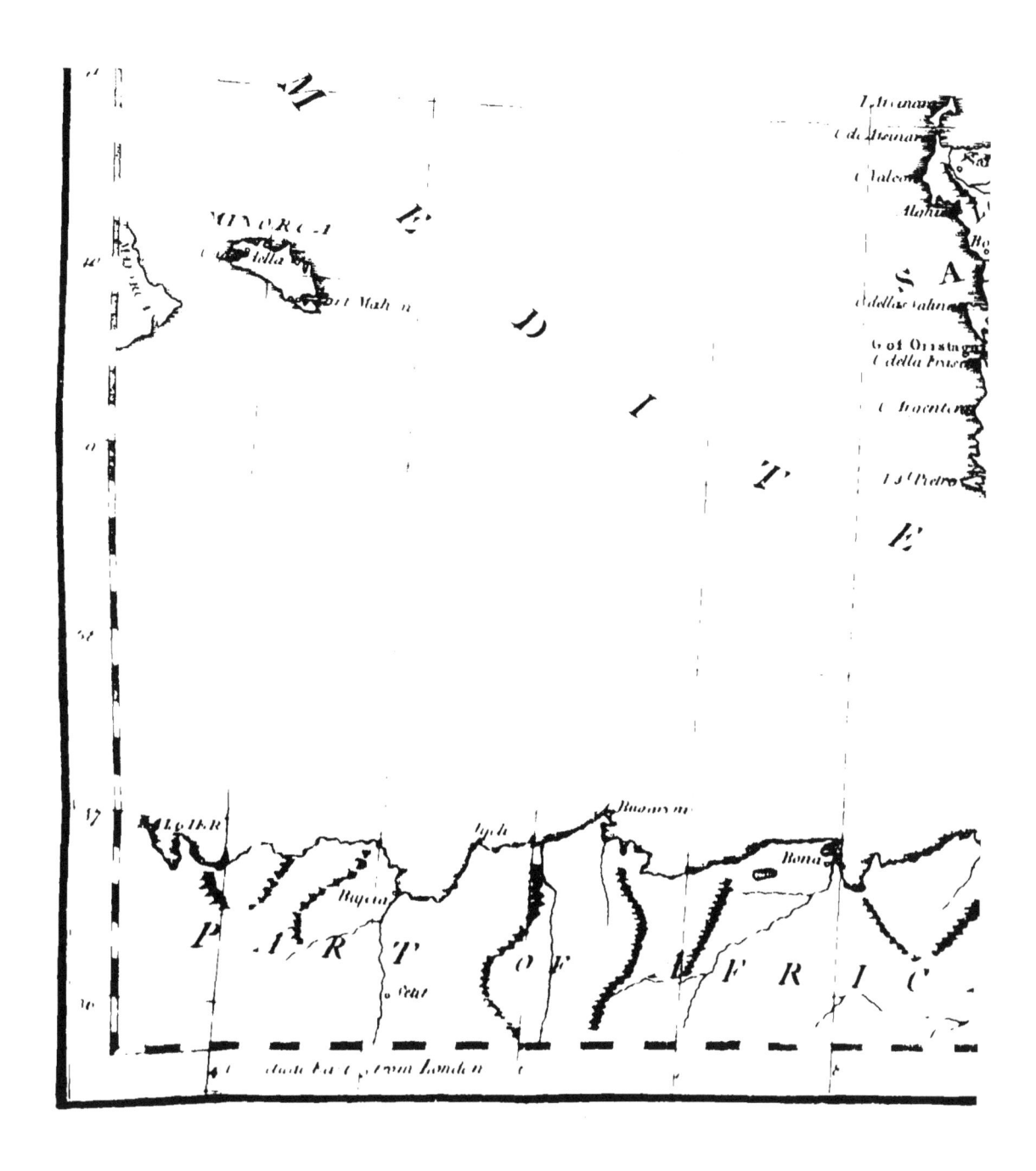

MINORCA

PART OF AFRICA

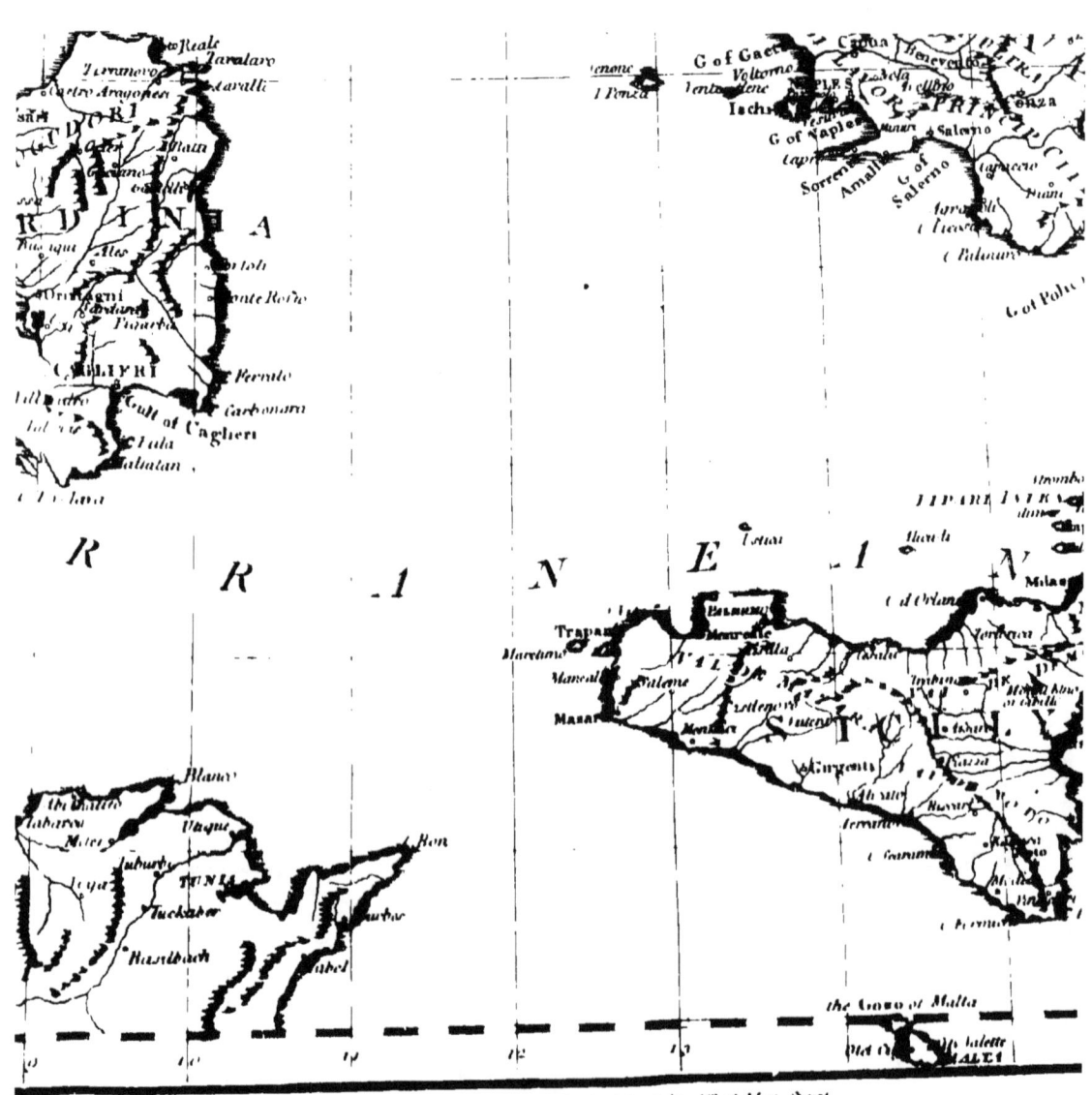

Publish'd Feb. 10 1787 by [illegible] No 16 Fleet Street

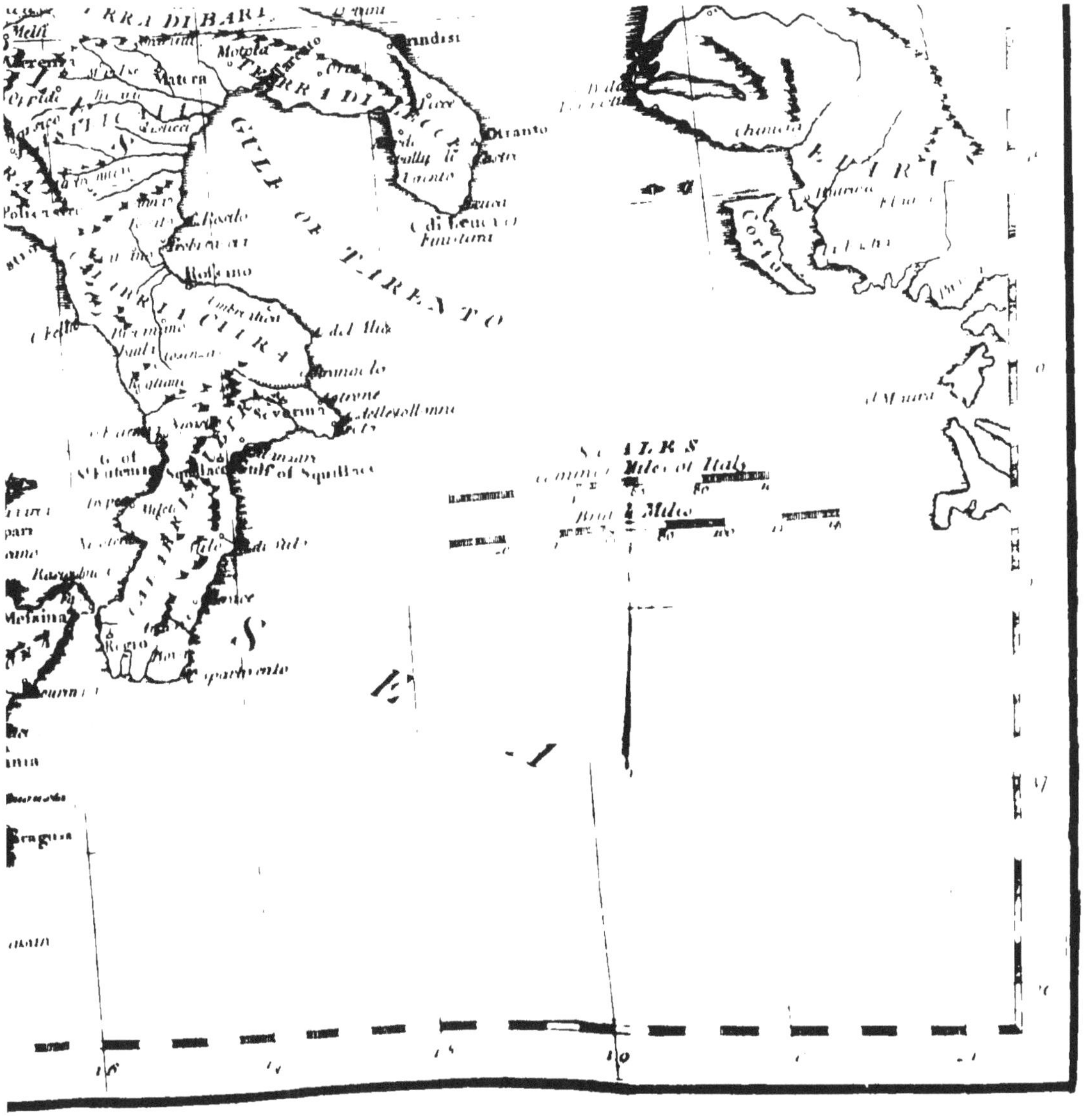
TERRA DI BARI
Matera
Motola
Otranto
GULF OF TARENTO
Corfu
EPIRUS
Squillace
Gulf of Squillace
Messina
Regio
SCALES
Miles of Italy
Miles

THE
GENTLEMAN's GUIDE
IN HIS
TOUR through ITALY.

SECTION I.

An Account of the different Ways that lead into Italy.

IF you enter Italy by the way of France, you will probably go to Lyon. From thence you have your choice, either to go by land through Savoy, and across Mount Cenis to Turin, or passing through Provence, to embark at Antibes or Nice, for Genoa or Leghorn. From Swisserland you may pass Mount S. Gothard; from the Valais

Mount

Mount S. Bernard; and from Germany you may go through the Tyrol. Carriages can pass only by the first and last of these routes; in crossing Mount Cenis they must be taken in pieces; but the whole road through the Tyrol is not merely practicable, but even excellent for a carriage.

From Lyon to Turin they reckon 35 posts, 64 leagues, or 193 English miles; the time 56 hours. The road passes through the Lyonnois, Savoy, and Piedmont, by Pont-Beauvoisin and Chambery over Mount Cenis.

Pont Beauvoisin, which is 15 leagues or posts from Lyon, is on the frontier; a little river separates it into two parts, one of which belongs to France, and the other to Savoy.

No sooner have you passed the frontier of France, than you perceive a change of country, climate, and people. The mountains of Savoy afford a new scene; woods, rocks, precipices, cascades and torrents, form views that charm an eye fond of rude nature; others find this journey dreary and disagreeable; the road however is safe and good, and in many places even beautiful. From Pont-Beauvoisin you go to Chambery, which, though the capital of Savoy, affords nothing worth seeing. The situation indeed is fine, wide, delightful valley, where there is the greatest variety of objects that a fine country and mountains can produce: but it is a poor dirty town; the houses dark, the streets narrow, the convents and other public buildings miserable. The remainder of the ducal palace is a castle; over the gate-way are the governor's lodgings, commanding the town and adjacent country. During the carnival they have plays and masked balls.

If instead of taking the direct route you go by Geneva, you will find it 19 posts, or 95 miles 3 furlongs from Lyon to that place: the time 21 or 22 hours. from Geneva to Chambery it is 7 posts, or 46½ miles; and the time 13 or 14 hours. This therefore is 72 miles out of the way, and will take 16 or 17 hours more in time. But if you have already seen Paris and Lyon, there is a road from Calais to Dijon, by S. Omer, Arras, Cambray, Laon, Rheims, Chalon sur Marne, Joinville, and Langres, which is 66 posts, or 351 English miles; and from Dijon to Geneva, by Auxone, Dole, Poligny, and from Morey across Mount Jura to Nyon, 21 posts: the time of the whole route about 81 hours; whereas by Paris and Lyon, it will cost you 102 hours,

102 hours, but during four or five months Mount Jura is impracticable.

From Geneva, your best way is to hire horses to convey you to Chambery, there being very few horses on the road till you come into the direct way from France. It is 7 posts from Geneva to Chambery, and the Voiturier will be at least 12 hours in going them, unless your carriage is light: if you think this too much for one day, you may set out in the afternoon from Geneva, lay at Frangy, and arrive easily at Chambery the next day, time enough to see that place.

Montmelian, which is only a post and half, or 9 miles from Chambery, is also most delightfully situated at the head of three vallies. The inn is not in the town, but half a league on this side of it, and the ascent from it is very steep. Having passed the mountain, the road lies in a very narrow valley, which winds incessantly. The wine made about Montmelian is much esteemed. After this you meet with nothing but wretched towns and villages, and a country of terrible poverty and filth. The honest, plain and thrifty Savoyards have very little land to cultivate, and look extremely unhealthy. Aiguebelle lies in a bottom closely surrounded by by mountains: it is but a poor straggling village: the water is clear, light and sparkling. After you have passed Aiguebelle, *goitres* or swelled necks become frequent. St. Jean de Maurienne was formerly the residence of the counts of this country; it is situated in the middle of the highest Alps, in a valley tolerably wide. The roads are pretty good, except through the towns, where they are ill paved, and barely wide enough for a carriage to pass: indeed they are in general narrow, which is no wonder, where there is so little land to spare: frequently you find no more than room for this confined way between the steep mountain and the torrent; and in some places they are obliged to hew it out of the rock itself. Whenever the valley widens a little, you find a miserable village, and some of these, as if it were to spare their useful land for cultivation, are placed in the very bed of the torrent, which occupies so large a portion of all that is not barren rock. The road is almost a continued ascent and descent by the side of the Arche, a river which rises in Mount Iserau, and joins the Isere near Montmelian. As you advance, the mountains grow higher and more steep, till at length the road closes in a narrow gorge, and a very long and heavy ascent to Lannebourg, which is at the foot of Mount Cenis. There are about 220 houses in this village, and about 100 porters on the Syndic's list, who are employed in their turns.

The inns are abominable on this road; it is therefore adviseable, if you can bear the fatigue, to go through without stopping. Chambery, Aiguebelle, S. Jean de Maurienne, and Lannebourg, are the best places to repose at. You should by all means have the whole day before you to cross Mount Cenis, that you may not be hurried in the double operation of taking your carriage in pieces, and putting it together again; and that you may have time in the evening to arrive at Suze; in which case, the next day you will easily reach Turin to dinner. The whole passage of the mountain from Lannebourg to Novaleze may easily be accomplished in four, or at most five hours; and has nothing terrible in it, at least from may to october. In a deep snow, in a violent tempest, and especially in a great thaw, there is certainly some danger; at all other times there is nothing but the inconvenience of taking the carriage in pieces, to send it over the mountain on mules; but

the

the people are so adroit in this operation, and restore it to its primitive state so easily, that the whole rather furnishes amusement than gives pain to the traveller. If you hire a Voiturier at Lyon or Geneva, you agree with him to pay all the charges of passing the mountain *. These men make their demands according to the number of travellers who are on the spot. The price for a pair of horses is from eight to eleven louis, besides a present of a louis, or half an one, at the end of the journey; but if there is no extraordinary demand, you may expect a pair of horses for eight louis. If you have no carriage of your own, and take the vetturino's chaise, he will carry you perhaps for seven louis, because he has a better chance at Tu-

* M Dutens says, that in 1761 he agreed, at the rate of twenty louis, and in 1770 of twenty-eight louis, for an English chaise and four horses, a two-wheel chaise and pair, a saddle-horse, the expences of two gentlemen on the road from Turin to Geneva, and the whole charge of passing the mountain.—Mr Sharp in 1765 paid thirty-one louis for six horses from Geneva to Turin. On his return a voiturin offered to take him back for twenty-eight louis; but staying some time he was obliged to pay thirty-six.

rin for a traveller to return with him. Fo[r] this sum he defrays your charges on the roa[d] except breakfast, and little presents to th[e] servants; he is also at the whole expence o[f] carrying you and your equipage over Moun[t] Cenis, except a little gratuity and drink t[o] your chairmen. These same men will fur‑ nish horses at four Savoy livres a day each, allowing seven days for going, and as man[y] for returning; that is, for a chaise and pa[ir] about 5l. 18s.; but this is much dearer tha[n] the other.

This road and that from Rome to Naple[s] are the only ones in which it is expedient t[o] travel by Vetturino, unless where it is ne‑ cessary for the state of a traveller's finances. I[f] you go post, you must be at the trouble an[d] expence of crossing the mountain: there is how‑ ever a tariff, fixing what you are to pay at th[e] different seasons, for mules to ride on, or trans‑ port your baggage, their conductors, porter[s] to carry the chairs, fellows who take the car‑ riage in pieces, &c. There is a Syndic bot[h] at Lannebourg and Novaleze, who appoint[s] a proper number of men to each service, [are] very useful and obliging, and not unwilling to accept a trifling gratuity.

You

You have your option to pass over on mules, or in *chaises-a-porteurs*, which are rush-bottomed elbow chairs, without legs; two men carry them by means of two poles, and they have a foot-board. These fellows are very strong and nimble, never missing a step, but treading firm in the roughest ways with the agility of goats: they relieve each other at proper intervals. In descending, they show great dexterity in the frequent windings of the mountain. From six to ten of these men are assigned to each person, in proportion to his size. Their pay is 50 sols of Savoy each, that is about 2s. 4½d. The price of a mule to carry the baggage is the same; of a mule to ride, 40 sols, or 2s. 1d. A mule is not obliged to carry above 350 lb. so that if the body of your carriage exceeds that weight, they may demand what they please. There is also one sedan chair at Suze, which may generally be had, by sending notice beforehand to the other side of the mountain: and lately they have provided other covered chairs. The ascent is not bad, and is easily performed in an hour and half. At the top is a plain, about five miles in length; it is a fine turf, and may be galloped over, not only with perfect safety, but with pleasure. There is a beautiful lake on this plain, with excellent trout in it. It is often related, as a wonderful circumstance, that there should be a lake on the top of Mount Cenis; but the truth is, that this plain is no more than a very high valley or gorge of the mountain; and though it be indeed the highest part which travellers pass over, yet there are lofty pikes, which rise at least 3000 feet above it. The lake is supplied from the snow that melts on these, and trickles through the crevices. It gives rise to the river Dora, and therefore may be looked upon as one of the sources of the Po. You may stop at a public house by the hospital to refresh the men; and having traversed the plain, you begin to descend into Piedmont. The prospect on each side of tall firs, larches, and chesnuts, of natural water-falls and roaring mountain rivers, affords a variety at once aweful and pleasing. From the plain of S. Nicola you have a view of a beautiful cascade; and half way between the great cross and Novaleze you pass a wretched village, called La Ferriere. You will be two hours at least in getting to Novaleze; the descent is steep, but no where dangerous.

Some adventurous people, who return from Italy by the way of Mount Cenis in winter, when the mountain is covered with snow, slide down on sledges. The descent towards Lannebourg is very steep, and it takes almost an hour to go down it, on account of the many turnings and windings you are obliged to make; but the whole side of the mountain being then covered with one solid smooth crust of snow, at the proper place you may put yourself on a sledge, with a guide on the fore part of it, who will conduct it, and change the direction of it with his foot, whenever it is necessary, and thus bring you to the bottom in ten or twelve minutes very safe; or if the sledge now and then overturns, they say it is without any bad consequence: this is called in French, *se faire ramasser*, and the place whence you set out, *les ramasses*. Novaleze is a poor place, with an indifferent inn, where is the first customhouse for Piedmont; and a stranger must take care not to have snuff, or any new foreign commodities.

You will quit this place if you had not time to reach Suze the evening before, by nine or ten in the morning, that you may have the day before you, and be sure to arrive at Turin before ten o'clock, after which hour the gates are not opened. The road to Suze is rough and bad, with a steep ascent and descent, and the town is not considerable. You will pass the formidable fortress of the *Brunetta*, along a narrow gorge of the mountain, which seems to close at the pass called *Pas-de-Suze*, but after that, opens sensibly wider. This is the barrier of Italy, and the key of Piedmont: the fortifications are said to be well worth seeing, but it is difficult to obtain the permission. At Suze, in the gardens of the castle, is a triumphal arch, erected in the time of Augustus.

At Rivoli, which is only two leagues from Turin, the King of Sardinia has a country house, where Victor Amadeus was confined and died; it is well situated, and commands a plain terminated by Turin. From hence to the capital is a handsome broad straight road, bordered by double rows of fine elms.

There are some wild and magnificent views between Mount Cenis and Turin; and the meadows in some seasons are equal in point of verdure to any in England; they are watered by the Dora, which descends with vast impetuosity from the Alps.

You

You may go from Lyon to Turin by post in three days and an half, or four days; by *Vetturino* in six or seven days, but then you must travel early and late. Many persons, however, prefer this latter mode of travelling, on account of its cheapness, the little trouble attending it, and the opportunity it gives of viewing the country with more leisure; but I give you notice to lay in a large stock of patience, for they go but two miles and three quarters an hour; and to run the hazard of being taken to second rate inns.

If you prefer a voyage by sea, you must go from Lyon to Avignon, Aix, Marseilles and Toulon to Antibes, unless you have seen Marseilles and Toulon before, in which case you may go directly from Aix to Antibes*.

Here

---

* This is the frontier of France towards Italy; it is pretty strongly fortified, and garrisoned by a battalion of soldiers. The town is small; vessels lay safely in the harbour, but there is not water enough at the entrance to admit ships of any great burden. The adjacent country is more pleasant than that on the side of Nice the ground is not so incumbered, it is laid out in agreeable enclosures, with intervals of open fields, and the mountains rise with an easy ascent, at a much greater distance from

Here you will hire a felucca for Genoa or Leghorn, as you please. This is an open boat with a *padrone* or master, and from eight to twelve rowers, who, partly by sailing, and partly by rowing, will convey you to Genoa in two days, if the sea be calm, otherwise they dare not stir; nor indeed is a felucca built for a heavy sea. The hire of this vessel will be eight sequins, or about four guineas. You will put in at MONACO, a small town, containing about eight or nine hundred souls, besides the garrison, built on a rock which projects into the sea, and making a very romantic appearance. The principality consists of three small towns, and an inconsiderable tract of barren rock. You pass *Ventimiglia*, where the Genoese territories begin, and several other places of less consequence, and come to *S. Remo*, a considerable town on the declivity of a gently rising hill, with a harbour for small vessels. The hills are covered with oranges

the sea than on the other side of the bay. Here are charming rides along the beach, which is smooth and firm. The corn is in ear before the end of april, the cherries at the same time are almost ripe, and the figs begin to blacken.

lemon

lemons, pomegranates, and olives. *Oneglia* is a small town, with some fortifications belonging to the King of Sardinia; the territory abounds with olive-trees, and produces the best oil of the whole Riviera. *Albenga* is a small town, the see of a bishop; it lies upon the sea, and the country produces a great quantity of hemp. *Finale* is capital of a marquisate belonging to the Genoese: the town is pretty well built, but the harbour is shallow, open, and unsafe; the country abounds with oil and fruit, particularly with excellent apples, called *pomi carli*. *Noli* is a small republic of fishermen subject to Genoa, but tenacious of their privileges: the town is tolerably well built, defended by a castle, and the harbour is of little consequence. *Savona* is a large town, with a strong citadel, and a harbour capable of receiving large ships, but partly choaked up. You pass Albisola, Sestri di Ponente, Novi, Voltri, and many villages, villas, and magnificent palaces belonging to the Genoese nobility, till you skirt the fine suburbs of St. Pietro d'Arena, and arrive at Genoa. The whole Riviera, where it will admit of it, is cultivated like a garden, and plantations extend to the very tops of th hills, interspersed with villages, castles, churches,

churches, and villas. When you are arrived at Genoa, you may perhaps not desire to proceed any farther by sea; but if you do, you may hire another felucca there for Leghorn.

You may also embark at Nice instead of Antibes: or you may go from thence by land along the *Corniche*, or *Col du Tende*; but that can be done only on horseback, or on mules, or in a chair carried by porters, along a very narrow path, by the side of precipices. As soon as you leave Nice, you climb the Scarena, a very high and steep mountain. *La Chiandola*, which is six posts from Nice, is in a very picturesque situation. a league from it is the bourg of *Saorgio*, so singularly placed on the top of a mountain, that it seems suspended in the air: from Chiandola to Tende you follow the bed of a torrent. *Tende* is the capital of a county, which gives name to this passage over the Alps; you are three hours in mounting, and two in descending it, unless the mountain is frozen, and then you may descend by a sledge to Limoni in less than an hour. Between Limoni and Coni you see Monte Viso 40 miles, and Mount Cenis 70 miles distant. *Coni*, called the maiden-fortress, because it was never taken, is situated near the confluence of the Stura and

and Geffo, which have deftroyed above 500 acres of land in the neighbourhood; thefe rivers, however, are greatly conducive to the general fertility of this part of Piedmont. From Limoni to Coni, the vale is watered partly by the Geffo, whofe ftreams are admirably conducted, and partly by the Varmenagna, which greatly contributes to the rich crops both of corn and grafs, with which this tract abounds. At *Poirino* you come into the high road from Turin to Genoa.

NICE is in a fmall plain, bounded on the weft by the river Var, which divides it from Provence, on the fouth by the Mediterranean fea, which comes up to the walls; on the north by the maritime Alps, which begin from the back of this plain, with hills of gentle afcent, rifing by degrees into lofty mountains, and forming an amphitheatre, ending at Montalbano, which projects into the fea, and overhangs the town to the eaft. The river Paglion, which is fupplied by the rains or melting of the fnows, wafhes the walls of the city, and falls into the fea on the weft.

The country about Nice is moft delightful and pleafant, the whole plain being highly cultivated with vines, pomegranates, almonds,

monds, oranges, lemons, citrons, and bergamots. The hills are shaded to the top with olive trees, among which are interspersed the cassines and white country houses. The gardens are full of rose-trees, carnations, and other flowers, blooming the whole winter. You will see the farmers at Christmas gathering their olives on the hills, and in the vallies getting their oranges and lemons, and mowing and making their hay, which they do four times a year. It is nearly as hot during the winter months here, as England is in May; and such is the serenity of the air, that one sees nothing over head for months together but the most charming blue expanse without clouds.

Nice, hardly a mile of circumference, is said to contain 12,000 inhabitants: the streets are narrow; the houses are built of stone, but the windows have in general paper instead of glass. The harbour is defended by a mole, on one side of which is a guard and a battery of seven guns; on the other manufacture for reeling silk, a coffee-house tavern, &c. for the sea-faring people. It is free port, and generally full of small vessel from Sardinia, Yvica, Italy, and Spain, loade with salt, wine, &c.

The walks are very pleasant and various; but the rides, which are much confined, are stony and disagreeable, except the two carriage roads, one by the sea side as far as the Var, about five miles; and the other about two miles only, from the new gate, on the Turin road, between two lofty mountains, by the side of the river Paglion.

The market is tolerably well supplied with fish, beef, pork, mutton, and veal; the lamb is small and often poor; poultry is very indifferent and dear; butter is good and rather cheap; bread very indifferent indeed *. Water is

---

* Butchers meat three sols a pound, and veal something dearer, but then there are only twelve ounces in the pound, which being allowed for, sixteen ounces come for something less than two-pence halfpenny English. Fish four sols, or three pence for sixteen ounces. A turkey, three shillings, a capon, a brace of partridges, or a hare, one shilling and six pence. Pigeons are dear, rabbits rare, and geese scarcely to be seen. All winter they have green pease, asparagus, artichokes, cauliflowers, beans, kidney beans, endive, cabbage, radishes, lettuce, &c &c. Potatoes from the mountains, mushrooms, and the finest truffles in the world. Winter fruits are olives, oranges, lemons, citrons, dried figs, grapes,

mostly drawn from deep wells, and is very hard; the only water fit for drinking, is that in the well of the convent of Dominican Friars in the great square, which being exposed a short time to the air, becomes soft and good. There are ten convents for men, and three for women. It abounds with nobleffe; but excepting three or four families,

grapes, apples, pears, almonds, chesnuts, walnuts, filberts, medlars, pomegranates, azarolle, and the berries of the laurel. There are caper-bushes wild in the neighbourhood, and some palm-trees, but the dates never ripen. In may there are wood strawberries, in the beginning of june cherries, and these are succeeded by apricots and peaches. The grapes are large and luscious. Musk-melons are very cheap, and they have water-melons from Antibes and Sardinia.

Wine is very good and cheap the merchants brew it a good deal; but both red and white may be had of the peasants, genuine, for less than three pence a quart, when taken in quantity. The wine of Tavelle in Languedoc, very near as good as burgundy, may be had for six pence a bottle. The sweet wine of S Laurent about eight pence or nine pence, and pretty good Malaga for half the money.

Wood for firing at eleven sols, or 6½d. a quintal consisting of one hundred and fifty Nice pounds

the

they are sprung from bourgeois, who have saved a little money, and raised themselves to this rank by purchase. There is a *conversazione* every evening at the Commandant's, and in carnival time a ball twice or thrice a week.

Insects, which are in vast abundance here, never sink into a torpid state, but are troublesome all the winter. Gnat-nets are fixed to all the beds, and without them there would be no sleeping. Lodging-houses are excessively dear, both in town and country *. Care must be taken to make the most particular agreements upon every occasion.

---

* Just without one of the gates there are two houses to be let, ready furnished, for about five louis d'ors a month. As for the country houses in the neighbourhood, they are damp in winter, and generally without chimnies; in summer they are hot and full of vermin. A tenement in Nice, consisting of hall, kitchen, two parlours, three bed chambers, and two or three servants' rooms, with a garden, will cost you about 20 l, and you must hire it for a year. You may hire furniture for about two guineas a month, or you may buy what is necessary for sixty guineas, but then you will sell it at going away only for one third of the money it cost.

The employments of the inhabitants of this country, are, besides agriculture and gardening, the making wine, oil and cordage, the rearing of silkworms, and fishing. They raise a great deal of hemp; some wheat, rice, barley and oats, and a considerable quantity of maize. Herbage is scarce; they have however some pleasant meadows in the skirts of Nice that produce excellent clover. All vegetables have a wonderful growth, and they have a great variety of sweet and aromatic herbs wild.

The air here is very dry and elastic, strongly impregnated with salt. The winds are very variable; and whilst the sun is so hot that you can scarce take any exercise out of doors without being thrown into a sweat, the wind is frequently so keen as to produce all the mischievous effects of pores suddenly stopped, such as colds, pleurisies, ardent fevers, rheumatisms, &c. East and north-east winds blow almost constantly during march, april, and may, and passing over mountains covered with snow, are very sharp and penetrating, when the snow begins to melt, the air grows more mild and balmy; and in a few weeks the heat becomes very disagreeable. The inhabitants are subject to fevers, scrophul-

Nice.

scrophulas, rheumatisms, scorbutic putrid gums, with ulcers and eruptions of various sorts; disorders similar to those of other towns on the sea coast of Italy; but the most prevailing distemper seems to be a marasmus.

Upon the whole the winter is warm and pleasant; in march and april it is dangerous for a valetudinarian to stir out on account of the cold winds; the autumn is usually very wet, and the summer intolerably hot; at this season a retreat may be found on the other side of the Var, about seven miles off, in or near the town of *Grasse*, pleasantly situated on the ascent of a hill in Provence. The air is certainly bad for such as have a scorbutic habit, particularly in summer, when the strong evaporation from the sea makes the air so saline, that the surface of the body is covered with a kind of volatile brine*.

* The whole journey from Calais immediately to Nice of four persons in a coach, or two post-chaises, with a servant on horseback, travelling post, will cost 120l including every expence. A travelling coach, or berlin, either at Calais or Paris, will cost from thirty to forty guineas.

If circumstances should induce you to enter Italy from the Valais, you will go by Bex, S. Maurice, Martigni, and across the mountain of S. Bernard. Were it not for the *hospice* or convent, it would be impassable in winter; and even with the assistance which that affords, many persons are lost in the snow, as the bones and corpses in the two chapels witness. As soon as a storm is over, the servants of the convent sally forth with wine, spirits, and provisions, to the assistance of the distressed, towards the Valais, as far as a building made for the refuge of travellers.

The convent is situated in the territory of the Valais, in the highest gorge of the mountain, 8074 English feet above the Mediterranean. You have still two hours to mount to it, after vegetation of trees ceases. The thermometer, even in summer, descends here almost every evening nearly to the freezing point; and below it, if the wind is northerly. M. De Sauffure has observed it below 0, the first of august at one p. m., though the sun was continually piercing through the clouds. Here the most sheltered situations will hardly afford a few small lettuces and sorry cabbages, a little spinage, and some sorrel; the whole

whole produce of the kitchen garden for these poor monks, who receive strangers with a hospitality that does honour to their order and to humanity. They have twenty horses, which are employed during summer in providing bread, wine, flour, cheese, dried fruits, and especially wood, which they fetch the distance of five or six leagues: they must bring in forage for the milch cows, and beasts which are fatted for the kitchen: as to the horses, they winter at Roche, in the government of Aigle, where the convent has a farm.

Not far from the convent are the remains of a Roman temple, where inscriptions, medals, and some bronze statues, have been found.

Though this situation is so high, yet it is overlooked by pikes 1500 feet higher, which therefore you will suppose are generally covered with snow, where they are not too steep for it to lie.

If you wish to pass into Italy by Mount Gothard, which, to a lover of rude and picturesque nature, will be highly interesting; you must go to Lucerne in Swisserland, and from thence cross the lake of that name to Altorf. The *hospice* at the top is inhabited

by

by two Italian friars, from the convent of Capuchins at Milan, who receive all strangers that pass through these inhospitable regions, where there is no other house for a considerable way. The weather is so cold here, as well as on S. Bernard, in the middle of august, that you will rejoice to find a good fire. The snow begins to fall the latter end of september, and the lakes about this spot are frozen three months of the year. The sources of the river Tesin, which runs into the Po, and of the Reuss which runs into the Rhine, are within two miles of each other. The source of the Rhine is within a day's journey, and that of the Rhone is about three leagues off. This habitation is 6790 feet above the level of the sea.

So few Englishmen go into Italy by the other passages, that it is scarcely necessary to describe them: as to the Tyrol, I shall suppose you to return that way, and shall inform you of it in its proper place.

SECTIO

SECTION II.

Description of Turin, and Journey to Genoa.

TURIN is the capital of Piedmont, and the residence of the King of Sardinia. It is situated in a fine plain, watered by the Po, and at the confluence of this river with the Dora. The approach to the city is magnificent, and the environs are beautiful: thick fogs from the two rivers are frequent in autumn and winter; so that the air of Turin is then very thick and moist. Its population is estimated at 80,000 [*]. The four gates are highly ornamental: the streets in the new town are wide, straight, clean, having plenty of water running through them; well built, in a good taste, chiefly of brick stuccoed, and generally terminating in some agreeable object. No inhabitant can rebuild or repair his house, but on an uniform plan laid down by government for the improvement of the city. The *Strada di Po*, leading to the Pa-

---

[*] According to Keysler the inhabitants were 4600 in the year 1728, in 1763, 63,000, in 1755, 64,298. De La Lande.

lace, is very spacious, and has handsome porticos on each side, *Strada Nuova* and *della Dora grossa* are also good streets. The principal square, called *Piazza di San Carlo*, is large, and decorated on two sides with porticos.

The fortifications of Turin are regular, and kept in excellent repair. The citadel is a regular pentagon, consisting of five strong bastions, and is reputed one of the strongest in Europe*. The glacis is planted with trees, forming three avenues; that in the middle very wide for carriages, and one on each side for walking, they extend to the Suze gate, between the fosse and the city. At the end next the new gate is the Arsenal, which, besides the armories, usually found in such places, contains a cabinet of minerals, a good chemical laboratory, a library of books in mineralogy and metallurgy, and furnaces for casting cannon: here also are mathematical, mechanical, and other masters, for the instruction of engineers, miners, &c. The garrison of Turin is always changed at the end of two years; and then there is a general review.

* Keysler has a very particular account of the citadel.

The University is in the *Strada di Po*. It consists of schools, wherein the twenty-four professors read lectures from the third of november to the twenty-fourth of june. Of the royal library, wherein are about 50,000 volumes of printed books, besides manuscripts*: this is open every day, except holidays, both morning and afternoon. Of the royal museum, which has a good cabinet of medals; and a collection of antiquities, found chiefly in Piedmont or Sardinia, and elegantly arranged. also of natural history— as shells and English minerals, polished marbles and hard stones, petrifactions, corals, zoophytes, and some minerals collected by Donati in the Adriatic; also some chests of natural curiosities, which Donati, during his travels in Egypt and Arabia, sent from Goa†. These are in no sort of order.

The military academy is to the east of the castle. Here young gentlemen, both natives and strangers, may be instructed in the exercises at a moderate expence, the King de-

---

* A catalogue of the manuscripts was printed 1749, in two volumes folio

† It is suspected that these chests were pillaged before their arrival.

traying a part of the charge attending this institution. The building is a large court, with porticos on three sides; the stables are handsome and spacious; and the riding-school is a very fine one.

The King's Palace is in a simple and noble style of architecture. The apartments are handsomely fitted up and furnished. the cielings painted by Daniele di Sancterre and others. They contain a great collection of pictures, among which are many good ones: great part of these were purchased from Prince Eugene's cabinet, by the late King. The statues and busts are part of the wreck of the Gonzagua collection, brought from Mantua on the pillage of that city. The celebrated Isiac table is in the chamber of the archives; where also are some antique statues, and an equestrian statue of Victor Amadeus; Pirro Ligorio's drawings in thirty-two folio volumes; many other drawings, among which is one by Michelangelo Buonarroti; an old picture of the crucifixion, said to be by Albert Durer, &c.

PICTURES*.

Gallery.

A large market. Baffano.
S. Sebaftian. Orazio Gentilefchi.
David with the head of Goliath. Guido.
Old man writing. Valentin.
A concert. Ditto.
Mofes faved by Pharaoh's daughter. Paolo Veronefe.
Martyrdom of S. Andrew. Spagnoletto!
S. Margaret, large as life. Pouffin.
S. Victor. faid to be by Goltzius.
S Jerom. Daniele.
Dead Chrift. Ditto.
The Ifraelites bringing their jewels to Aaron. Calabrefe.
Four pictures. Pompeio Battoni.
Cupid. Guido Reni.
Apollo flaying Marfyas. Guido Reni.
The Virgin in glory. Guido Cagnacci.
Virgin, child, and S. John. Lorenzo Sabattini.
S. Peter and S. John, two pictures by Valentin.

* Cochin has given little more than a general account of this collection.

Baccha-

Bacchanals. Calabrese.

Solomon and the Queen of Sheba. Paolo Veronese.

S. Margaret. Rubens.

Christ and the woman of Samaria. Lanfranco.

A Concert. Lanfranco.

Rape of the Sabines. Bassano.

S. Sebastian dead, and two women pulling out an arrow. Gentileschi.

Second Gallery.

A Hermit in a hollow tree. Salvator Rosa.

Portrait of a Scotch nobleman, whole length. Rubens.

Portrait of a man with a picture before him. Holbein.

Painter contemplating the portrait of a lady.

Charles I. Mytens: architecture by Steenwyck.

Head of Vandyck, with the sunflower; by himself.

A Nymph or Venus. Carlo Cignani.

Adonis. - - - Ditto.

Head of Rembrandt; by himself.

Portrait

Portrait of a man with a glafs of wine. Pourbus.

Lucretia, half figure; by Guido.

Entombing of Chrift. Baffano.

Three children of K. Charles I. Vandyck.

Prince Tommafo di Carignano, on a white horfe, large as life, in armour. Vandyck.

A man in armour with a woman, lefs than half figures. Rubens.

Two boys. Carlo Cignani.

S. Jerom; and S. John Baptift, half figure; both by Guido.

Repofe in Egypt. Albano.

Charity. - Ditto.

Sir Thomas More's daughter with her father's head.

Virgin and child. Vandyck.

Portrait of a woman in a ruff, and another, younger; both by Pourbus.

An old man, half figure. Guercino.

Another. Spagnoletto.

Portrait of a man. Bronzino.

Two pictures of animals.

An old man, half figure, almoft naked. Spagnoletto.

Another, half length, in a chair. Rembrandt!

A man, half length, sitting. Pourbus.

An old man and an angel, less than half figures.

A young woman with a glass.

Holy family, half figures, from Rubens.

Orpheus with animals.

Virgin, child and S. John; dark but good.

Lucretia. Domenichino.

Incantation. Teniers.

Portrait of a woman in a ruff.

Another by Pourbus.

In the next room.

The four elements, four oval pictures, by Albano.

Four subjects from the Old Testament, by Solimene; the best is the Queen of Sheba offering presents to Solomon.

Three pieces of peasants, by Teniers!

Small battle-piece. Wouvermans!

Cattle. Potter! 1649.

Woman and two children, small. C. d Moor.

Two insides of churches.

Four landscapes, by Greffier; one larger and two others very fine.

Visitation of Elisabeth. Rembrandt.

Landscape, with the baptism of Christ. Salvator Rosa.

Two landscapes. Greffier.

Virgin and child in the style of Rubens: perhaps by Willibert.

A large picture with many figures. Bassano.

Another Room.

Pope Paul III. half length, sitting. Tiziano.

Flower-piece. De Heem.

Picture-shop. Franck, 1618.

Holy family in a landscape. Brueghel and Rottenhamer.

Venus and Adonis. Ditto.

The Salutation of Elisabeth. Orazio Gentileschi.

The return of the Prodigal. Guercino:— both large.

Luther and his wife. Holbein. Repaired, or copies.

Virgin and dead Christ. Carracci.

Landscape. Greffier.

Martyrdom of S. Laurence; figures large as life. Bassano.

A warm landscape. Both.

Two landscapes, with naked women. Polembourg.

Head of an old man with a white beard. Rembrandt!

Adam and Eve weeping over Abel. Vanderwerff.

Country Attorney and his Clients; said to be by Quintin Matsys. It is like that engraved by Boydel.

Inside of a church, large. Peter Nefs.

Holy Family with angels. D. Calvaart. 1579.

Another Room.

A dropsical woman with her physician; finished with the most exquisite Dutch nicety, by Gerard Douw.

Two landscapes, by Jan Brueghel.

Landscape, by Hellish Brueghel.

Dead Christ. Daniele.

Battle at a bridge. Wouvermans!

Resurrection of Lazarus. Rubens.

Moses bringing down the red sea on the Egyptians. Jan Brueghel.

Christ sitting on the sepulchre, and treading on death. Rubens.

Eight single heads, studies from nature, by Rubens.

Slight sketch of Henry IV.'s apotheosis. Rubens.

Landscape. Jan Brueghel.

Martyrdom of a female Saint. Polembourg.

Another Room.

Magdalene weeping, large as life. Rubens.

Fruit, by Claude Mignon.

Virgin and child after Raffaelle. Saffa Ferrata.

Two old heads, by Guercino.

Portraits of a man and woman sitting, Vandyck

The descent of a hero into hell — and a small landscape: both by Hellish Brueghel.

Two landscapes by Jan Brueghel.

Adoration of the shepherds. Pietro da Cortona.

Two pictures with two heads in each. Schidone.

Flower-piece. De Heem.

A little room.

A small piece of horses. Wouvermans.

Landscape with S. John preaching: very old.

Two

Two landscapes, by Greffier.

Erasmus, by Holbein; and an old head its companion.

A medley, said to be by Rubens.

A small portrait of Schalcken, by himself.

Boy, girl, and dog, at a window. Gerard Douw.

Two landscapes. Claude Lorrain: perhaps copies.

Two sketches. Rubens.

Rinaldo and Armida. Vandyck.

Two small pictures. Albano.

Landscape with a pleasure-boat, and another with carriages: both by Jan Brueghel.

Another room.

Old man with a glass, half figure. Ostade.

Magdalene with a lamp. Schalcken.

Old man and a young woman. Vanderwerff.

Three pictures of women. Vanderwerff.

Six landscapes, by Greffier.

S. Frances of Rome, large as life. Guercino.

Christ receiving penitents. Rubens. The same at Dusseldorff, but finer: engraved by Lauwers.

Moonlight

Moonlight winter landscape.

The salutation of Elisabeth; large. Gentileschi.

Holy family: school of Rubens.

Long room near the Chapel.

Inside of a room, with fruit, &c. 1765.

Large round landscape, romantic. Jan Brueghel.

Four landscapes by the same: 1. sea shore; 2. hunting; 3. village feast; 4. good Samaritan.

Small moonlight landscape. Peter Nefs.

Two small landscapes. Jan Brueghel.

Old man, and old woman; small whole lengths: both by Rembrandt.

Two insides of churches. Peter Nefs.

Virgin and child. Francis Francia.

Two small landscapes. Jan Brueghel.

Two pictures of horses. Wouvermans.

Small landscape! Jan Brueghel.

Its companion, with a river and ships. Jan Brueghel.

Moses bringing back the red sea. Jan. Brueghel.

Man and woman sitting; said to be Ostade.

Savoyard

Savoyard with a cymbal. Teniers.
Woman with two children. Ditto.
Village feast. Greffier.
Small portrait of a man in a hat!
Landscape with cattle. Berghem.
Landscape, by Greffier.
Two landscapes, by Jan Brueghel.
Ruined temple, small, by the same.
Horse shoeing, small. Wouvermans.
A young woman, with a brass pail and dead fowls. Gerard Douw!
Landscape, with S. Hubert. Jan Brueghel.
Noah entering the ark, small. Bassan.
Landscape with boats. Jan Brueghel
Woman counting money. Gerard Douw.
Small landscape with ruins. Greffier.
Old man reading, and old woman with hands on each other; both small. Rembrandt.
Young woman with grapes. Gerard Douw.
Landscape with a sacrifice to Cupid. Jan Brueghel.
Young woman writing. Schalcken.
Old woman in a cap. Gerard Douw.
Old woman with a reel. Ditto.
Old man with bottle and glass. Ditto.

Young

Turin. Palace. 41

Young woman. Gerard Douw.
Shoeing of horses. Wouvermans.
Village feast, with many figures. Jan Brueghel
Cows and sheep. Teniers.
Landscape, with S. John Baptist
Holy Family, with Joseph at work. Albert Durer.

Small closet, hung with looking-glass.

Seventy-two miniature portraits; fifteen half length; the rest ovals.

Little room.

Adam and Eve, large as life. Guido.
Salmacis and Hermaphroditus. Albano.
Man and woman, small. Corregio.
Man and woman in the water, probably Salmacis and Hermaphroditus. Mieris!
Cleopatra, large as life. Guido.
Nymph and shepherd. Vanderwerff.
Landscape, with Diana and nymphs. Brueghel.
Child asleep. Guido.
Woman on a bed. Tiziano.

Room

Room near the last.

Boors fiddling. Teniers.
Boors smoking. Ditto.
Fragment of a woman. Tiziano. head and breast only remaining.
Purse and book. - Gerard Douw.
Hour-glass and ink-horn. Ditto.
Battle. Giulio Romano.
Landscape with horsemen. De Momper.
S. Catherine with a lamb; large as life. Guido.

The King's Theatre, or great Opera house, adjoins to the royal palace, and is reckoned one of the finest in Europe. It is 96 English feet wide, and 126 in length. Six rows of boxes rise above the pit; each big enough to hold eight persons with ease, but only three in front. The king's box is opposite to the stage, and occupies the width of five boxes, but the height only of the second and third rows: the back part is covered with looking-glass, and there is a moveable partition, which is taken down on high festivals. thus the room is doubled in size, and being grandly illuminated, with the whole theatre, makes a very handsome appearance. The machinery and

and decorations are magnificent. The king is at the chief expence, they who have boxes paying only two or three guineas for the season as a kind of fee, money being taken at the door only for sitting in the pit. The serious opera begins on the sixth of January, which is the king's name-day, and continues, except on fridays, till lent; and this interval is called the *Carnival*.

There is also a little theatre, called *Teatro Carignano*, which has five rows of boxes, and twenty-four in each row. A company of *burletta* performers exhibit here from october to christmas; and, during summer, some *buff* comedians present every night, except friday, a farce, with a musical interlude, which they continue till the burlettas begin.

The *Corso* is usually in an avenue of elms about a mile in length, leading from *porta nuova* to the Po, and the king's villa of the Valentine: here all the city parades in carriages between five and seven in the evening, when they change their ground for another avenue near the citadel; and this they leave at eight for the theatre, or some assembly, in summer; but in short days the theatres open between five and six. During the Carnival the Corso is in the Po street.

The

The buildings which are most esteemed in point of architecture are, the palace of the duke of Savoy, called *Castello Reale*, by Filippo Giuvara; the Carignano palace, by Guarini; the buildings of the university, and the town house.

The most remarkable of the churches are, 1. The cathedral, dedicated to S. John Baptist; a gothic edifice, restored in 1498. The chapel *della santissima sindone*, or S. Suaire, by Guarini, is much noticed, rather for its singularity than its beauty. It is quite circular, wholly incrusted with black marble, heavy and dismal, resembling a melancholy mausoleum, the dome is a very singular structure. A symphony is commonly played here every morning between eleven and twelve o'clock, by the king's band, divided into three orchestras, placed in three separate galleries. The royal family are constant in their attendance. On festivals there is other music, and motets are sometimes performed with voices. 2. San Filippo Neri, by Giuvara. 3. The church of the Carmelites in the great square, by the same architect, in which is a statue of S. Theresa in ecstasy, by Le Gros. Several other churches are much decorated,

decorated, but rather extravagant in their style of architecture.

The principal paintings in the churches are—in that of the Jesuits: S. Paul, by Fred. Zucchero. In S. Dalmatius: the burial of Christ, by Molineri. In S. Domenico: Virgin and Christ in the clouds; and S. S. Domenico and Rosa, by Guercino. In S. Filippo Neri: pictures by Solimene, Carlo Maratti and Conca.

In the Pertengo palace are many small pictures, among which that of the dying officer at confession has great merit.

The Bezozzis have, among others, a fine picture of Christ bearing his cross, by Lodovico Caracci. Cavalier Gelosi has the Virgin, child, and St. John, a capital piece, by Andrea del Sarto.

A league and half from the city is the *Superga*, a handsome church, richly ornamented, built on the top of a mountain, after the designs of Giuvara, in consequence of a vow made by Victor Amadeus in the year 1706, when Turin was besieged by the French. The building was begun in 1715, and finished in 1731. On the 8th of September in every year, the king and royal family go to this church, to commemorate the delivery of the city.

city. The view from the dome is very extensive.

Les Vignes de la Reine is a small palace of the king's, near Turin, on a height, from whence there is a view of the city, of the plain as far as Rivoli, and the course of the Po for three leagues. There are some cielings here by Daniele.

Veneria Reale is the palace where the late king chiefly lived. In the guard-chamber are ten large hunting-pieces by Jean Miel. The chapel is by Giuvara: at one of the altars is a picture of S. Sebastian, S. Roch, and S. Eusebius, by Sebastian Ricci. The orangerie is beautiful, about 540 feet long, and 96 wide. The stables are spacious and handsome. The gardens are large, laid out in the French taste, with a sylvan theatre, a labyrinth, &c. It is full of quarters planted with brushwood, intersected by narrow allies, forming stars, in which the king used to post himself, to shoot the game, which was driven out of the coppices by the piqueurs.

The parish church also is by Giuvara.

Moncalieri is preferred by the present king for his residence. It is pleasantly situated on the Po, and being farther removed from the Alps, is warmer than La Veneria or

Stupenigi

Stupenigi: another palace, where the king breakfasts when he hunts, which is twice a week. He lives much in the country, and does not come to reside at Turin till christmas. The queen, princesses, and younger princes, attend the chase of the stag, in two-wheeled post-chaises, with post-horses.

Valentino is a small palace of the king's, a little way out of town, on the banks of the Po: it has a large garden, in which the royal family walk, and it is open to strangers. The university have also here a small botanic garden, well furnished with alpine plants.

The convent of the Camaldules is in a fine situation, on a hill five miles from the city; it was founded by Charles Emanuel in 1599. The best picture here is a large one, filling the end of the refectory, by Br. Mattheus of Antwerp; the subject is the last supper. The road to this convent is romantic.

There is a literary society at Turin, who have published memoirs, under the title of *Miscellanea Philosophico-Mathem. ca.* Padre Beccaria is professor of natural philosophy. Ignazio Somis is professor of physic, and physician to the king. Dr. Allione, the professor of botany, has a good museum of dried plants,

plants, insects, petrifactions, and minerals. Dr. Giov Pier Maria Dona is professor extraordinary of botany, and inspector of the museum of natural history. Dr. Charles Louis Bellardi is a learned physician. S. Bartoli is professor of eloquence. Father Gerdil is a celebrated mathematician. Cavalier Terini has the custody of the royal museum. M. Grafion is professor of the mine academy, and has the direction of the mines of Savoy. The Bezozzis and Pugnani are univerfally known in the musical world.

The chief trade of this city and country is in thrown silk, which is sent to England and Lyons: they manufacture, however, some of it into excellent stockings, and good silk for furniture. They are famous for rosoli, millefleurs, snuff, chamois gloves, and some other trifles. They import broadcloths and linen from Great Britain; some woollens and Lyons goods from France, linens from Swifferland and Silesia; also iron, copper, fugar, and drugs of all forts. Their chief export is cattle, some hemp, thread and cordage: they reckon that upwards of ninety thousand bullocks are annually sent out of Piedmont. Several manufactories are carried on for the king's account, as to

bacco

bacco, bottles, lead, shot, &c. All the salt used here comes from Sardinia: the king disposes of the produce of the salt springs in Savoy to the Swifs. A great deal of wine is made in Piedmont, but it is not all good: the principal attention of government has been bestowed on the cultivation of mulberry trees. Rice also is a great object of culture in some provinces. They abound in good fruit, particularly chesnuts; and are remarkable for fine truffles.

Piedmont is 150 miles in extent from north to south, but much less from east to west. It is flat, and well watered by rivers and brooks. They have the good sense to make the best use of these for the improvement of their meadows. From the Alps to the Venetian lagunes there is very little uncultivated land. A ridge of low hills, called *la Collina*, beginning not far from Turin, and continuing along the banks of the Po, for forty or fifty miles, is covered with houses and vineyards, and enjoys delightful and extensive prospects. The Val d'Aosta is interesting to a naturalist, it its copious quartz veins with plenty of native gold; fine-grained lead ore, containing , &c.; red antimony; green lead ore, &c. This

&c. This is also the country of the *Stein-bock*.

The Piedmontese language has a great mixture of French; and the nobility, who are numerous, affect french fashions and manners. They are fond of outward show, but not being in general rich, are obliged to be oeconomists. The people are said to be addicted to play, and have the reputation of being sharp and crafty. They make very good soldiers; and the peasants and artisans are industrious, and not unskilful. The inhabitants are supposed to exceed two millions; and the king's revenues are estimated at little more than a million sterling: with this his houshold is well supported and paid, his troops well cloathed, and always complete.

By setting out early from Turin, you may get to Alessandria the first day, and arrive at Genoa the second, before the gates are shut. The road to Asti is bad, and the country uninteresting. *Asti* is built of brick stuccoed, the streets are narrow, and the people poor, without trade or industry; there are some large palaces that have a deserted appearance, and several churches and religious houses.

The fortifications and castle are in ruins; but there is a garrison and commandant.

From Ash the road is sandy all the way to Alessandria, and in some places very indifferent. The products are corn, mulberry-trees and vines. *Alessandria* has a strong citadel, and a garrison consisting of five regiments of infantry, and a detachment of cavalry. There is an opera here during the two fairs, in april and october; but the place is neither large nor remarkable. The principal building is the town-house in the great square, by the cathedral, a gothic edifice, which contains nothing to detain a stranger.

Immediately after quitting the town, you cross the river Tanaro in a boat, which is so contrived as to carry passengers over, without getting out of their carriages. The soil to Novi is gravel, and the country level; the road pretty good, but narrow: there are vines all the way in rows, with corn between. *Novi* is the first town in the Genoese territories, and contains about 6000 inhabitants: the republic keeps a considerable garrison here, and a governor. Between Alessandria and Novi is the abbey del Bosco, belonging to the Dominicans. In the prior's lodgings is a curious picture of the life of Christ, by Albert Durer. The church has a great deal of fine sculpture in marble, by Michelangelo, &c.*

From Novi to *Ottaggio*, or *Voltaggio*, the road is uneven, but chiefly descending: the products are vines, mulberries, chesnuts, and a little corn. The white mountains have a barren appearance, and are bare of trees. They consist of a fine hardened marl, mixed with glimmer and small blunted pieces of gabbro.

The fortress of *Gavi*, between Ottaggio and Campo-Marone, is remarkably situated on the top of an isolated rock, in the middle of a plain. There is a small garrison here, and a commandant. The passage of the *Boccketta* over the Apennines is agreeably varied with pretty hills and vallies. The mountains consist of black undulated slate, green gabbro or serpentine-stone, polzevera or gabbro with calcareous veins, argillaceous slate, and gray limestone: they are covered in many places with fine lofty chesnut trees. The whole road from Novi is paved, and very good: the ascent and descent

* Keysler 363.

are both extremely steep, but not dangerous. From the top of the Bocchetta there is a fine view of Genoa, and of the valley, through which the torrent of the Polzevera runs. Travellers were obliged to cross it above forty times between Campo Marone and Genoa, and were stopped whenever it rained two days succeffively; but now there is a fine, wide, folid road, made along the eastern bank of the torrent, at the fole expence of the Cambiafo family. The country is fine, and full of country houfes, as you approach towards Genoa; and there is almoft one continued ftreet, long before you enter the city by the fuburb of *St. Pietra d'Arena*, which is magnificently built, but narrow.

SECTION III.

Defcription of Genoa.

GENOA is built on the fide of a mountain, in a femicircle round the harbour. For magnificent buildings, and beauty of fituation, it may vie with any city; but it has no large fquares, and the ftreets are fo narrow, as not to admit of viewing its many grand

grand palaces to any advantage: several of them are only six feet wide; even the two best, strade Balbi and Nuova * are very narrow: they are however all admirably well paved and clean. Two palaces of the Balbi family, the Jesuit's college, and palazzo Durazzo, 140 paces in front, are the great ornaments of strada Balbi; as the Doria palace is of strada Nuova. Piazza Doria, at one end of this street, is not so remarkable for its size, as for the beauty of its buildings. The square of the Annonciata is the largest in Genoa.

The city is about six miles in circuit, and is surrounded by a double wall; one encompassing it immediately; the other taking in all the rising grounds that command it. There is a most agreeable walk round the ramparts, from the convent of S. Antonio to the *fanale* or light-house. A good bird's-eye view of the city may be taken from the top of the Carignano church; but it is seen to most advantage, by traversing the harbour in a boat, or a quarter of a league out at sea.

* The latter is twelve paces broad.

The opening of the harbour between the two moles is about 750 yards; vessels of 80 guns can ride in it, before the new mole; a light-house is built at the point of that and the old mole; and they are both provided with brass cannon. When the wind blows from S. or S. W., a great sea rolls in, and is troublesome to the shipping. There is a smaller harbour for merchant vessels to unload in; and by that is the *Dorsena*, or wet dock, for the gallies of the republic.

At the bottom of the harbour to the eastward is the *Porto Franco*, containing the warehouses of the merchants, admirably disposed in a separate enclosure, opened only at certain times[*]. All merchandize must be lodged here, and pays no custom at entrance: whatever is sold for the consumption of the city pays eight or ten per cent. upon the value; but all that is exported pays only a slight duty. They do not suffer ecclesias-

[*] From the 15th of September to the end of March, from eight in the morning till two in the afternoon, and during the rest of the year, from eight to one, and from four to six; during June and July it continues open till seven.

tics, officers, women, or livery servants, to enter without particular permission.

The *Cathedral*, dedicated to S. Laurence, is a gothic building, very dark. It is incrusted both within and without, and also paved with black and white marble. There is a picture in it of the crucifixion, by Baroccio; some other paintings of no great account; and also some sculpture by Guglielmo della Porta. In the treasury is a curious hexagon bowl, pretended to be of emerald, fourteen inches and an half in diameter, given to the Genoese by Baldwin king of Jerusalem[*]. It is kept under several keys, and cannot be seen without a decree of the senate.

S. Ambrogio joins to the palace of the Doge, and it is in this church that he goes to hear mass. Here are three of the best pictures in Genoa—the circumcision, by Rubens: S. Ignatius exorcising a demoniac, and raising children to life, by the same painter: and the Assumption of the virgin, by Guido.

The church of the *Annonciata*, built at the sole expence of the Lomellino family, is one

---

[*] M. de la Condamine has entered deeply into the controversy concerning the material of this famous bowl.

of the moſt rich in marbles, gilding, and paintings; among which that of the laſt ſupper, by G. C. Procaccino, is the moſt curious; it is over the door, and is much blackened.

The church of *S. Ciro*, which was the firſt cathedral, and now belongs to the Theatins, is very richly adorned and incruſted within. At the high altar are angels and boys in gilt bronze, by Puget. The pictures are, the nativity, by Cambiaſo. The annunciation, by Gentileſchi. S. Andrea Avellino, by Sarzana. The adoration of the ſhepherds, by Pomerancio. The beheading of S. John Baptiſt, by Carlo Bonnone.

S. Domenico, a church belonging to the convent of Jacobins.—Beheading of S. John; by Lorenzo Bertoloto, a Genoeſe painter. Aſſumption, by Cappucino; who alſo painted the cieling of the ſanctuary in freſco. Circumciſion, by G. C. Procaccino. Virgin preſenting Jeſus to Simeon, by Borzone, a Genoeſe painter. S. Peter martyr, our lady of Loretto, and S. Jacinto before the virgin, by Domenico Fiaſella, commonly called Sarzana. S. Franceſco d'Aſſizi, by Piola.

S. Filippo Neri is alſo handſomely ornamented. The cieling is by Franceſchini. S. Francis de Salles, by Parodi. S. Catherine fine and S. Francis d'Assizi: both by Piola. S. Filippo Neri; marble group; by Dom. Guidi.

THE oratory adjoining to this church has a statue of the virgin with angels, by Puget. *Concerti spirituali* are performed on the evenings of festivals, from all Saints to easter, at the expence of the fathers.

S. Francesco in Castelletto, a convent of the Cordeliers. The church large and gothic. Virgin and saints, Perino del Vaga: much hurt. S. Jerom, Bern. Castello. S. Catherine, Andrea Semino. Adoration of the shepherds, by the same. Death of the virgin, Sarzana. S. Francis, Cam. Procaccino. Conception, Tintoretto. Nativity, Vencini. Statues and bas-reliefs in bronze, Giovanni Bologna. Marble tomb of Andrea Spinola, with the virgin, by Cambiaso.

S. Luca. Painted by Piola the elder. At the high altar, the Conception, by Filippo Parodi. In a chapel on the right, a picture by Benedetto di Castiglione.

S. Maddalena. All painted in fresco by Sebastiano Galeotti. The chapel of the virgin, by Domenico Parodi. Assumption, the style of Vandyck. The Magdalene,

Paggi. The altar of S. Nicolas, by Gio. Battista Parodi.

S. Maria di Carignano is built in a style of architecture very different from all the other churches, and in form of a greek cross, by Alexio Galeazzi of Perugia, who planned the strada nuova, and built most of the palaces. The paintings are—the virgin, S. Francis and S. Charles, by G. C. Procaccino. S. Francis, by Guercino. S. Peter and S. John curing the paralytic, by Piola. Martyrdom of S. Basil, by Carlo Maratti. S. Mary the Egyptian, receiving the communion from S. Maximin: by Vanini of Siena. A Pietà, by Cambiaso. Here are also statues of S. Alessandro Pauli, and S. Sebastian, by Puget.

In coming out of this church you pass over a lofty bridge, above the tops of the houses, made to join the two hills of Carignano and Sarzano: it consists of three large arches, and one small one; is 90 feet high, 45 wide, and 160 or 170 paces long.

S. Stefano is remarkable for the stoning of S. Stephen, a painting at the high altar, the lower part of which is by Raffaelle, and the upper by Giulio Romano.

The *Albergo* is a large building, serving at the same time for the reception of the poor who are unable to work, and as a house of correction. In the chapel is a fine alto-relievo of the virgin contemplating Christ dead, commonly called a Pietà, by Michelangelo; and the assumption of the virgin, by Puget.

The great Hospital is on a very extensive plan, and receives the sick of all nations and religions. The Conservatory for educating and portioning three hundred poor girls, is an immense building, and was founded entirely by a nobleman of the *Fieschi* family, who died without children.

The palace of the Doge is very large, without any exterior decoration. On each side of the door is a statue of Giovanni Andrea, and Andrea Doria, larger than life. The walls of the great council-chamber are painted in fresco by Franceschini, with the principal occurrences in the history of Genoa. In the little council-chamber are three large pieces, by Solimene.

The Arsenal, which is in this palace, is said to contain arms for 25,000 or 30,000 men. In the little arsenal there is the prow of a roman galley, and a cannon of a very ancient form*.

* Commonly said to be of leather; others say of wood lined with brass. I neglected to examine it

The palaces of the nobility at Genoa are univerfally celebrated for their magnificence. The principal of them—1. that of Francefco Balbi and Giacomo Balbi; in each of which is a numerous collection of valuable pictures. 2. The Brignole palace, called Palazzo Roffo; remarkable for the diftribution of the apartments, the richnefs of the furniture, and the number and excellence of the pictures. 3. Palazzo Doria, fituated at the gate of S. Thomas, is the largeft of all the palaces. It was begun by the celebrated Andrea Doria. The principal front is to the harbour. In the gardens is a ftatue of Andrea Doria, in the character of Neptune. 4. The palace of Marcellino Durazzo has an immenfe front, and fuperb apartments well furnifhed. You enter a hall 40 feet cube; on one fide is a handfome room 24 feet by 20, and three rooms beyond it, 22 by 15; on the other fide a room 24 by 20, and a gallery 80 by 15—towards one end a dreffing room, and towards the other five fmall rooms that go out on a terrace, with a lovely view of the harbour. The furniture is rich damafk or velvet, with gilt chairs; the cielings gilt and painted in ornaments, but crouded. The collection of pictures, both of italian and

flemifh

Flemish masters, is very fine. One of the most esteemed is a large piece by Paolo Veronese, of the Magdalene at the feet of Christ in the pharisee's house. There is also an antique bust of Vitellius. 5. The palace of Marcello, late Giacomo Filippo Durazzo, has many excellent paintings, particularly of the Bolognese school, and of Vandyck. The Carrega, Palavicini, and several other palaces, are full of good pictures*. The most esteemed with respect to architecture, where the style of architecture, it must be confessed, is not good, are that of the duke of Tursi; the two Brignole palaces, called Palazzo Rosso and Bianco; that of Palavicino di Castelliano, and of the duke S. Pietro Spinola; the two Balbi palaces; the two Durazzos; and that of Andrea Doria. Those which are best fitted up and furnished are—Marcellino Durazzo's, Francesco Maria della Rovere's, Palazzo Rosso, Carrega's, and that of Bartolomeo Saluzzo.

* I have not given the catalogues, since they may be found in a book which may be purchased on the spot for three livres. It is entitled *Description des beautés de Genes, et de ses environs*, and has a plan and view of the city, plates of the principal buildings, &c.

The

The Genoese have sumptuous country houses or villas: the principal of these are those of Marcellone Durazzo at Cornigliano, of the Imperiali, Spinola, Doria, Grimaldi, and Palavicini families, at S. Pietra d'Arena; of Brignole, Saluzzo, and Giustiniani, at Albaro; of Maria Spinola, at Sestri, &c. They have gardens, with abundance of orange and lemon trees, hedges of myrtle, fountains, jet d'eaus, statues, &c. The first mentioned is by far the largest of these villas: it has fifteen windows in front, with a court, offices, stables, &c. on each side; built by a Frenchman; good and very plain, all of rough stone stuccoed; the walls tinged yellow, the ornaments white, which, with the green jalousies, has a pretty effect. You enter a large square hall, one side of which has open arches to the great staircase; on the other side are two tolerable rooms and two closets. From the hall you enter the salon, about forty feet square, having on each side the same number of rooms: the height of this story is twenty feet. This is the ground floor. That above is 24 feet high, and distributed nearly in the same manner. This villa is furnished in a neat but plain manner, with printed linens of different colours; and the rooms and cielings

are

are stuccoed with light foliage, coloured to suit the linen. It has an excellent mezzanine full ten feet high. Behind is a garden like a French parterre. This may serve to give an idea of the Genoese taste in their villas. From Genoa to Sestri there is a continued chain of country houses for six miles together.

The Genoese state is well peopled, considering the nature of the territory. The inhabitants are estimated at 400,000, of which 80,000 are in the capital. The government is mild, the habitations roomy and clean, and the face of the country often romantically beautiful. The nobility have scarcely any tincture of literature: though they are generally educated in Tuscany, scarcely any of them are able to speak pure Italian; but all talk the same wretched patois, which is in use among the lower people. In general they are said to live with great parsimony in their families; and since they always appear in black, are at little expence in the article of apparel. Some of them however have five or six palaces; and others, much to their honour, have expended prodigious sums in public works of great magnificence or utility: witness the house for 300 girls; the foundation

tion for the maintenance of 340 nuns; the church and bridge of Carignano; Durazzo's college for twelve noble youths; the fine road from Campo Marone, &c.

The people are laborious, industrious, and brave: they, with the Piedmontese, pass for the most crafty nations of Italy.

The state is poor, its annual revenues not amounting to 300,000 pounds sterling. The regular troops are only 2500, but they have 30,000 militia, which are exercised every month.

Genoa is most brilliant at the coronation of a Doge*. At other times there is no resource for the idle, but the assemblies or conversaziones; and during the carnival, the opera, which is played in the theatre of S. Agostino, or di Falcone, alternately; and plays in the *theatrins*.

Their trade consists in their manufactures of rich silks, velvets, brocades, stockings,

---

* He holds his office only during two years. His dress of ceremony is a long robe of crimson velvet or damask. his ordinary dress is red, stockings, shoes and all; with a large cravat of lace, and a prodigious periwig. The procurators and senators wear robes of black damask.

gloves,

gloves, artificial flowers, and gold filagree; together with their own produce of wine, oil, fruits, dried mushrooms, anchovies, and sweetmeats: they also build ships for foreign powers.

Genoa has the face of business, though their trade is not considerable; for the vicinity of Lombardy brings some merchant ships, and a great quantity of goods is brought here by foreigners. The streets are crouded, the shops are well furnished, and the markets abound in excellent provisions. Bread is white and good, but dear: the beef, which they have from Piedmont, is juicy and delicious, but twelve fols, or near sixpence a pound. The poorest sort live chiefly on chesnuts, macaroni, dried fish, and cheese. Fish is far from plentiful; and wood for fuel is dear. The wine made in the neighbourhood is in general indifferent. The state has the monopoly of this, and also of bread and oil. The climate is so moderate, that there is abundance of garden stuff, as peas, artichokes, &c. great part of the winter; as also of flowers, as roses, pinks, and carnations.

The whole range of rocks on the Genoe[se] coast is either flate or marble; they are ver[y]

stee[p]

steep both towards the sea and the land. The industry of the inhabitants has in many places made amends for the want of fertility in the mountains, which are in general covered with olives, vines, pomegranates, orange and lemon trees; or shaded with carob-trees and evergreen oaks; and adorned with buildings and gardens.

SECTION IV.

Departure from Genoa. Description of Pavia and Milan.

IF you purpose to go immediately to Rome, Florence, and Naples, you will hire a felucca at Genoa for Leghorn. You may have a large one, manned with ten hands, for about five guineas: the distance is about 160 miles, and if the wind and weather are favourable, you will arrive at Leghorn in two days. You may make an agreement with the *padrone*, to set you down at Lerici, in case of bad weather; which he will do for three or four guineas: and from thence you may take the post. The road however from
Lerici

Lerici is mountainous and indifferent: but you will have pleasure in seeing the mountains covered with olive trees, and abundance of vines in the low lands, running up the poplars, and stretching from one tree to another; with myrtles, pomegranates, &c. growing wild along the road-side. *Massa* is the only place between Lerici and Pisa, where it is safe to repose; the other towns being in a flat country, near the sea. It is at Carrara and Seravezza, in the principality of Massa that the fine white marble is dug, which is so much coveted by the sculptor. The grain of the Seravezza marble is yet finer than that of Carrara. The marble of Porto Venere is yellow mixed with black, and extremely beautiful: and near Sestri, &c. different coloured marbles are dug.

It is a journey of ten or eleven hours from Lerici to Pisa, the gates of which are shut two hours after sun-set; but they will readily open them at any time.

If however you are not in haste to be at Rome, I advise you rather to go from Genoa to Milan. To do this, you must return by the road you came, as far as Novi, and then go by Tortona and Voghera to Pavia, from whence it is only two posts to Milan.

PAVI

PAVIA from a metropolis is become a mere country town, with little or no manufactures. It has some large buildings, and wide streets; but all looks gone and neglected. In spite of a fine plain, a good river, and hills within a few miles distance, it is an unpleasant situation. There are several squares; that in the middle of the town is the most considerable; it is surrounded with open porticos, and has an antique bronze equestrian statue in it, said to be Marcus Aurelius; the horse admirably done, but the emperor a mean figure.

The cathedral is rebuilt; by what remains of the old church it was a heavy gothic building. The pictures are of little consequence. The church of S. Peter, with the Convent, are handsome structures. That of the Dominicans is large, neat, and has some paintings. King Luitprand, Boetius, Lionel duke of Clarence, Francis duke of Lorrain, and Richard de la Pole, the pretended duke of Suffolk, are all buried in the convent of the Augustinians. This city is most famous for its University, founded by Charlemagne, and re-established by Charles IV. in 1361. The Borromean seminary is remarkable for its buildings, which within are neat and elegant,

gant, and for some paintings. The late empress put the University upon a respectable footing; and the names of Scopoli and Spallanzani alone, are sufficient to insure it celebrity.

The river Tesin (*Ticino*) is wide and deep at Pavia: it is navigable for large barques, in which they export grain, hemp, cheese, and some wine. There is a bridge over it, 340 paces long, built by Galeazzo duke of Milan, of brick, partly covered with marble.

The grand and beautiful *Chartreux*, or convent of the Carthusians, is five miles from Pavia. A handsome avenue of trees leads to it from the Milan road. The church is a gothic structure much ornamented, the front being of white marble with sculpture, and most of the altars being adorned with florentine work, of the finest hard stones, inlaid in marble. Giovanni Galeazzo Visconti, the first duke of Milan, founded the convent, and is buried in the church, where his monument still remains: there was an equestrian statue over it, which has been long destroyed. The principal pictures are — Virgin, child, and an angel. S. Michael standing in complete armour. The Deity surrounded by twelve cherubim

cherubim. The Annunciation in two pieces, by Pietro Perugino.

Virgin, child, and four angels. S. Anselmo. S. Hugo. The resurrection. Two old men writing. An old man writing, and another reading—the two last pieces probably the four evangelists. All by Macrino d'Alba.

Christ on the cross, virgin, &c. Ambrogio Fossani.

Virgin and child, S. Peter and S. Paul. Guercino.

Annunciation. Camillo Procaccino. 1616.

Virgin, Magdalene, &c. with the holy handkerchief: by the same.

Adoration of the Magi. Cav. Pietro Negri.

Virgin and child, S. Catherine, &c. Cav. del Cayro.

Virgin and child, S. Charles and S. Bruno. Cirino.

Virgin and child, with the rosary. Mazazone.

Seven Saints, half figures. P. Bonelli.

S. Paul and S. Antony; fresco. Dan. Crespi. Other frescos by him are mentioned in Cochin; but this is the best.

A curious

A curious ivory altar, with three neat gothic arches, and small basso-relievos.

In the nave are several statues.

In the Convent is an old copy of Leonardo da Vinci's last supper, in oil, as large as the original.

MILAN.

The city of *Milan* is supposed to be not less than six miles and two thirds in compass; like Rome it has many large gardens, and like Rome too it is well peopled in the parts that are built. In general the buildings are wretched; very large palaces, with roman or neapolitan windows, and execrable architecture, mostly of brick stuccoed, with granite architraves round the windows and doors. All the squares are poor and mean. The inhabitants are reputed to be about 140,000. The number of churches, monasteries, seminaries, penitential chapels, colleges, brotherhoods, and schools, is prodigious.

The *Duomo* or *Cathedral* is a gothic building of an extraordinary kind*, with a gre-

---

* Over the capital of each column is a fillet of eight niches.

cian front, by Pellegrini*; and next to S. Peter's is the largest church in Italy †. It was begun in the year 1386. The outside is loaded with sculpture ‡. The roof is exquisitely well wrought, and supported by 160 vast columns of white marble. The dome, by Brunelleschi, is in the middle of the cross, and immediately under it is an opening, surrounded with rails, to give light to the subterraneous chapel, where reposes the body of S Carlo Borromeo, in a case of crystal set in silver gilt.

This great church is built of brick, cased

---

* Designed by him, and executed by Bassi.

	Height.	Length.	Breadth.
† Duomo at Milan.	180	249½	148⅞
S Paul's at London.	174	256	127½
S. Peter's at Rome.	221½	321½	230½

Milanese Braccia.

‡ Above 260 statues larger than life, and upwards of 4400 within and without, when Addison reckons them to be 11,000, he must comprehend the figures in the relievos. The most celebrated of the statues is that of S. Bartholomew, by Marco ... io, called Agrati. It is within the church, near the sacristy.

L   without

without and within with marble. It consists of a nave and four ailes, but the transept has only two ailes. The outside is not near finished; many of the pinnacles are not erected; and great part of the west front remains still rough brickwork.

In the sacristy is a considerable treasure, with some good pieces of sculpture. From the top of the tower there is a very extensive view of the vast plain of Lombardy, and of the Alps.

Of the other churches, those most worthy of observation are:—

S. Alessandro, belonging to the Barnabites; the paintings are indifferent; but the high altar, pulpit, confessionals, &c. are covered with a profusion of lapis lazuli, agate, jasper, and other hard stones.

S. Ambrogio is remarkable for its antiquity. The high altar, supported by four porphyry columns, is rich in precious stones.

S. Antonio, a church of the Theatins. Virgin and Christ bruising the head of the serpent. Annunciation, by G. C. Procaccino. Virgin and child, S. Paul and S. Catherine by Bernardino Campi. S. Andrea Avellino dying. Francesco del Cayro.

S. Fd

S. Fedele is a handsome church by Pellegrini.

S. Francesco. Virgin and two angels, by Leonardo da Vinci. Two upright pictures with whole figures and architecture, by Bart. Bramantino of Milan.

S. Giovanni in Conca. A very ancient church, in which is the monument of Barnabo Visconti, with an equestrian statue of him.

S. Lorenzo, built by Martino Bassi. It is an octagon, and in a singular style of architecture.

The portico of this church is the only monument of antiquity remaining at Milan. It consists of sixteen fine fluted columns of the corinthian order: the proportions show that they are of a good age. They are of marble found near the lake of Como; and are generally thought to have been a temple or public bath dedicated to Hercules.

S. Marco. S. Ambrose baptizing S. Augustin, by Cerano! Dispute between S. Ambrose and S. Augustin, by Camillo Procaccino.

Madonna della Scala. Dead Christ, &c. by Procaccino.

S. Maria presso san Celso. an old heavy gothic, modernized; the front said to be by Bramante. Statues of Adam and Eve, on each side the great door, said to be by Artaldo di Lorenzi, probably Astoldi Lorenzi. Over the door, two Sibyls, by Annib. Fontana.

Paintings in the church: Virgin blessing Christ, Carlo Procaccino. Assumption, Cam. Procaccino. Virgin, child, and S. Jerom, Paris Bordone. Martyrdom of S. Narno and S. Celso, by G. C. Procaccino. The Resurrection, by Campi. S. Renato, by Camillo Procaccino. Assumption, by Carlo Procaccino. Baptism of Christ, by Gaudentio di Ferrara. Conversion of S. Paul, by Alexander Morettus, commonly called Alessandro Bonvicino. Dead Christ with the virgin, &c. by G. C. Procaccino. Martyrdom of S. Catherine, by Cerano.

In the sacristy: Elisabeth with S. John and S. Ann, by Leonardo da Vinci: and a holy family, with S. John, by Raffaelle.

S. Maria delle grazie. A chapel painted by Gaudentio di Ferrara. S. Paul, by the same. Virgin, child, and two portraits, by Leonardo da Vinci. Christ crowned with thorns, Tiziano.

In the refectory of the convent—the last supper, in fresco, one of the most famous works of Leonardo da Vinci, but probably repainted.

S. Maria della Vittoria.

The assumption, at the high altar, with thirteen figures large as life, by Salvator Rosa! S. Peter delivered out of prison by the angel, Domenichino. S. Carlo Borromeo giving the sacrament to persons infected with the pestilence; by Giacinto Brandi. Two landscapes, by Gaspar Poussin, one representing S. John in the wilderness; the saint is by Francesco Mola.

Santa Marta, a nunnery. The statue of Gaston de Foix, with the remains of his monument, by Agostino Busti.

La Passione. Dead Christ. Bern. Luino. Christ holding his cross; the battle of Constantine; and the finding of the cross, by the same: under the other.

The last supper, by Gaudentio di Ferrara.

In the Refectory—Abraham and Melchisedeck, a large picture, by Paolo Lomazzo. Daniel in the lion's den; by Joseph. Vermilius.

San Vittore, a church of the Oliverans. S. Bernardo

Bernardo Tolomei visiting the sick of the plague, by Pompeio Battoni. S. Antony with the body of S. Paul the hermit, by Dan. Crespi, called Cerano. Procession of Pope and bishops to the castle of S. Angelo, Camillo Procaccino. Two other pictures by him. Destruction of Pharaoh and his host in the red sea, by the same.

In the gallery of the Archbishop's palace are some good pictures: as—

The Virgin and child with a lamb. Leonardo da Vinci.

David with the head of Goliath; and Judith cutting off the head of Holofernes. Guercino.

Christ with the woman taken in adultery, by Marazone. Cochin says, Tintoretto, and De La Lande, Palma vecchio.

The Holy Family. Pompeio Battoni.
Prodigal returning. Ditto.

Besides these, Cochin has—
Adoration of the Magi. Tiziano. De La Lande says, Marazone.

A picture by Giorgione.—Moses saved from the water. *De La Lande.*

A picture by three different painters. S. Rusiena ready to have her head cut off: G. C. Procaccino. S. Secunda, with her head cut

cut off: Cerano—and a gentleman with a black: Marazone.

A Magdalene, with an angel—and a holy family: both by Cerano.

A little S. John, by Guido.

In the Archbishop's apartments, several pictures by Giov. Paolo Pannini and Canaletti.

De La Lande adds:

S. Sebastian, by Caravaggio.

Marriage of S. Catherine: by Procaccino.

A drawing by Michelangelo; and two by Leonardo da Vinci.

The *Ambrosian Library*, founded by Cardinal Frederic Borromeo, archbishop of Milan, and nephew of S. Charles, is perhaps the largest and most valuable foundation that any private person ever planned and executed, in favour of the arts and sciences, since the restoration of learning. The entrance is by a room 60 feet long, 24 wide, and 36 high, which is filled with books, to the number of thirty-five or forty thousand; exclusive of the manuscripts, which amount to fourteen or fifteen thousand volumes. This is open every day for public use, during two hours, both morning and afternoon. Hence by a portico, surrounding a small court, you come to the rooms of the academy of painting and sculpture: the first full of performances of the greatest painters; the second furnished with casts of the best antique statues, &c. There is also a cabinet of natural history, antiquities, medals, &c.: and behind these buildings is a botanic garden belonging to the univerfity.

Besides the plaster casts of the antique statues, and some of the best of Michelangelo's, are three models in alto-relievo for the tomb of Gaston de Foix.

Descent from the cross, small basso-relievo in wood—and the burial of Christ: both by Baccio Bandinelli.

Bust of Guido's wife.

Paintings and Drawings.

The school of Athens, black chalk: by Raffaelle.

Holy family, ditto, by Baroccio.

S. Peter consecrating S. Ciro. ditto, by Ant. Busca.

Burial of Christ. Ditto. Camillo Procaccino.

Christ on the cross. Pietro da Cortona.

Sixteen

Sixteen drawings executed in windows of the cathedral. Pellegrino Tibaldi.

Miracle of the loaves and fishes, by Ant. Busca.

Three drawings of boys. Carlo Cignani.

Two upright drawings, single figures. Campi.

Second room.

S. Hubert or Eustachius. S. John Baptist's head in a charger. Christ, a head. Mater dolorosa. Eleven small uprights of the life of Christ, one of S. Benedict: all these by Albert Durer.

Virgin, child, &c. and Virgin and child its companion: by Lucas van Leyden.

Christ bearing his cross. David with the head of Goliath on glass, in brown; both by Lucas.

S. Mutius in a landscape; said to be by Paul Brill; the figure by De Vos.

Seven other landscapes, by Paul Brill.

Four elements, by J. Brughel.

Daniel in the lion's den.

S. Paul the first hermit in a landscape.

S. Antony. Destruction of Sodom and Gomorrha.

A winter snow landscape, with a view of Antwerp. Landscape with a hermit.

Landscape with birds. Hell. Landscape with a hermit, the figure by De Vos. Apostles waking Christ in the storm. Flora, &c.

A rocky landscape, with a small figure of a hermit. Landscape with water and ducks. These six, and the six former ones, each in one frame. Virgin and child in a garland of flowers. A glory of boy angels. Garland of flowers, round a virgin and child, by Rubens. A pot of flowers. A glass of flowers, smaller. 1608. Winter piece, and a procession of capuchins, very small, figures not a quarter of an inch high. A storm at sea, its companion. Christ bearing his cross, and the crucifixion; both very small, in one frame with two small heads, by another hand.—All these by Brueghel.

Inside of a church, by Steenwyck.

Virgin and child, with monks and saints by Andrea Mantegna.

Head of Pope Paul III. by Michelangelo.

John Baptist, half figure, less than life.

Head of Christ.

Beatrice dutchess of Milan, wife of Louis

Head of a duke of Milan; young, in a red cap.

Old man, with a long dark beard.

These by Leonardo da Vinci.

Copy of Leonardo's famous last supper, by Giov. Battista Bianchi.

Holy family, Elisabeth and S. John, figures to the knee. Magdalene, head and hands, large as life. S. John Baptist, a boy, with a lamb; head and hands, small. These by Bernardino Luino.

A very fine portrait of a man. Head of a boy, small: both by Andrea del Sarto.

Christ washing the apostles' feet; by Perino del Vaga.

Head of a young man. Bramantino of Milan.

Head of a boy, a round picture, by Giorgione.

Burial of Christ. Adoration of the Magi. Holy family, with S. Catherine, half figures. Another, smaller. Portrait of a general of the Medici family. Portrait of himself with a long beard, near as large as life. S. Jerom, half figure. Ecce homo, half figure, less than life. A night landscape.—All by Tiziano.

Holy family, by old Palma.

Christ with a globe, half figure, large as life. Virgin, Christ, and Elisabeth, half figures,

figures, large as life. Adoration of the shepherds: all by Palma.

The transfiguration, Paolo Lomazzo.

Ecce homo, half figure, by Corregio.

Magdalene, half figure, said to be Corregio.

Virgin and child, whole figures, sitting under a tree. Corregio.

Virgin and child, whole figures. Adoration of the Magi; both by Schidone.

An old man, by one of the Caraccis.

A basket of fruit, by Caravaggio.

Nativity and burial of Christ, and S. John preaching; small pictures, by Baroccio.

Head of the virgin, by Scipione Gaetano. Lucretia. Magdalene. Head of a man. Temptation of S. Antony. All by Dan. Crespi, called Cerano.

Much has been said of twelve volumes in folio of drawings, by Leonardo da Vinci, as manifesting his accurate knowledge in anatomy, optics, geometry, architecture, sculpture, and mechanics. And we are told, that for his mechanical designs in 399 leaves, containing 1750 original drawings, our king James I. commissioned the earl of Arundel to offer 3000 pistoles to Galeazzo Arconati; but that he rather chose to make a present of
th

the volume, to the Ambrosian college. These drawings however were probably studies, done when he was very young, and by no means merit the reputation they have acquired.

The *Seminario*, founded by S. Charles, is a handsome building, with a double row of porticos round a square court: the lower order doric, and the upper ionic.

The *Swiss College* is another of S. Charles Borromeo's establishments. This has two courts, with double porticos. The architect is Pellegrino Pellegrini.

The *College of the Jesuits*, called *Brera*, is large and handsome; the staircase is particularly spoken of. Here is a library, a cabinet of medals, and an observatory, planned by Boscovich.

The *Hospital* is large and grand, the great court is fine, surrounded like the others with double arcades, forming two galleries one over the other, ionic and composite. Here are 1200 beds for the sick, and 4000 foundlings are brought up. The whole was built at the expence of a merchant named *Cottoni*.

The *Lazaretto*, a large quadrangle with cloisters round it, supported by clumsy pillars,

lars, probably taken from some ancient building.

Il Foponè, or the cemitery to the great hospital, at a considerable distance from it, is a space of ground almost circular, surrounded by a cloister, and in the middle a church. The cloister is vaulted for burying. It was all built by S. Annone, a silk merchant of the city.

The *Prisons* are magnificent, and the portal in a good style of architecture.

The Palace of the Archduke is elegantly fitted up and furnished; the ball-room is one of the finest in Europe.

Good pictures are to be found in several of the palaces. The marquis di Peralta has many, particularly by John Stommer, a German.

Milan stands in the middle of a plain, without any natural defence. Though an inland city, it is possessed of the chief advantages that can promote commerce or agriculture, in its canals from the Tesin and Adda, leading to the Po. It is one of the most agreeable cities in Italy to reside at, on account of the excellent society which is to be found there.

In the neighbourhood are some beautiful country houses: as *Castellazzo*, where there is a fine a fine statue of Pompey. *Lainate*, belonging to the marquis Lita, &c.

At *Casa Simonetta* is an echo which will repeat the human voice forty times, and the report of a pistol 56 or 60 times. The Milanese are fond of rural sports, and pass part of the summer, and the whole autumn, in the country. Monte di Brianza, on which many of their country-houses are situated, is delightful for the variety of landscapes, and for being well watered *.

Every part indeed of the state of Milan, except to the northward, which is mountainous, bears testimony to the beneficial effects of irrigation. There are generally five crops of hay every season, in the neighbourhood of Milan, and in the province of Lodi, where the meadows are watered once a week, during the summer, if necessary.

This dutchy is 120 miles in length, and 100 in breadth. The soil is in general fertile, and the climate moderate and healthful. Its many lakes abound in fish. Their commodities are grain, cattle, cheese, cloth, silk, linen, stockings, gloves, handkerchiefs, rib-

* See Symonds, in Young's annals, v. 3.

bands,

bands, artificial flowers, steel, crystal, agates, jewels, gold and silver lace and embroidery, tinsel and thread lace, glass and pottery. They are also carriers of goods for Swisserland, France, Germany, and Italy, both on mules and by water.

The Carnival continues till the sunday after ash-wednesday; during that time there is a serious opera, every evening, except friday. The new Theatre, built instead of that which was burnt down some few years since, is handsome and commodious. In winter, people of fashion parade in their coaches on the esplanade between the town and the citadel, and in summer upon the ramparts.

Whilst you are at Milan, you will probably make an excursion to the *Lago maggiore* and the Borromean islands. Of these *Isola bella* is small and pretty; it has a magnificent palace, with four fronts, not half finished; few palaces have better rooms, or worse executed, both within and without: in the garden is terrace upon terrace, with orange, lemon, and citron trees; shrubs, flowers, and statues; grottos paved with mosaic, and hanging over the lake. *Isola madre* is larger, irregular, and more rural. The one is dressed, the other wild. Thus they set off each other
mutually

mutually, and conspire to adorn this superb basin, which is 65 italian miles long, and from 6 to 9 or 10 broad.

Returning by Varese, you may visit Como, whose lake is the pleasantest of all those which are at the foot of the Alps. There are large plantations of *agrumi* on the borders of it, particularly in the sweet environs of Tremenzina, whither many of the noble Milanese retire during the heats of summer.

If you leave Genoa to the end of your tour, and go directly from Turin to Milan, you pass by Vercelli and Novara. In this route you have frequently rivers to pass, and pay a paul for ferrying over your carriage; these ferries are a great impediment in travelling; but the roads are good, even, and well planted.

At Vercelli, in the treasure of the cathedral, is a manuscript in latin, of S. Mark's gospel, which they pretend to be in the hand writing of the evangelist himself; and in the church of S. Maria maggiore, a fine marble pavement, representing the history of Judith. In quitting Vercelli you enter the state of Milan.

SECTION

SECTION V.

From Milan to Bologna, and account of that place.

ON leaving Milan, you have your choice either to go to Venice or Bologna. If you take the former route, you will pass by Bergamo, Brescia, Verona, Vicenza, and Padua. But I shall suppose you to take the route of Bologna, because I shall carry you to Venice hereafter.

In this journey you will go through Lodi, Piacenza, Parma, Reggio, and Modena.

LODI is a small town, walled round, with a few large, good palaces, and a tolerably pretty square with porticos; upon the whole neatly built, and containing about 14,000 inhabitants. The most remarkable building is an octagon church, called *Incoronata* of which Bramante was the architect; painted partly in fresco, partly in oil, by Callisto, scholar of Tiziano.

The whole *Lodesan* can be irrigated by means of canals. The number of cows kept in this little province is about 30,000, and the inhabitants receive commonly 70,000 pounds a year for cheese exported. Some of their cheeses weigh above 500 pounds, and are the best of what is called Parmesan. A great deal however is also made in the province of Pavia, and in some parts of the Milanese.

From Lodi there is a road by Cremona and Mantua to Bologna; but the other by Piacenza and Parma is the pleasantest, and the most frequented. From Lodi also there is a road to Venice, by the same towns and Verona. But you are probably impatient to be at Rome: since however Cremona is only ten leagues from Lodi, and six from Piacenza, you may perhaps be induced to visit it, from one of those two places.

CREMONA is on the north side of the Po, and a quarter of a mile from it: from the river there is a canal, which runs through the city, fills the ditches, and forms a communication with the Oglio. It is about five miles round, with some wide streets, and small squares; some considerable palaces, but almost all gothic, of a bad kind. It is remarkable for its towers; all of them however have the appearance of overgrown chimnies,

nies, except one, which is very high. In the cathedral, which is very large, and tolerably handsome, is a good picture of the crucifixion, by Pordenone. There are a few handsome churches and convents; and no less than twenty-two nunneries. The inhabitants are about 20,000.

Cremona belonged formerly to the Venetians; but now makes part of the dutchy of Milan. The castle and fortifications are ruinous.

PIACENZA is about 200 yards from the Po, a town of great note and antiquity, but of late much decayed and depopulated. It has no architecture, long ugly streets, and paltry squares.

Most of the churches are embellished with paintings of the Bologna school, the Caracci and their disciples.

Duomo or Cathedral· at the high altar

Sick man in bed, by Camillo Procaccino.

Virgin and angels, large, above it; by the same.

Angels, over that; by Lodovico Caracci

Burial of a saint; tomb after his assumption; and two prophets, single figures, by Lod. Carracci.

The choir and cupola are painted by Guercino.

Death of S. Alexis, by Lanfranco.

Hermit, single whole figure, by the same.

La Madonna della Campagna.

The Nativity. Adoration of the Magi. S. Catherine disputing with the doctors. All by Pordenone.

S. Francis on his knees before the virgin, Christ in the clouds: by Camillo Procaccino.

S. Sebastian and S. Roch, whole figures? said to be by him.

Marriage of S. Catherine. S. Peter and S. Paul. Three boys. All by Pordenone.

S. Augustin and boy Angels, by the same.

S. George and the dragon. Cam. Procaccino. Cochin mentions the ruin of a fine fresco by Parmegiano, on the left at entering.

S. *Sisto.* The virgin, child, saints, &c. after Raffaelle: the original is in the gallery at Dresden; and the king of Poland is said to have given 20,000 roman crowns (near 5000l. sterling) for it in the year 1753.

S. *Agostino* is built by Vignola.

The

The *Palazzo Publico*, or town-hall, on the Piazza, is a curious building.

In the same square are the equestrian statues in bronze of Alessandro I. and his son Ranuccio Farnese; either by Giovanni Bologna, or his pupil Moca.

The *Ducal Palace* is by Vignola: it is of brick, and only a third of it finished. The Theatre adjoins to it.

PARMA.

Parma is about four miles in circuit, and contains 37,000 inhabitants*. It is walled, but the fortifications are in a ruinous condition. You enter by a broad street, which conducts you over the bridge, and through the square, to the end of the town; this is tolerably handsome for its breadth; but bad as to its buildings, and notwithstanding what has been done of late years, it is a poor-built town. No church, palace, or convent, that is worth seeing, and no appearance of a court

* De La Lande says 30,000, Richard 45,000, others 60,000, but they exaggerate greatly, or rather tell us what the population was, than what it now is.

or capital: brick stuccoed in the new houses, and sometimes so in pannels as to look like wood. The river Parma has a vast bed, and little water; a wooden bridge, and two stone ones over it, none of which are handsome.

The *Cathedral* is a curious, heavy, dark, gothic building. The famous painting by Corregio in the dome, is much damaged.

Annunziata. S. Sebastian, a decayed fresco, by Corregio. Virgin and child, S. Jerom and S. Bernard, by Parmegiano.

I Cappucini. S. Francis receiving the marks, by Sisto Badalocchio. Christ on the cross, S. Catherine, and S. Francis, by Guercino.

S. Giovanni Evangelista. The famous cupola, by Corregio.

Transfiguration, by Parmegiano.

Dead Christ, Magdalen, &c. Corregio.

Martyrdom of S. Eulalia, and S. Benedict companion, by the same.

Holy Family, by Jerom Mazzuolo.

Adoration of the shepherds. Giac. Fran-

S John, half figure, fresco. Corregio.

S. Roch. Virgin and child, two saints and angels. Giuseppe Crespi

Christ

Christ in the clouds, S. Sebastian and S. Roch below. Paolo Veronese.

S. Sepulcro. Repose of the holy family, by Corregio!

Virgin and child, S. John and two angels, by Parmegiano.

Steccata. Marriage of the virgin, by Giulio Cesare Procaccino.

Flagellation of Christ, by Lionello Spada.

Sibyl, by Jerom Mazzuolo.

Three Sibyls, and a Moses, by Parmegiano.

S. George and the dragon, by Franceschini.

S. John Baptist, by Spada.

The monument of Ottavio Farnese.

The *Ducal Palace* is now in great part pulled down. The Farnesian collection of pictures, gems, &c. was removed to Naples when the king of Spain went to take possession of it, and is still in confusion there, Capo di monte.

In the Academy is a fine antique statue of a woman. A young Nero with the bulla.

Virgin and child, Magdalen, S. Jerom, and two angels. 1518. Corregio.

Entombing of Christ. Schidone.

Ador

Adoration of the magi. Parmegiano. Brought from the Carthusians.

The Theatre is all of wood, and in general finely imagined; it has not the defect of Palladio's, where a part of the spectators cannot see: here also every body can hear, a low voice being audible from one end to the other, and a loud one making no echo. It will hold commodiously 9000 spectators*, but has not been used since the death of the last duke. There is another theatre for the Opera.

The dutchies of Parma and Piacenza have undergone the same revolutions, and are now in the Spanish family, by their marrying the heiress of Farnese. Their extent is 50 english miles from east to west, and 44 from north to south. The soil is fertile; the pastures and cattle fine; salt-works and minerals abound, and there are mines of copper and iron in the Apennines. Castello vecchio, on the Taro, which gave name to

---

* De la Lande says 12,000, Wright 14,000, I have been assured by some Italians that it will not be above 4000, but I believe the number given in the text.

the party of the Guelphs, is in this territory.

The road from Parma to Modena is along the ancient Emilian way.

The city of REGGIO has about 17,000 inhabitants.

Duomo or *Cathedral*. Virgin and child in the clouds, angels and saints; by Ann. Carracci.

La Madonna della Giarra. Christ on the cross, Magdalene and S. John, by Guercino. S. Francis on his knees, to Christ and the virgin in the clouds, by Spada.

Adoration of the Magi, by old Palma.

La Capella della morte. Descent into hell by Capuccino del Castel Franco.

Christ appearing in the garden. Luc. Masari.

Christ seized in the garden. Sisto Pallocchio.

Burial of Christ; by the same.

Resurrection of Christ, by Bononi Ferrerese.

Finding of the cross. by Cav. Guidotti

The Crucifixion, by Aleffandro Tiarini.

Dead Christ, by Franc. Vellani Modenese.

The baptism of Christ, by Guercino.

A Saint, by Carlo Barbieri

The Annunciation, by Guercino; in two pieces over an arch.

Virgin and child, by Francesco Vellani.

The flagellation, by Giacomo Palma

There is a Theatre; and an Opera during the Fair.

The famous poet Ariosto was born here in ——.

Between Reggio and Modena, the road passes within a league of Correggio, which gave birth and name to the great painter.

MODENA.

Modena, a city of 23,000 inhabitants, has been really improved of late. small, but neat and regular, arcades which are really noble, to walk under, in the chief streets. the churches for the most part in a very bad state, as well as the ducal palace, which for some time is not finished. the library is a very handsome room, well furnished with useful, though not with very curious books, and a very comfortable public room to study in.

Of the fine collection of pictures formerly in this palace, one hundred of the best were sold by Rossi, for Augustus King of Poland

and Elector of Saxony, who paid 50,000 pounds, which was very cheap, since they were the choicest pictures in Italy.

There are some pictures yet remaining.

The *Cathedral* is a heavy, dark, gothic building; with the presentation of Christ in the temple, a capital picture, by Guido.

There is a *Theatre*, in which the steps rise one above another, as in the ancient amphitheatres; it is adorned with columns, and the proscenium, tribunes, &c. are well decorated. They have also another Theatre, which is nothing extraordinary.

The *secchia*, or bucket, immortalized by the poem of Tassoni, who was born here, was a trophy of an advantage gained by the Modenese over the Bolognese, within the very walls of Bologna, about the middle of the tenth century.

The dukedom of Modena is a fertile plain, watered by the Po, Panaro, Secchia, and Lenza; 56 miles in extent from north to south, and from east to west between 2 and 56.

The inhabitants of Modena are noted for wearing masks and veils. The women wear the *zendado*, which is a piece of black silk covering the head, falling down and over before, and finally tied behind the waist. What little trade remains is from their fairs, and their connection with those of Bologna, Siniglia, and Alessandria.

BOLOGNA.

Bologna is a large, rich, and populous city, two miles long, about one broad, and five miles in circuit, with fifty or sixty thousand inhabitants*. It is surrounded only by a wall, without bastions, ditch, or citadel. There are twelve gates, and the streets have porticos or open arcades, commodious to walk in but very irregular. They have very little good architecture or sculpture in Bologna; but next to Rome it boasts the most capital paintings in the world: the Caraccis and their scholars having carried this art to the summit of perfection.

The number of Churches is upwards of two hundred, some of them well built, and richly decorated, but few without good pictures. Fortunately the air and situation of

* Others say seventy, eighty, and even ninety thousand, the numbers I have given are from M. Dutens.

this city is favourable to the preservation of them. It has none of the saline moisture of Venice, nor the penetrating fogs of Rome.

The *Cathedral*, dedicated to S. Peter, has been entirely rebuilt in the modern style, from designs of Torregiani, by funds given or secured by Pope Benedict XIV. In the choir is the Annunciation, in fresco, the last work of Lodovico Carracci. In the cupola, S. Peter kneeling to the Virgin, and condoling with her on the death of Christ. Lodov. Carracci *.

After this, the principal churches are—
S. Agnese. S. Antonio.
S. Bartolomeo di Porta.
S. Bartolomeo di Reno.
S. Bernardo.
Le Cappucine. I Cappucini.
La Certosa. Corpus Domini.
S. Cristina. S. Domenico.
S. S. Fabiano e Sebastiano.
S. Francesco.
Gesu e Maria.

* I have not remarked the pictures in the other churches, since they are to be found in Zanotti of Bologna. These are marked with

S. Gregorio

Duomo maggiore.
S. Giorgio.
S. Giovanni Batista.
S. Giovanni in monte, in which is the famous S. Cecilia, by Raffaele.
S. Gregorio. S. Leonardo.
Madonna di Galiera.
Madonna di S. Luca.
Madonna di strada maggiore.
S. Maria nuova.
S. Margherita.
S. Martino maggiore.
Mendicanti di dentro.
S. Michele in bosco.
S. Niccolò di S. Felice.
S. Paolo. S. Petronio.
S. Pietro Martire.
S. Salvatore.
I Servi.
S. Tommaso del mercato.
S. Tommaso di strada maggiore.
S. S. Vitale ed Agricola.

Bologna has been famous for cultivating the sciences, ever since the restoration of learning. Besides the ancient University, or Scuole, here is an Academy, called *Instituto*, or the arts and sciences. It contains an ample library, with the manuscript collections of Marsigli the founder; of Aldrovandi the naturalist, in 187 large folio volumes; of Colpi; of Pope Benedict XIV. &c.; some oriental manuscripts; and a collection of prints and drawings *. This library is open to the public every morning, except Wednesday. Here are also several rooms for the public meetings of the Institute, and the academy of sciences which is a part of it. In the vestibule are statues of Benedict XIV. and Hercules: the walls are covered with inscriptions, bas-reliefs, &c. Here is a room for antiques, medals, and casts of the most celebrated statues, &c. at Rome and Florence. Another for turning instruments. A third for dioptrics. A fourth for chemistry. A fifth for military machines, arms, &c. Three rooms are assigned to experimental philosophy and the physical apparatus. In the anti-room is the portrait of Benedict XIV. executed in mosaic at Rome. The apartment for natural history consists of six rooms, very well furnished. A room for geography and the marine, has maps, charts, instruments, books, and models of vessels.

* Richard says there are 50,000 volumes in it, De La Lande gives it 115,000.

The

The Anatomy room is amply furnished with figures of the human body and its parts finely executed in wax by Ercole Lelli and his wife Anna Manfolini. The Institute includes the Clementine, or academy of drawing and painting; in which they design from the human figure, as well as from models.

The Academy of sciences and belles lettres, consisting of twenty-four members, meet here every thursday; and from these the professors of chemistry, military architecture, physics, natural history, geography, and astronomy, are taken, who give public lectures in the Institute.

The building is a large palace, purchased by the senate in 1714, at the instance of general count Marsigli, who originally furnished the apartments, under the protection of Pope Clement XI. But the Institute owes much to the munificence of Benedict XIV. He furnished the Observatory with instruments; employed Ercole Lelli to make the anatomical preparations in wax; and gave the models of statues, &c. from the antique. He also left by will his private library and manuscripts.

The architects of this palace were Pellegrino Tibaldi and his son Domenico. Pellegrino

grino also painted the room where the Academicians meet, and some others, on the ground floor. Niccolo dell' Abate painted one of the rooms now used for the museum. The chapel is painted by Vittorio Bigari and Stefano Orlandi; and the annunciation is by Marc' Antonio Franceschini.

The Botanic garden is a dependance upon the Institute.

With such encouragements and opportunities, it is no wonder that Bologna has always men of learning.

It furnishes also musicians and singers for many of the Italian theatres. The principal Theatre here was built on the ruins of the Bentivoglio palace in 1760, by Bibiena. It is elegant, and has five rows of boxes, twelve or thirteen on a side.

Palazzo Publico, or the town-hall, is an ancient building of brick, wherein the legate, vice-legate, gonfaloniere, and senators, inhabit; and in which are the courts of justice.

The principal palaces of the nobility are the Aldrovandi, Bovi, Magnani, Ranuzzi, Sampieri, Tanari, Zambeccari. In all these there are fine collections of pictures; especially in the Sampieri, where is the famous S. Peter and S. Paul, by Guido, and several

other

other admirable pieces, in the highest preservation. The Caprara palace is handsomely furnished; and the gallery is ornamented with turkish spoils, the share of marshal Caprara, at the raising of the siege of Vienna by Sobieski, in 1683. In the Malvezzi palace is a collection of the original masters of the Bolognese school. Many of the other palaces have been most cruelly pillaged of their best ornaments.

The *Asinelli* tower built in 1109, is 327 english feet and a quarter in height: De La Lande says it is three feet and an half out of the perpendicular. The *Garisinda* tower, which was built the year following, is only 153 feet in height, or according to M. Dutens, no more than 140; but this is eight feet, eight or nine inches out of the perpendicular. These brick towers were common in Lombardy and Tuscany; being domestic citadels, or watch-towers, which in times of anarchy were equally necessary to peaceable and turbulent citizens.

The Bolognese put themselves voluntarily under the protection of the Pope, in the year 1506, on condition of being governed by their senate; of nominating an auditor of the *Rota*; and having an ambassador at Rome.

Rome. A cardinal legate constantly resides here, and has for his guards a company of Swifs halberdiers, and another of light horse.

Citizens wear a cloak when they walk abroad: women wear a kind of close gown buttoned, with sleeves down to their wrists; when they go out they cover themselves with the *zendado*.

The manufactures are damasks, sattins, taffaties, velvets, crapes, gauzes, and paper. The goldsmiths work curiously in gold ornaments, and make a kind of gold crape. They export hemp, flax, wax, and honey. Their macaroni, tobacco, and snuff, are highly esteemed; and their breed of lap-dogs has been long and generally known. The markets are plentifully supplied with provisions, good in their kind: hog-meat is particularly excellent; and their hams and sausages are generally in repute. They also excell in soap, perfumes, and artificial flowers. They have abundance of walnuts; and their quinces, grapes, melons, and truffles, are remarkably fine.

The Bononian stone, which by a chemical process becomes phosphorescent, is a sort of *gypsum* found at *monte Paterno*, three miles from Bologna.

The

The territory is bounded to the south by the Apennines, to the east by the Romagna or the legation of Ravenna, to the north by the Ferrarese, and to the west by the Modenese.

SECTION VI.

From Bologna to Rome.

YOU will be determined by particular circumstances, and the arrangement you have made, to go from Bologna to Rome, by the way of Florence or Ancona. The only difference will be, that if you go by the one, you will return by the other. I shall suppose you to take the route of Ancona.

The road from Bologna is flat, straight, and good.

Near three miles from Cesena you pass the Pisatello, commonly supposed to be the Rubicon: but it is so small, that you may pass it without observing it.

Imola, Faenza, Forli, and Cesena, have nothing in them to detain you; except that at *Forli* the cupola of the cathedral is

painted

painted by Cignani; and at *Cesena* there is a curious library belonging to the minor conventuals, containing manuscripts collected by the last of the Malatesta family, before the invention of printing.

Forli is the only one of them whose inhabitants appear to have any industry: their chief employment is in wax, linen, and umbrellas. *Faenza*, as if satisfied with the honour of having given the french name (*fayence*) to earthen ware, makes at present very little, and that very bad.

These towns of the *Romagna* are well built. Some of the churches have good paintings; and there are also some palaces with courts and fountains. Romagna even boasts a school of painting, with Baroccio at its head.

You will enter *Rimini* over the bridge of S. Giuliano, all built of blocks of the finest white marble, in the time of Augustus and Tiberius.

At the Capuchins are remains of the amphitheatre of Publius Sempronius; and in the market-place a pedestal, which they pretend to be the *suggestum* of Julius Cæsar. At the oratory of S. Jerom is a picture of the saint writing, and an angel blowing the trumpet,

trumpet, by Guercino: and at the church of S. Giuliano, the martyrdom of that saint, by Paolo Veronese. Count Gambalonga's library is kept in good order, and the building is elegant.

On quitting the town you will pass under a triumphal arch of Augustus.

From hence you may make an excursion to *Ravenna*, which is distant only four posts. It was the seat of empire under Theodoric; and afterwards was governed by Exarchs, under the greek emperors, from whom it was conquered by the Lombards. It afterwards came into the hands of the Venetians; and was by them finally ceded to the Pope in 1529.

This city is thinly inhabited, the streets are wide, straight, and regular; most of the sacred edifices are stately remains of its ancient splendor. It has neither trade nor manufactures; but many idle gentry, and twenty-four convents; the inhabitants are scarcely 15,000.

Ravenna is famous for its mosaics, antique marbles, sarcophagi, and some buildings of the lower ages: there are also some good pictures in the churches, of the Bologna school, but hurt by the damp.

The

The *Cathedral* is good, and modernized. The cupola of the Aldobrandini chapel is painted in fresco by Guido; and there is also a picture in it by him of the Israelites gathering manna. The Baptistery is in its old state; an octangular fabric, with eight large arches at bottom, and over each three gothic ones: the front is a vast basin of white grecian marble.

In the church of *S. Apollinare*, belonging to the Camaldules, in the suburb, is a double row of columns of grecian marble, twelve in each row, brought from Constantinople: the altar is enriched with verd-antique, porphyry and oriental alabaster, and the tribuna is supported by four fine columns of *nero e bianco*. The cieling is one of the most perfect mosaic now remaining; the figures hard and dry but with strong expression and colours.

S. Vitale, a church of the Benedictines, is a very ancient fabric. It is an octagon; supported by fine columns of greek marble, and on a singular plan: the columns have their bases within the ground. The pavement is very beautiful; some of the bas-reliefs, and the mosaics in the choir are extremely curious. In the sacristy is a picture of the martyrdom of the saint by Baroccio.

Th

The church of *S. John the evangelift*, built by *Placidia*, has been modernized; yet the old cipolline columns, twenty-four in number, are remaining; there is also much porphyry and verd-antique in repairing it they found the old mofaic pavement of the fourth or fifth century, now all preferved in a chapel; it is figures and animals.

S. Maria del porto. The martyrdom of S. Mark by old Palma.

S. Romualdo, belonging to the Camaldules. The annunciation by Guido.

A faint, with an angel driving the devil from him; by Guercino.

S. Nicholas, with two children at his feet; by Carlo Cignani.

In the refectory; the entombing of Chrift, by Vafari.

In the *fquare* are two lofty granite pillars, a marble ftatue of Clement XII. by Pietro Bacci, and a bronze one of Alexander VII.

On a fountain before the Pope's palace, is an antique ftatue of Hercules, with a globe on his fhoulder, ferving for a fun-dial.

In the public ftreet, at one corner of the Francifcan convent, is the tomb of Dante.

Without the city, towards the ancient haven, ftands the tomb of Theodoric. It is a rotunda, divided into two stories, each serving for a chapel: the roof is one single piece of granite, four or five feet thick, and thirty-one feet two inches in diameter; forming a dome. On the middle of this, four columns supported the sarcophagus, a single block of porphyry, eight feet long, and four feet deep and broad. It had a bronze cover of most curious workmanship. This is gone, but the sarcophagus is fixed in the wall of the convent belonging to the *Zoccolanti*; where the ancient palace of Theodoric, within the city, is supposed to have stood. This tomb was once a stately sea mark; but is now near twelve miles from the sea, and yet the lower chapel is submerged at high water.

In the neighbourhood of Ravenna, is a large forest of pines, belonging entirely to the Benedictines, twelve miles in length, and three or four in breadth, called *Pigneta*, and furnishing *pigroli*, or kernels of the pine, for the deserts of a great part of Italy.

Hence also you may make an excursion to the little republic of *San Marino*. A mountain, and a few neighbouring hillocks scattered about the foot of it, form the whole circuit of their dominions. They have three castles, three convents, and five churches;
and

and reckon about 5000 souls. This republic has subsisted near 1400 years. All that are capable of bearing arms are exercised, and ready at a moment's call. The government is in a council of sixty, as it is called, though it consists only of forty members; but the *arengo*, or general council, is assembled in cases of extraordinary importance. The chief magistrates are two *Capitaneos* a Commissary, who is always a foreigner, is joined in commission with them, and is the judge in all civil and criminal matters.

The winter is very severe at San Marino; the snow laying on the ground six or seven months, to the depth of two feet or more.

Pesaro was dismembred by Pope Julius II. to make a fief for his own family, but devolved again to the holy see, on the extinction of it. The elegant court of Urbino used to spend the winter here, in palaces, of which little more than melancholy remains are now to be seen. It had a bad character anciently for the malignity of its air in summer; but the draining of the neighbouring marshes has long since removed it.

There are some good pictures here by Baroccio.

In the great square is the statue of Pope Urban VIII.

The antiquities of Pesaro have been engraved, with explanations, in folio, under the title of *Marmora Pisaurensia*, well printed here.

From the mountain of Pesaro the country is flat, and the road, by the side of the Adriatic all the way, very good, through well-built towns, and a cultivated country. Some of the scenes are uncommonly beautiful, and there is a succession of the most lovely green hills imaginable, with the prospect perpetually shifting. Severe weather however sets in the beginning of december, and lasts till the middle or latter end of february; and the snow often lies four months upon this coast.

The silk of the dutchy of Urbino, and the upper part of the Romagna, is bought up at Rimini and Pesaro, and trafficked raw with the English for mohairs, silks, cottons, &c.

At *Fano* are the remains of a triumphal arch of Constantine, and part of a building in a good style: there is also a theatre, and a library.

Half a league from Fano, the road crosses

the river Metro, anciently *Metaurus*, famous for the total defeat and death of Asdrubal.

At la Cattolica, between Rimini and Pesaro, you quitted the Romagna, and entered the dutchy of Urbino; which you quit between Fano and Sinigaglia, for the marc of Ancona.

Sinigaglia is a flourishing town, almoſt new built of white brick; has a little port, and ſome trade in corn, hemp, and ſilk. During the fair, which is in the laſt week of July, there is a conſiderable reſort of ſtrangers.

Ancona has a beautiful and convenient harbour; and being a free port, and the only conſiderable one which the Pope has in the Adriatic, there is a flouriſhing trade here. The chief exportation is of grain, wool, and ſilk. The town is built on the ſide of a hill, and extends now to the water's edge. The cathedral ſtands on the ſummit of the promontory, where was anciently a temple of Venus, and this was the original ſite of the place. Ancona appears well from the ſea, but is a moſt wretched town within, full of trade and ſtench: in the chief ſtreet there is room but for one carriage to paſs. The mole

mole is a very fine work, 2000 feet long, 100 feet broad, and 68 high from the water edge: it is adorned with an antique triumphal arch, of white marble, of good proportions, and well preserved, erected in honour of Trajan. There is also a modern arch, in honour of Pope Benedict XIV. by Vanvitelli, who built the mole, and finished the Lazaretto, which is a pentagon, and a work little inferior to the mole itself. This was built in the time of Clement XII., who first declared Ancona a free port.

Of paintings, in the church of S. Domenico, Christ on the cross, the virgin, S. John, and S. Domenico, said to be by Tiziano.

At S. Francesco della Scala, S. Francis, and another religious praying in the desert, by Porcini da Pesaro.—A virgin holding Jesus between two Franciscans, by Tiziano.

At S. Palatia, the saint of that name, with an angel, by Guercino.

From Ancona to Loretto the road is hilly and runs through a fine country, well cultivated and populous.

Loretto is on the top of a hill, near three miles from the sea, commanding a delightful and extensive prospect; and containing about 6000 inhabitants. It is but indifferently
bu lt

built; the principal street consists mostly of small shops for rosaries, crucifixes, madonnas, agnus deis, medals, little works in fillagree, small bells, broad figured ribbands, and such trifles.

The church was gothic, and however modernized, has no pretensions to beauty. The front is by Giacomo della Porta, and on one side of the court are double arcades, said to be finished by Bramante. Over the portal is a statue of the virgin by Lombardi; by whom also are the bas reliefs upon the bronze gates, the lower of which are almost effaced by the kisses of the pilgrims. Within the church are about twenty chapels, in which are pictures by Baroccio, Zucchero, &c. In the cupola are the four evangelists, by Pomerancia.

The holy house, or chapel of our Lady, stands in the middle of the church. It is an oblong room, 31 feet 9 inches in length, 13 feet 3 inches in breadth, and 18 feet 9 inches in height; incrusted with Carrara marble, of beautiful architecture, designed by Bramante; and ornamented with sculptures by Sansovino, San Gallo, Bandinelli, &c. representing the history of the blessed virgin. The walls of the holy house (as may easily be seen on the

the inside) are of brick, with some flat bits of stone intermixed. Towards the east end there is a separation made, by the grate-work of silver, this they call the sanctuary; and here stands the holy image of the virgin, in a nich of silver; made, as they pretend, of cedar of Lebanon, and carved by S. Luke: her dark complexion, as well as the glitter of her robe entirely covered with diamonds, bespeaks her an Indian Queen: she has a triple crown on her head, and holds the image of Christ, covered also with diamonds, in her left hand she carries a golden globe, and two fingers of her right are held up, as in the act of blessing. The other part of the house has an altar at the upper end, at the lower a window, through which the angel is supposed to have entered, at the Annunciation. The sanctuary is perfectly crouded with sixty two great lamps of gold and silver; one of the golden ones, which was presented by the republic of Venice, weighs thirty-seven pounds. There are also Angels waiting about the holy image, one of massive gold, and two of silver, and the walls are covered with plates of silver. The sacred bowl, out of which the holy family used to eat, is preserved here. As who enter the chapel armed are excommunicated. Poor wretches are continually crawling round it on their knees, and wear two deep grooves in the marble pavement*.

But the jewels of the holy house are nothing in comparison with the treasury; where the number, variety and richness of the vestments, lamps, candlesticks, goblets, crowns, crucifixes, images, cameos, pearls, gems of all kinds, &c. is prodigious. They are locked up in seventeen large presses, in a spacious room, the cieling whereof is painted in compartments by Pomerancia: the altar-piece is a crucifixion, by the same hand. Here also is a holy family, by Raffaelle; and the birth of the virgin; by Annibal Carracci.

If the treasure within the holy walls be surprising, the poverty without is no less so: such shoals of beggars, and so excessively importunate!

The country is delightful and well cultivated, washed by two rivers, and distributed into hills and vallies bounded by mountains,

* A pamphlet may be had here, giving an account of the treasures, and all the wonders of the *Santissima Casa.*

from Loretto to *Macerata*, which is pleasantly situated on a hill. It is the capital of the marc of Ancona, a bishop's see, and the residence of the governor or legate of the province. There are good crops of corn about it, and the fields are enclosed by flourishing hedges of white thorn, planted and preserved with great skill and attention.

At *Tolentino* you enter the Apennines. Hence to *Valcimarra* the country is almost covered with fine oaks. From Valcimaria it is a continued ascent to the narrow pass of *Sorravalle*, an impregnable post, separating the marc of Ancona from Umbria. From *Cafe nuove* to *Foligno* the ascent and descent are formidable. Before you go down the last hill to the town, a little out of the road, in the village of Palo, there is a curious stalactitic cavern, really worth seeing, but the key is kept at Foligno. This town is seated in a delicious vale, of a fertile soil, with immense pastures, watered by the Clitumnus. Here are some manufactures of paper, and a fair of great business *.

* See the country from Ancona to Foligno beautifully described by Dr Symonds, in Young's annals of agriculture, vol. V. p. 325, &c

In the church of a convent of Franciscan nuns, called *la Contessa*, is a picture by Raffaelle, of the virgin in glory holding the infant Jesus; and below, S. John Baptist and S. Francis on one side, S. Jerom and a Cardinal on the other. In the *Duomo*, a gothic building, is a statue of S. Feliciano in silver, by Le Gros; a baldacchino, or pavilion over the high altar, in imitation of that in S. Peter's at Rome; and the cupola is by Bramante.

The road from hence to *Spoleto* is good, through a delightful plain, laid out into beautiful enclosures, and watered by the pastoral streams of the Clitumnus, which takes its rise in three or four rivulets, issuing from a rock near the highway. Several towns appear on rising grounds, as *Assiz*; and a little town named *Trevi*, that produces the prettiest effect imaginable. Just before you come to the post of *le Vene*, is a little antique temple, now christianized, called the temple of Clitumnus.

At *Spoleto*, the capital of Umbria, are some remains of antiquity: as a roman building, called a temple of concord, at the church of the crucifix: there are three doors which seem to have been very fine: four columns, two large ones of the composite order, twenty feet high; two of the corinthian order almost as high, and ten others: these have been brought from other places, and put here as it were by chance: fragments of a temple of Jupiter, at the convent of S. Andrea: of a temple of Mars, at the church of S. Giuliano; and of a castle built by Theodoric. The aqueduct, out of the town, said to be a roman work, was evidently built in the later ages; the arches are gothic, without any kind of proportion, and intolerably ugly. In the cathedral and S. Filippo Neri are some good pictures.

About three miles beyond Spoleto, the road begins ascending to the highest point of the Apennines on this side, which therefore is called *la Somma*.

Terni is situated in a pleasant valley, between two branches of the river Nera, whence it had the name of *Interamna*. Here you get on horseback, or into a calash, in order to see the famous *Caduta delle Marmore**.

---

* They charge five pauls for a horse, and a sequin for a calash. A Cicerone will endeavour to fasten himself on you, and demand ten pauls, but he will take five, and indeed is of no use.

It

It is about four miles from Terni, and the road is up a steep ascent of the *Monte di Marmore*. This cataract is formed by the fall of the river Velino into the Nera: it does not make one leap, like the *Staubbach*, but consists of three cascades: first falling about 300 feet upon rocks with so much violence, that a considerable part of the water is dashed into vapour, which mounts again almost as high as the top of the cascade; the rest at the same time forming a second fall, and thence a third; after which, in conjunction with the Nera, it rolls boiling and foaming along the deep valley. The roaring is heard from a considerable distance*. This cascade

---

* M. Dutens says that the fall is 1083 roman palms, or near 800 feet; that it is the highest cascade known; that the cataract of Niagara, so famous for its vast bulk of water, falls only 150 feet; and that the whole fall of the Velino, from the level of its bed, to that of the Nera is 1364 feet. It is remarkable that the French writers make the fall to be only 200 feet. Kircher says he measured it 300 feet, but Montfaucon will not allow it to be more than 100. Smollet makes it only 160 feet. But these all certainly mean to speak only of the first leap Staubbach in the valley of Lauterbrunn, takes one

cascade is, I believe, generally viewed only from above, where it is most easy of access; but the view from below is infinitely the most picturesque. This cannot be approached on horseback, but it is not a great way to walk from the road.

The valley of Terni, watered by the Nar or Nera, for this is its name after the turbulent junction of the two rivers, was famed in ancient times, and is so still, for the richness of its soil. Pliny says that the meadows were mowed four times in a year: and two ancient aqueducts made for flooding the lands, are still used for that purpose. As I returned from the cascade after dark, in a delightful still evening, the grass in the meadows was covered with myriads of *Lucioli* or little fire-flies.

At *Narni* you will see the remains of the bridge of Augustus, built of vast blocks of marble.

---

leap of 930 feet Terni owes its celebrity in great part to its situation. Such cascades are common in the Pyrenees, and in the way from Baretge to the source of the Gave, are fifty at least comparable to that of Terni. Symonds in Young's Ann.

Here

Loretto to Rome. Narni.

Here you quit the Apennines, and descend all the way to *Otricoli*: near this place the views are picturesque, and there are hamlets and country houses on the sides of the mountains. The ruins of the ancient *Ocriculum* are near the banks of the Tiber, about half a mile out of the road; but there is nothing among them worth seeing.

At *Otricoli* you quit Umbria and enter Sabina; passing the Tiber over a beautiful bridge of three arches, built under Augustus, and repaired by Sixtus V., whence it has the name of *Ponte Felice*.

All the country from hence to Rome is volcanic. The situation of *Civita Castellana*, by some supposed to be the ancient *Veii*, is remarkably strong. You perceive from the road, that the hill on which it stands is composed of breccia and rolled pebbles; these appearing under the volcanic tufo, immediately over which the town is built. About two miles before you enter Rome, you pass the Tiber again, over the Milvian bridge, now *Ponte Molle*. The last five leagues of country are the worst cultivated of any on the whole road; and majestic Rome lifts her towering head amidst a wide waste.

G 4 SECTION

SECTION VIII.

Description of Rome.

NOTHING can be more magnificent than the entrance into Rome by the *Porta del Popolo*. The road is fine, the approach beautiful, the gate handsome. The traveller immediately enters a large area, from the farther side of which he sees the three principal streets of the city diverging, and flanked by the fronts of two handsome churches. In the middle is a noble egyptian obelisk, and a fountain.

Rome is about thirteen miles in circuit [*], measuring round the wall; which is single, and without any ditch, defended only by some towers and bastions. The ancient wall of Aurelian yet in great part remains; the city therefore is still of the same extent, though the present population is only about 160,000 [†].

---

[*] Some say fifteen.

[†] In the reign of Claudius, the inhabitants were 6,968,000; but the people of the suburbs must have been taken into this account.

Before the time of Aurelian, the city was no more than nine miles in compass, and had undergone very little alteration from Servius Tullus's time.

The numerous *gates* of the city are by no means handsome or ornamented. The Flaminian gate, or Porta del Popolo, is the best of them: the outside by Buonarroti, and that next the city by Bernini.

The inhabitants of modern Rome have in a manner left the seven hills to villas, convents, gardens, and vineyards, in order to inhabit the lower parts; and the Campus Martius is become one of the most populous quarters of the city. These hills are much less considerable than they were anciently, since the vallies have been filled up with enormous quantities of rubbish.

The seven hills are, the Aventine, Capitoline, Celian, Esquiline, Palatine, Quirinal, and Viminal: and besides these there are Monte Celiolo and Citorio, the Janiculum and Vatican, the Pincian, and monte Testaccio.

The *Aventine* hill is formed almost entirely of volcanic materials. The prospect from it is truly beautiful, especially from the gardens of the Priorato.

The *Capitaline* hill has been always famous for the Capitol, from whence it takes its name.

The *Cælian* commands a most extensive prospect, and yields only to the Palatine.

The *Esquiline* is the highest of all the hills, and was inhabited by the principal families of ancient Rome. The church of S. Maria maggiore now stands on it.

It is well known that the *Palatine* hill was the site of the fabulous palace of Evander; of the city of Rome in its infancy; of the palace of the Emperors, in the time of its greatest power and magnificence; and now of kitchen gardens. The Roman Emperors could not have chosen a finer situation: it was about 125 feet higher than the *via sacra*, and commanded every part of the city, as well as the river and all the adjacent hills.

The *Qurinal* hill is very lofty, of good extent, and now enjoys the best air in Rome.

The *Viminal* is much the smallest of the seven hills, and is a long, narrow slip of ground. The chief antique building of consequence was the baths of Olympias, some very little remains of which we see in the convent of S. Lorenzo in Pane e Perna.

Monte Citio is very inconsiderable: there
was

was a temple on it sacred to Mars, on the ruins of which the church of S. John is built.

Monte Citorio is raised chiefly by rubbish.

The *Janiculum*, or *Monte Gianicolo*, is of great extent, and reaches from the Ponte Molle along the villas Madama, Mellini, Pamfili, aud Corsini, quite to the flat part of the Campagna, in the way to Ostia.

Monte Vaticano is only a part of this, and at the foot of it is the Vatican palace, and the church of S. Peter.

Monte Pincio commands some delightful views. Salluft's gardens were here, and Villa Ludovisi is now on that site. Villa Medici is in a delicious situation on this hill.

Monte Testaccio is 160 feet high, and half a mile in circumference, composed wholly of potsherds. There are vaults under it, in which wine is kept remarkably cool, and in summer there is a great resort of people to drink it. Some years since they found some tombs under it, done in the best ages, and paved with mosaic.

Some of the principal streets of Rome are of considerable length, and straight. That called the *Corso* is most frequented. It is above a mile in length. Here are the horse-races; and here the nobility display their equipages during the carnival, and generally in the evenings, when it is fine weather. The palaces, of which there are many in this street, range in a line with the other houses; having no court before them like many of the great hotels at Paris; nor being shut up like Burlington house in London, within high, gloomy walls; but contributing greatly to the ornament of the city.

Strada Felice, in the higher part of Rome, from Trinità de' Monti to S. Maria Maggiore, is above a mile in length, and thence to the church of S. Giovanni in Laterano, is near another mile; all in one line, only with the view interrupted by the fine church of S. Maria Maggiore. This street is crossed by another straight street, called *Strada Pia*, considerably above a mile in length, terminated at one end by Porta Pia, at the other by the colossal statues at Monte Cavallo. The intersection of these streets is one of the noblest points of view in Rome.

It would be difficult to convey any idea of the smaller and less regular streets. In general, however, we cannot avoid observing the strange mixture of interesting and magnificent with common and beggarly objects; palaces, churches, fountains, and the finest remains of antiquity, with rags, poverty, and filth.

There are many *Piazze*, or *Places*, as the French call them; and we improperly *Squares*. 1. *S. Apostoli*. 2. *Barberini*, wherein are two fountains by Bernini. 3. *Del Campidaglio*. 4. *Campo di Fiore*, wherein is the corn market; and on mondays and saturdays a market for horses. Persons condemned by the inquisition are burnt here. 5. *Piazza Copranica*, a small square, on which is one of the theatres, that takes its name from it. 6. *Colonna*, with the Antonine column in the middle of it. 7. *Farnese*. 8. *Di S. Maria Maggiore*. 9. *Piazza Mattei*. 10. *Montanara*. 11. Before the Quirinal palace, or Monte Cavallo. 12. *Monte Citoria*, a handsome square, in which is the pedestal of the true Antonine column; and on one side of it the *Curia Innocenziana*, or palace of justice. 13. *Piazza Navona*, a fine area, with some handsome buildings round it, and a magnificent fountain by Bernini, in the middle. Every sunday in august this square is flooded by means of the

the fountain, and the nobility and gentry drive round in their carriages through the water. Here also is one of the principal markets, especially on wednesdays. 14. *Piazza di Pasquino*, a small square, in which are many booksellers' shops; but chiefly remarkable for the antique mutilated statue of a greek soldier, well known under the name of *Pasquin*. 15. *Di S. Pietro*, the fine area before S. Peter's church, surrounded by Bernini's portico, supported by 286 columns, and supporting 138 statues. 16. *Del Popolo*, at the entrance of Rome from Florence, &c. 17. *Della Rotonda*, where is the famous Pantheon, now generally called *Rotonda*; and a fountain with an obelisk, set on an elephant's back. 17. *Piazza di Spagna*, where is the palace of the Spanish ambassador, il Collegio della propaganda, Bernini's fountain of the Barcaccia or boat, and the fine flight of steps up to Trinità di monte. 18. *Piazza della Colonna Trajana*, a small square, remarkable chiefly for the famous pillar.

The principal ornaments of the Piazze, or open areas of Rome, are the *Fountains*. That in the Piazza Navona, is the most magnificent in the whole world. It is a vast rock, pierced through and through, so as to be divided.

vided into four parts which unite at the top, where the obelisk is placed: towards the bottom of each part of the rock is seated a colossal figure, representing the principal rivers, with their attributes.

The Fountain of Pope Paul V. near the church of S. Pietro Montorio, is in a very bad style. The water is so rapid as to turn several mills; it serves all the Trastevere, and is even carried along the Ponte Sisto; but it has a bad taste. It was brought by Augustus from the lake of Bracciano, 35 miles from Rome, to supply his Naumachia, and there are now great remains of the aqueduct near the villa Pamfili.

Fontana di Termine receives the *Acqua Felice*; it is a despicable piece of architecture by Fontana. Here are three bas-reliefs, representing Moses striking the rock; and in the middle is a colossal statue of Moses by Prospero Bresciano: here are also two Egyptian lions of basalt, formerly placed under the portico of the Pantheon. Sixtus V. brought this water from Colonna, twenty miles from Rome.

Fontana di Trevi receives the *Acqua Vergine*. It is a noble fountain. This is the only water which now comes to Rome by an ancient

ancient aqueduct: it is for the moſt part under ground, which is the reaſon why it has been ſo much better preſerved than any other. This is alſo the beſt water in Rome; and all the lower parts of the city being furniſhed from the fountain of Trevi, thoſe who prefer good water to good air, live in thoſe parts. It was brought from the Sabina by Agrippa, to ſupply the Campus Martius.

The abundance of fountains in Rome gives an air of coolneſs, life, and motion, to the whole city; but it is a great miſtake to conclude from thence, as many have done, that it is plentifully ſupplied with good water; for the reverſe is really the caſe.

The river Tiber divides the city, properly ſo called, from the *Tranſtevere*, or quarter wherein is the church of S. Peter and the palace of the Vatican. This river is about 315 feet wide, at the bridge of S. Angelo, and is navigable for great barques: the water is yellow and turbid.

There are now three Bridges at Rome—

1. That of S. Angelo, anciently *Pons Aelius*, leading to the caſtle, S. Peter's and the Vatican. It is 300 feet long; all the upper part of it is finiſhed by Bernini, in a
good

good taste; the statues on it are heavy and disagreeable.

2. *Ponte Cestio*, or of S. Bartolomeo, to pass from the Isola Tiberina to Transtevere; and *Quattro Capi*, anciently *pons Fabricius*, to go from the same island into the city.

3. *Ponte Sisto*, anciently *pons Janiculensis*, rebuilt by Sixtus IV. in 1473.

Ancient Rome had six bridges.

There are some small remains of the *Sublician* bridge *, which was the only one, when Horatius Cocles defended it so valiantly. It was then only of wood; but was afterwards built of stone by Lepidus.

There are more remains of the Senatorian bridge, now called *Ponte Rotto*, which show it to have been very noble. It was repaired by Julius III; but falling soon to decay, it was again repaired under Gregory XIII. in 1575: but in 1598 a flood carried away two of the arches, and it has remained ever since in a ruinous state.

Part of the *Pons triumphalis* is to be seen, opposite to the church of Spirito Santo; and from the bridge of S. Angelo some small remains of the piers.

* They may be seen from Ripa grande.

Ponte Molle, anciently *Pons Emilianus*, and then *Milvius*, is out of the city, above a mile from the *porta del popolo*, on the Flaminian way *. It was built in Justinian's time, and rebuilt by Nicholas V. on the old foundations. The river here is full 400 feet over. The old bridge, where the battle was fought between Constantine and Maxentius, was 200 feet higher up the river.

Cicerones and Books † are by no means wanting at Rome. To put yourself under

the

---

* Near this is the Rotonda of S Andrea, by Vignola, perfectly chaste, and perhaps the best modern building about Rome.

† Famiani Nardini, Roma antica. 1666. In Grævius's collection.

Insignium Romæ templorum, &c. prospectus, a Jacobo de Rubeis. 1683

Studio d'architettura civile de Rossi 1702, 1711, 1721.

Descrizione topografica delle antichità di Roma. 1763 4° — and di Roma moderna, 1766, dell' Abbate Ridolfini Venuti

Le antichita Romane, di Piranesi &c &c.

There is a great plan of Rome by Noli, in nine sheets, with a description. And variety of smaller plans.

The

the conduct of one of the former, will be the least trouble, if you do not regard the expence; and the surest way of seeing every thing according to rule. If you commit yourself to the books, you will find every thing described with almost the same degree of admiration. I have endeavoured to select, from my own observation, whatever seems to me most worthy of attention; and to dispose it in such a manner as may most easily catch the eye, and offer itself when it is wanted. The city is divided into fourteen quarters or wards, called *Rioni*. In most of the guide books the churches, palaces, &c. are to be found under these divisions. I have preferred another method; and have thrown every thing into a few classes or general heads, placing the particulars under each, for the most part, alphabetically. A

The common guide-books are,

Il Mercurio errante, di Pietro Roffini, 1760. 12°.

Descrizione delle pitture, sculture, &c. di Filippo Titi 1763 12°.

Roma antica e moderna, in 3 volumes, 8°. 5.

Vasi itinerarie instructif. 1773. 12°. he also has published views of Rome.

person

person of taste will always quit Rome with regret; but it is impossible to view the principal things there to any purpose, in much less than three months.

Let us begin with ancient Rome.

In *Antiquities* the COLISÆUM takes the lead. It obtained this name from an enormous colossal figure of Apollo with the head of Nero, sixty feet high. It was also called the *Flavian Amphitheatre*; Flavius Vespasian having begun it, after his triumph over the Jews. It was finished and dedicated by Titus. The area is an oval of 598 feet by 519; the height is 162; and the circumference measured on the outside 1741 feet. It is now in general 25 feet within the ground. There are three rows of columns one above another; doric, ionic, and corinthian, all remarkably plain: the pilasters over the upper row of corinthian pillars are corinthian, not composite. When complete it had 80 arches; 56 are now remaining, together with the whole superstructure on the north side. It has been pillaged at various times; but is still a most stupendous and picturesque ruin. It is generally said that this Amphitheatre held 100,000 spectators; others say 85,000, 80,000, and 50,000; but according to Fontana's tana's measurement, allowing a foot and half to each person, no more than 34,000 persons could sit in it; so that in order to have held the great numbers which it is said to have done, we must suppose that there were galleries at the top, which were probably of wood.

The *Arch of Constantine* is all of marble, and still entire; the architecture is beautiful. There are some excellent bas-reliefs on it, taken from the arch of Trajan, which compared with the others of the time of Constantine, serve to show how miserably the art of sculpture had fallen in the latter period, whilst architecture still kept its ground.

The *Arch of Titus* is by far the first at Rome in point of architecture; and is remarkable for the inscription, which yet remains, but especially for the excellent sculpture, of Vespasian and Titus carrying in triumph the spoils of the temple at Jerusalem, among which are the golden candlestick, and the table of shew-bread.

The *Arch of Septimius Severus* is of saline marble, and ornamented with fluted columns of the composite order, and bas-reliefs, in a bad style. It is at least 25 feet in the ground, and

and the two side arches are almost entirely buried.

The principal of the ruins in the Campo Vaccino are—1. Three beautiful fluted corinthian columns, at the foot of the Capitoline hill, buried 35 feet in the ground, so that the elegant frieze is in a manner level with the eye. these are supposed to be part of the temple of *Jupiter tonans*, built by Augustus. 2 Eight columns, seven of gray, and one of red granite, of different sizes, and not handsome: part of the portico of the *temple of Concord*. 3. A single pillar with a corinthian capital. 4. The *temple of Antoninus and Faustina*, of which ten columns are remaining, fifty feet high, and each one block of numidian marble, in a fine taste · they stand before the church of S. Lorenzo in Miranda. 5. The *temple of Romulus and Remus*, now the church of S. S. Cosmo and Damiano *. The old bronze doors of the temple are entire:

---

* It is probable that the church of S. Theodore, at the foot of the Palatine hill, is the site of the ancient temple of Romulus, since the famous bronze wolf in the Capitol was found in it. The present building is of much later ages. There is a little altar at the entrance, which is antique.

the pedestals, the porphyry pillars, and entablature, are all likewise antique. They were taken up, and replaced in their present situation, near 20 feet higher than the floor. 6. Two columns near this, buried half way in the ground, against the Oratory of the Confraternity of *Via crucis*. 7. Three vast arches of the *Temple of Peace*, finished by Vespasian, after the reduction of Judæa, partly out of the famous golden house of Nero. This was much the largest temple in old Rome, and quite different in form from the rest. The columns were very fine, as may be seen by the only one remaining, now before the church of S. Maria maggiore. 8. The remains of two square rooms, within the convent of S. Maria nuova, generally supposed to have been the *temples of the Sun and Moon*. 9. Three great columns before the church of S. Maria liberatrice, not far from the Palatine hill; supposed by some to have belonged to the building where the *comitia* were held, but commonly called the *temple of Jupiter Stator*. The capitals of these columns are the richest in Rome, and the frieze is plain. 10. From the *Campo Vaccino* is the principal entrance into the *Orti Farnesiani*, by a rustic portal of Vignola's. These occupy a considerable

siderable part of the Palatine Hill, where the ruins of the Imperial Palace may be seen. It was 1700 feet long, and 1200 broad; but little of it now remains, except some vast arches and foundations of brick. The great hall was traced out by Bianchini. Two baths were also discovered, incrusted with marble, and with most curious painting and gilding on the cielings. The greatest curiofities are some elegant capitals of columns. The whole ground, which is now a kitchen garden, is full of ancient marbles. The statues found here were many, but not very fine. There is now a good one of Commodus, and a very particular one of Esculapius.

The Emperors displayed much of their magnificence in *Thermæ* or hot-baths for public use. They were not merely for bathing, but for academies, and the gymnastic exercises: and contained libraries, musæums, &c.

The *baths of Titus* were about 790 feet by 684. All the rooms had a communication with the large one in the middle, where the youths performed their exercises in bad weather. The remains of them are immense vaults and corridores under ground, painted with arabesques, from which it is said Raffaello elle took the idea of his paintings in the *loggie* of the Vatican; but little or nothing of them is now discernible.

Near these are the *sette sale*, or reservoirs of water for these baths.

The *baths of Caracalla* are at the foot of the Aventine mount, and immense ruins of them still remain. There were two vast rooms, which they could lay together; one was 310 feet long, and the other was much bigger. They contained 2300 cells *, wherein as many persons might bathe at the same time, without seeing each other: they were also rich in statues and other ornaments †.

Diocletian's Baths were 1200 feet square, and yet not so large as those of Caracalla. They occupied all the gardens of the Carthusian convent, the public granaries, the great square before them, and the church of S. Bernardo, which is circular and antique. A

---

* De La Lande says 3000. There were 1600 marble seats those in the cloister of S. Giovanni in Laterano are supposed to have been two of them.— *Wright*

† The Toro and Hercules Farnese, &c. were found here.

part of these *Thermæ* is converted into the church of S. Maria degli Angeli *.

There were no less than fifteen *Circuses* at Rome. The *Circus maximus* occupied all the valley between the Palatine and Aventine hills. According to Pliny it was three stadia long, and one stadium and an half broad †; and held 385,000 spectators. It is calculated that 280,000 might sit there; the rest must have been in temporary galleries. Nothing of it now remains but the site, and some large arches on the side of the Palatine hill: the area is chiefly occupied by gardens.

The *Circus of Flora* was in Piazza Barberini, and grew into disuse upon the building that of *Sallust*, in the vale opposite to what is now Villa Ludovisi. It was about 1600 feet long. Near it are some ruins, perhaps of the temple of Venus Erycina.

Circus Flaminius, extended from the foot of the Tarpeian rock, as far as the Altieri palace. The remains, which are trifling, may be seen in the vaults of the convent of the nuns of S. Ambrogio.

---

* Palladio has given plans of these three Thermæ
† The Stadium was 625 feet, or near a furlong

That which is now Piazza Navona, was the *Circus Agonalis*.

The *Circus of Caracalla*, as it is called, is about two miles from Rome, near S. Sebastian and Capo di Bove. The length is 1630 feet, the breadth 330, a covered gallery ran round it, and over that were feats, on three sides; on the fourth, where the *carcer* was, the Emperor had a portico. This is the most entire of all the Circuses, for the walls and the two *metas* are still standing. The Egyptian Obelisk, which is now in the Piazza Navona, stood in the middle of it. It probably served for the suburb, which was considerable hereabouts.

The two noble Columns of Trajan and Antoninus are well known. That of *Trajan* stands in a small square, the base near 15 feet under the present level of the ground about it. The height is near 128 english feet, the column alone 92½. The shaft is of 23 pieces, admirably carved in bas-relief, in a spiral line, with the actions of the Dacian war. There is a commodious staircase within, to ascend to the top; on which now stands a colossal statue of S. Peter.

The *Column of Antoninus*, or more properly of *Aurelius*, far inferior in merit to Trajan's, stands to more advantage, quite clear of the ground, and in the middle of a large square, called from the pillar *Piazza Colonna*. It is higher than Trajan's, the column alone being 106 feet high, and the pedestal very lofty. The shaft is carved in bas-relief, with the actions of Marcus Aurelius in the war against the Marcomanni, but the execution is poor. On the top is a colossal statue of S. Paul, placed there when Sixtus V. restored the column in 1589.

This column has been improperly named; for Antonine's column was an immense one of granite, about seven feet in diameter, part of which is now to be seen behind Monte Citorio. It stood on a pedestal, ornamented with bas-reliefs of the funeral games and apotheosis of the Emperor, which is to be seen on Monte Citorio.

The *Roman Forum* was the vale between the Capitoline and Palatine hills, where the Campo Vaccino or beast-market now is; but the area of this is much larger than the ancient Forum, which was probably about 750 feet in length, and 500 in breadth *.

* For the buildings, see the article *Campo Vaccino*.

There were several other Forums in the city; as those of *Augustus*; *Antoninus Pius*, in the middle of which the Antonine column stood; of *Nerva*, wherein are the remains of a temple of Mars, built by Augustus: there are two corinthian fluted columns, of greek marble, of a vast size, but in two pieces; with beautiful foliage, and a Minerva in bas-relief. The wall, which was probably the boundary of this Forum, is 60 feet high, and entire for a long space. But the Forum of *Trajan*, where the column now stands, was the finest in Rome, and was built by the famous grecian artist Polidorus, who also made the column.

The Mausoleum of Augustus is by the palace of the Marquis Correa, near the church of S. Carlo, between the Corso and the river. It is a miserable remain of the magnificent structure erected by Augustus to receive the ashes of the Cæsars. The inner wall, which is circular, is still entire; it was surrounded by three other circular walls, which rose 30 feet one above another, and the top was covered with a dome. The area was left open, and the vaults for sepulture were in small rooms under the corridores. The area is now converted into a garden. There is much of the *opus reticulatum* in this building, but no remains of columns, and only a small piece of the frieze. This mausoleum was one of the chief ornaments of the *Campus Martius*, which at that time extended from hence to the theatre of Marcellus, and from the foot of the hills to the Tiber. Soon after it was so crouded, that there was not room for the troops to exercise, in Nero's time therefore it was extended to *Ponte Molle*.

The *Mausoleum of Hadrian*, now the Castle of S. Angelo, from one of the most beautiful buildings in the world, is become one of the most ugly ones. It was incrusted with white marble, surrounded with fine columns, and enriched with statues and other ornaments. It is now not only the citadel of Rome, but the arsenal, treasury, and state prison. A covered way extends to it from the Vatican, in order that his Holiness may get into this place of safety, in case of an insurrection, or a sudden attack. In the great room which occupies the centre of the building, and two others, are admirable arabesques by Giulio Romano, Perrino del Vaga, and other scholars of Raffaelle; also some antiques, as a bust of Antoninus Pius, a statue of Roma triumphans, &c.

Some

Some columns in the church of S. Paolo fuori were taken from this building: and the large pine fruit of bronze, which Dante mentions, and which is now in the garden of the Belvedere, was once on the top of it.

The tomb of Caius Cestius is a beautiful Pyramid, and the only one in Europe, near the Ostian gate, or porta di S. Paolo. It is a hundred feet high, but being in a hollow, the base being buried, and the ground rising near twenty feet round it, the building does not appear so high as it really is. Within there is a room, adorned with paintings, but they are now almost effaced. On the outside is an inscription. Two antique fluted columns stand near it, which bear no proportion to the pyramid. Heretics are permitted to be interred on the spot just by.

All along the Appian way, for many miles together, are the foundations of sepulchres; but the only one which deserves attention is that of Cecilia Metella, the wife of Crassus. The lower story, which is square, lies within the ground; over it is a round tower, which was covered with a dome. The tower is pretty perfect, built entirely of Tivertine stone, and put together without cramps, or cement; the frieze has bull's heads in relievo, whence

whence it took the modern name of *Capo di bove*. This is the handsomest building left of the times of the Republic.

There are nine Egyptian Obelisks set up at Rome, and three on the ground—

1. That which stands in the midst of the vast area before S. Peter's is 72 feet high, and reckoning the base, 108; it is plain, or without hieroglyphics. This is the only obelisk which was found entire.

2. The Obelisk before S. Giovanni in Laterano is covered with hieroglyphics, and having been thrown down by the barbarians, was broken into three pieces. The height, including the pedestal, which is the best of any in Rome, is about 138 feet.

3. The Obelisk behind S. Maria maggiore was taken from the Mausoleum of Augustus. It is plain, and much smaller than the others.

4. That in the Piazza del Popolo is 66 feet high, and covered with hieroglyphics.

5. The obelisk of the Piazza Navona stood in the circus of Caracalla. It is about 55 feet high, and has one row of hieroglyphics.

6. A small one before the church of the Minerva, set upon an elephant's back, by Bernini.

Bernini. It belonged to a temple of Isis, and was found in the garden of the adjoining convent.

7 Another small one, by the church of S. Ignazio: it has hieroglyphics on it, and was in the Campus Martius.

8. A third small one, with hieroglyphics, is in the garden of the Villa Medici.

9. A broken, pieced one at Villa Mattei.

Besides these which are standing, there is one very large one prostrate in the back court of a palace, called *la Vignaccia*, not far from the *Ripetta*. It is of red granite, like the rest, but the hieroglyphics are better executed. It is much to be lamented, that it is so much broken, as to have discouraged the government from setting it up; since it seems to be the most curious of any of the Obelisks, as well as the largest. There is another by the Scala Santa; and a third, in several pieces, at the Barberini palace.

Of all the Temples, and indeed of all the buildings, which ancient Rome has left us, the *Pantheon* is certainly the most noble and perfect. The portico has eight pillars in front, and three pillars with one pilaster on the sides, all of granite, with corinthian capitals and basements; but none of them ex-

H 5 actly

actly of the same size. The inscription is on the frieze. The bronze door did not belong to it, but the door-case of white marble, in the proportion of 40 to 20, is quite complete, as it was originally. The outside of the whole building was incrusted with marble. The portico and body of the edifice were probably built at different times. The inside is exactly 143 feet and an half in diameter without the recesses, a complete circle, and as much from the pavement to the hole which lets in the light; this hole is 25 feet in diameter. The dome is very plain, but in its glory was probably covered with plates of silver. The pavement is of porphyry and giallo antico, bordered with other precious marbles. The inside is handsomely fitted up, opposite to the door is the great altar, and on each side of that, four other altars; the pillars giallo-antico and pavonazzo alternately; on the altars themselves granite or porphyry pillars, with larger ones of giallo-antico. The room is extremely well lighted by the aperture.

Several famous artists are buried here, as Raffaelle, Perrino del Vaga, Annibale Carracci, Taddeo Zuccheri, Flaminius Vacca, and the famous musician Corelli.

The

The elegant Temple of *Fortuna virilis* is now a church of the Armenians, under the name of S. Maria Egizziaca. It was probably built in the times of the republic; as the columns, which are of a chaste ionic, are only stone stuccoed. the frieze, though but of stucco, is well preserved. half the columns only projected from the walls.

Near this is a building, in a bad style, of the lower ages, patched up out of the ruins of better edifices, vulgarly called Pilate's palace.

In this neighbourhood is the little elegant round Temple of *Vesta*, now the church of Madonna del Sole. There is an open portico round it of corinthian columns the walls are of greek marble. It is situated low, and near the Tiber. In a manner under it, is the opening of the *Cloaca maxima*, or great common-fewer of the city, 14 feet high, and as many wide, built of vast stones, and in perfect repair, though said to have been made by Tarquinius Priscus.

S. Maria in Cosmedin is built on the ruins of a temple, said to be that of *Pudicita* or Modesty. At one end of the portico is a great antique mask, or perhaps a sink to let

water

water through, with a wide mouth, called *la bocca della verità*.

Some will have the church of *S. Stefano Rotondo* to have been a temple of Faunus. It is round, bigger than the Pantheon, and perfect. It has many faults; so that one can hardly suppose it of genuine antiquity. Two corridores run round it, supported by granite columns, of different diameters, and with various capitals; some have the cross on them, which shows that part of it at least was done in christian times.

The church of *S. Urban alla Caffarella*, at some distance from the city, was a temple, some say of Mars, Piranesi thinks of Bacchus; perhaps it was the temple of the Muses. It is entirely of brick, except the columns, which are white marble, and corinthian: the frieze is plain, and the brick cornice is better preserved than the marble capitals.

At the foot of the eminence on which this building stands, is the *Fountain of the Nymph Egeria*, Numa's favourite retreat. There are some remains of the building over this spring, with much reticulated work about it; three niches for statues on each side, and in the front a large recess, wherein is a cumbent statue

statue of the nymph, broken and much worn. The water is very clear and sweet.

All this side of Rome abounds with remains of Antiquity. Not far from the fountain of Egeria is a small building of brick, said to be the temple which the Romans erected to *Ridicule* when Hannibal quitted Rome, without having accomplished any thing answerable to his reputation: or, as others will have it, to the god *Rediculus*, a reditu or redeundo. However this may be, it is clearly a building of later times, from the trivial ornaments with which it is loaded.

Near the circus of Caracalla is a round temple, with an ante-temple, through which you must pass to enter the other: and this is supposed to be the temple of *Virtue* and *Honour*.

Here also are the ruins of the temple of *Mars* [*], where the victors waited for leave from the senate to enter the city. It was a large square, with a rotunda in the middle, of about 108 feet diameter. The lower part is exactly in its ancient situation; vaulted,

---

[*] Venuti thinks it was a place for the horses to be in, before they entered the circus.

with

with several recesses, and a vast pier in the middle, to support the floor of the rotunda.

To return into the city. In a vineyard near the church of S. Bibiana, is the picturesque ruin of the temple of *Minerva Medica*. It was a decagon, covered with a dome; not lighted from the top, but from ten windows placed over ten niches. The whole is 75 feet diameter. The sides were incrusted with porphyry and serpentine, of which there are still some fragments. The whole dome was brick; the ribs remain, but the interstices have fallen in.

The famous temple of the *Sun* was built by Aurelian, on the top of the Quirinal hill, now the site of the Colonna gardens, where there is a piece of the cornice and frieze, from whence we may form some judgement of its magnificence. The columns must have been 70 feet high, and the workmanship is exquisite.

The temple of Janus, as it is improperly called, has no appearance of ever having been a temple; it was more probably an exchange or market-house. It is all of white greek marble, some of the blocks of an immense size. It has four equal fronts, with a large opening in the middle of each; and on each
side

side are six niches for statues. It is a curious, solid edifice, but by no means handsome the materials too good for the times of the republic; the workmanship too bad for the times of the Emperors.

Near this is an arch, called the arch of the silversmiths, because it was erected by that company, to the honour of Septimius Severus and his son Caracalla, in the old *foro boario*. It is small, and in a bad taste, full of useless ornaments

In a square called *Piazza di Pietra*, is the *Dogana di terra*, built on the site of what is called Antonine's Basilica; though more probably a Temple. The columns are of white marble, fluted and corinthian, with handsome capitals. Eleven are now entire.

The *Portico of Octavia*, on the *Pescaria* or fish-market, is an oblong building, in which the two principal fronts have each four columns, and two pilasters, of the corinthian order. Over against this, in the court of a house, are three composite columns, said to be part of a temple of *Juno* by some; of a temple of *Bellona*, by others. And about twenty paces farther, are two fluted columns, thought to be part of a temple of *Mars*.

In

In the convent of S. Niccolò de' Cesarini are some pillars, part of one of the temples belonging to the circus Flaminius, and the only one that remains of them. It was dedicated to Apollo, and probably was of the times of the republic, since the pillars are of tufo, and the building a small one.

The *Theatre of Marcellus* is one of the most beautiful remains of ancient architecture. What is now to be seen, is in the dependencies of the Orsini palace, towards the Piazza Montanara. There is an order of doric, with an ionic over it, both of half columns; and probably there were corinthian pilasters above: these are the most perfect columns of the doric and ionic orders. Different accounts say it held 22,000, 30,000, and 60,000 spectators.

Of the vast *Theatre of Pompey*, which is said to have held 80,000 persons, and to have been the first built with stone, the ruins are but inconsiderable, and so environed with houses as to be distinguished with difficulty. There is only a little piece of the semicircle, and some cunei, that serve now for stables.

After the Antiquities, the Churches and Palaces

Palaces are the great objects of a stranger's attention at Rome.

Of the first, there are seven which are called *Basilicas,* or Royal Churches; the principal of which, for size and beauty, richness and elegance, is S. Peter's, called *San Pietro in Vaticano.* This noble edifice was above a century in building, and cost forty-five millions of roman crowns *. The original architect was Bramante, and the first stone was laid on the 18th of April 1506; but the greatest part of the plan was Michelangelo Buonarroti's, who raised the enormous cupola. Several succeeding architects worked after his plan, till Maderni finished the towers in 1621. As to Bernini's colonnade, it was not begun till forty years after.

The height of St. Peter's, to the top of the cross, is 435 feet, english measure; the length on the outside 704, within about 622; the breadth within 291 feet, and the length of the cross aile or transept 493 feet †.

The

---

* It is supposed that there has been as much more expended, in the fitting up, &c. &c.

† The measures are given very differently in different writers, the above are the most authentic I could

The immense area, the circular periſtyle or double colonnade, the two magnificent fountains or jet-d'eaus, and the Egyptian obeliſk, all together form an approach to this fine church, which is truly ſuperb. From the entrance into the area, to the end of the building, is near 1800 feet, above one third of a mile.

Giotto's moſaic, called the Navicella, is in the portico, oppoſite to the great door; and over it is a great bas-relief in marble by Bernini, of Chriſt commanding S. Peter to feed his flock: at one end of the portico, is an equeſtrian ſtatue of Conſtantine, by Bernini, and at the other, of Charlemagne, by Cornacchini.

On entering the church, the ſpectator will remark, that the proportions are ſo well obſerved, that nothing diſtinguiſhes itſelf ſo far above the reſt, as to hurt the eye: and that the ornaments are in ſo good a taſte, that nothing appears peculiarly gaudy or ſplendid.

After a general view, the firſt object that attracts notice is the vaſt *Baldacchino*, ca-

could procure, and I believe are near the truth. The dimenſions of St Paul's at London are—height 340, length 500, breadth 250 feet.

nopy or pavilion, supported on four bronze wreathed columns, 122 feet high. This covers the altar and confession of St. Peter, and is placed immediately under the centre of the great cupola, which is larger than the Pantheon, and is covered entirely with mosaics.

Beyond this, the church is terminated by the great Tribune, in which is the chair of S. Peter, enclosed in gilt bronze, and supported by the four doctors of the church. The Mausoleum of Urban VIII. on one side, is by Bernini; that on the other, of Paul III., is by Guglielmo della Porta.

Amidst the variety of superb ornaments with which the church of St. Peter is enriched, the Mosaics are not the least curious. These, which are intended to immortalize the best performances of the first masters in the art of painting, are executed very near S. Peter's, and the whole operation may be seen there.*

Beginning

---

* The material is a semivitrified substance, which they call *fritta*, mostly manufactored at Venice, and of about a thousand different colours. It is cut with a diamond, and then with an iron hammer broken

into

Beginning on the right hand; over the *porta santa*, which is closed up, and opened only in the year of jubilee—S. Peter from Ciro Ferri. In the first chapel, the mosaics of the cupola are histories of the old testament, sybils and prophets, from Pietro di Cortona and Ciro Ferri, by Fabio Cristofori. In this chapel is the famous Pietà of Michelangelo, when he was only twenty-five years old. The frescos are by Lanfranco. In the little side chapel is S. Nicola di Bari, in mosaic, by Cristofori.

The cupola in the side aile, opposite to the first chapel, is in mosaic, from Ciro Ferri, and is one of the best in the church.

2. S. Sebastian's. Cupola from Pietro di Cortona: at the high altar, martyrdom of S. Sebastian, from Domenichino, by P. P. Cristofori. Cupola opposite, from Pietro di Cortona.

3. S. S. Sacramento. Cupola from Pietro di Cortona by Abbatini. The rich tabernacle, or *ciborio* of lapis lazuli, after the plan

into cubes of different sizes; these are ranged in drawers, according to their size and colour. A strong plaster is made, in which these *fritias* are immersed.

of the temple of Vesta, is by Bernini. The picture of the Trinity is by Pietro di Cortona. S. Maurice is by Bernini. On the altar opposite is a mosaic of the communion of S. Jerom, from Domenichino's famous picture in the church of S. Girolamo, by Cristofori.

S. Basil celebrating mass after the Greek rite, from Subleyras, by Ghezzi.

The martyrdom of S. Processus and S. Martinianus, from Valentin, by Cristofori.

The martyrdom of S. Erasmus, from Nicola Poussin, by Cristofori.

La Navicella, or S. Peter sinking, and Jesus saving him, from Lanfranco.

The archangel Michael, from Guido.

S. Petronilla, from Guercino, by Cristofori.

S. Peter raising Tabitha, from Placido Costanzi.

The cupola of the Clementine chapel is from designs of Michelangelo, and is covered with arabesques and foliage in mosaic; in the angles are four doctors of the church; these and the other mosaics are by Marcello Provenzale from designs of Roncalli. There is an admirable picture at the altar, by Andrea Sacchi.

Against one of the pillars, the death of Ananias and Saphira, by Pietro Adami from Cav. Roncalli.

The famous transfiguration, from Raffaelle.

Chapel of the choir, or Siſtine chapel.

Aſſumption of the virgin, with ſaints, from Pietro Bianchi.

Chapel of the preſentation: moſaics in the cupola, &c. to the honour of the virgin, from deſigns of Carlo Maratti. Preſentation of the virgin, at the high altar, from Romanelli. Portrait of Maria Clementina Sobieſki; all by Criſtoforo.

In the baptiſmal chapel, or baptiſtery, which is the firſt on the left hand entering the church, are three moſaics—S. John baptizing Chriſt, in the middle, from Carlo Maratti; that on the right is from Giuſeppe Paſſari, and that on the left from Cav Procaccini. In this chapel is the ancient baptiſmal font, which is a large porphyry ſarcophagus.

There is a great deal of good modern Sculpture in this church. The beſt piece are the Pietà already mentioned, and a moſt excellent bas-relief by Algardi, repreſenting Pope Leo I. going to meet Attila, with S

Peter and S. Paul appearing in the air. Of the numerous superb Mausoleums, those which have the most merit are, that of Paul III by Giacomo della Porta, that of Gregory XIII. by Camillo Rusconi, and those of Urban VIII., Alexander VII., and the Countess Matilda, by Bernini. The best statues are, S. Domenico, by Le Gro, S. Bruno by Michelangelo Slodtz, and particularly S. Andrew bearing his cross, by Francesco Fiamingo. The bronze statue of S. Peter sitting, though without merit, attracts all the homage of the faithful; it is said to have been made by Leo. I. from the statue of Jupiter Capitolinus.

The walls of this famous church are incrusted with the finest marbles; the pilasters are ornamented with children in alto-relievo, and medallions of some of the ancient Popes, in white marble. The columns in the chapels, except those in the arches of the side ailes, and four of red marble in the transept, which came from the forum of Trajan; all belonged to the ancient church, and many of them are very fine ones. In short, though none of the wonders of ancient or modern art are to be found here, yet there is much to admire, and very little to blame. The whole of of this stupendous edifice is most highly finished, without any gaudiness or superfluity of ornament: and it is singularly fortunate, that during more than a century, no doating Pope, or vain Architect, desirous of outdoing their predecessors, or envious of the fame which Bramante and Buonarroti had acquired, stepped in at some unlucky moment, to mar the whole.

The church of *S. Giovanni in Laterano* ought to have had precedence, as the mother church of all christendom, where the Pope takes possession of his papal charge. The principal front is by Alessandro Galilei, and is pretty well, considering that the architect was forced to have two enclosed porticos, in order that there might be a balcony from whence the Pope was to bless the people. The inside of the portico is excellent. The rest is by Borromini; and is a series of absurdities in architecture. The nave was divided from the ailes by antique granite columns. Borromini took away every third pillar, and covered the two others on each side, so as to change them into piers. Between these are twelve niches, in which the twelve apostles are placed between columns of verd-antique; S. Andrew, S. John, S. James,

James, and S. Matthew, by Rusconi, are good ones. S. Thomas and S. Bartholomew are by Le Gros.

The Corsini chapel is probably the most elegant in Europe, both for its proportions, and the disposition of the marbles. The architecture is by Galilei. The picture of the altar is a mosaic after Guido. The beautiful porphyry sarcophagus, under the statue of Clement XII., being found in the Pantheon, is supposed to have contained the ashes of Agrippa.

Before one of the side altars are some fluted pillars of gilt bronze, antique and very magnificent, the capitals modern, and well executed.

The organ is the largest in the city, was built in 1549, and has thirty-six stops and pedals.

In the sacristy is the Annunciation by Michelangelo, a crucifix of the same master, and a drawing in black chalk of the holy family by Raffaelle.

In the cloister is the tomb of Helena, mother of Constantine: it is of porphyry with bas-reliefs. Here also are two seats of *marmo rosso*, which were used in the baths.

Near this church is the *Baptistery* of Constantine,

stantine, of an octagon form. On the outside are two large porphyry columns. The inside is a sort of dome, with two ranges of pillars, one above another; the lower of eight porphyry columns, with different capitals, two corinthian, the other six ionic and doric. The cieling is painted with the history of S. John, by Andrea Sacchi; below also are several frescos; the destruction of idolatry by Carlo Maratti, &c. The font in the middle is of porphyry.

The *Scala Santa* is opposite to this church; it consists of twenty-eight marble steps, said to be brought from Pilate's palace at Jerusalem; and in the spacious area before it stands a great Egyptian obelisk.

The papal palace here is converted into an hospital or conservatory for girls, who are taught different sorts of work.

S. Maria Maggiore is on the highest part of the Esquiline hill. The front was built at the expence of Benedict XIV. from designs of Cavalier Fuga, in a very bad taste. The nave is supported by forty antique columns of greek marble, they are ionic, and belonged to the temple of Juno Lucina. The roof is flat, and gilt with the first gold which came from Peru. The arch which
separate

separates the nave from the choir is covered with mosaics of the fifth century; at the end of the choir are other mosaics of 1289; and in the vestibule, is a mosaic of God, accompanied with many figures, by Gaddo Gaddi.

The chapel of Sixtus V. by Fontana, is a heap of absurdities. Opposite to it is that of Paul V. immensely rich in jasper, oriental alabaster, lapis lazuli, agate, amethyst, &c., but so heaped together as to hurt the eye.

The Sforza chapel is by Michelangelo. And in the church are some monuments by Guglielmo della Porta and Algardi.

The high altar is a large antique sarcophagus of porphyry. The paintings are by Guido.

In the square is one of the columns, belonging to the ancient famous temple of peace; it is fluted and very beautiful, but has been repaired. And behind the choir is a plain obelisk.

S. Paolo fuori, or fuila via Ostienfe, is a full mile from the gate, and if not built by Constantine, is certainly as old as Theodosius. There are two ailes on each side of the nave. The roof is of wood, the beams of an immense length, and joined by iron cramps:

this church is very ugly, and like a huge uncomfortable barn; it deserves, however, the attention of the curious, on account of the ancient columns and mosaics.

Of the first, there are not less than 140; 34 of porphyry, 20 of pavonazza marble from the mausoleum of Hadrian, with rich corinthian capitals; the rest of greek white or dove-coloured marble, or granite. The pavement is a chaos of precious marbles, and inscriptions. Over the arch of the high altar is an ancient mosaic, representing Christ in the midst of the twenty-four elders of the apocalypse, made at the cost of Placidia Galla. Round the middle aile, above the pillars, are portraits of all the Popes, from S. Peter to Benedict XIV. The three gates are of bronze, with historical subjects on them: they were made at Constantinople in the year 1070. The Convent belongs to the Benedictines.

S. Lorenzo fuori le mura is a very old church, with an open portico, and four wreathed columns. Three narrow ailes within, supported by eleven columns on each side. The pavement is in mosaic; and there are two pulpits of white marble, with porphyry, serpentine and mosaic, coeval with the church.

There are two ancient sarcophagi of marble, one with grapes, and the other with the ceremonies of marriage, in basso-relievo.

S. Croce in Gerusalemme has been repaired and adorned by Benedict XIV. It has very little remarkable, except some fine ancient pillars of granite. The statue of S. Helena was doubtless a Juno, and very dexterously metamorphosed into a saint. The frescos of the tribuna are by Pinturicchio. The chapel where the holy earth is deposited has frescos by Pomerancia, and mosaics by Peruzzi. In the gallery leading to the sacristy are three pictures by Rubens.

S. Sebastiano, a mile without the porta Capena, on the Appian way. The portico is supported by six antique granite columns of the ionic order. The only thing observable in this church, is a cumbent statue of S. Sebastian, supposed to be just shot to death: it is by Algardi's scholar, Giorgetti, who was Bernini's master.

Under this church are the Catacombs. They are very narrow in comparison with those at Naples, but are commonly said to extend forty miles. To make this out they must measure all the branches, and there is a disposition in mankind to lengthen out in imagination all these dark subterraneous passages. They were originally quarries of puzzolana, then served for burial places of the heathens, and afterwards of the christians.

Other Church's are—

S. *Agnes* on Piazza Navona; begun by Rainaldi, but finished by Borromini: the front and dome are by him. It is one of the most adorned in Rome, particularly with modern sculpture, among which the most remarkable is a bas-relief of the Saint, naked, except that she is covered with her hair, by Algardi. This is in the *soutterains*, which are said to have been the *Lupanaria*, whither S. Agnes was dragged in order to be defiled, had not her chastity been miraculously preserved.

S. *Agnese fuori delle mura*, is about a mile from the city, by the *porta Pia*. It was built in the lower ages, and is now almost under ground. Some of the columns are beautiful, but ill disposed. There are several of granite, breccia, and two of pavonazza marble. Four porphyry pillars support the great altar, and are esteemed the finest in or about Rome. In a little chapel, is a bust in white marble of

our

our Saviour, by Michelangelo; it is a masterpiece for character, and has served as a model to sculptors.

Close to the church of S. Agnese is a Rotonda, which probably was the burying place of Constantia. It is now called the church of *S Costanza*, and is commonly supposed to have been a temple of Bacchus, because the sarcophagus has carvings on it, of children playing with bunches of grapes, and there are allusions to Bacchus in the mosaics; but at that time they frequently mixed heathen with christian ornaments, were not nice about the propriety of them, and borrowed from other buildings at random. The dome is supported by twenty-four granite columns, of different sizes, with poor capitals. The porphyry sarcophagus is the largest about Rome, but ill wrought, and by no means elegant.

S. Agostino is remarkable for a painting in oil of the prophet Isaiah, as large as life, by Raffaelle; it is in his last manner, and in a very bold style, but the colouring is almost gone. There is also the coronation of the Virgin by God and Christ in heaven; S Augustin and S. Guglielmo are looking up from below: one of Lanfranco's best pictures.

In the convent is the Angelica library, lately augmented by that of Cardinal Passionei, and reckoned one of the largest in Rome.

S. Andrea del Noviziato, a beautiful little church by Bernini. In the chapel of S. Stanislaus Koska, is a picture of S. Francis adoring the virgin, by Carlo Maratti. the two columns of the altar are of the best oriental alabaster.—In S. Stanislaus's chamber, now converted into an oratory, is an admirable statue of this saint expiring, by Le Gros. S. Andrew adoring the cross, by Andrea Sacchi. A holy family, by Giulio Romano from Raffaelle.

S. Andrea della Valle, by Carlo Maderni. The great cupola is painted by Lanfranco: four evangelists in the angles, with great force of colouring, by Domenichino. The tribuna is by him and Calabrese.

The Strozzi chapel was designed and fitted up by M.chelangelo.

S. Bartolommeo, on the island in the Tiber, built on the ruins of a temple to Esculapius, where his statue was found, which is now in the Farnese gardens. Here is an antique porphyry sarcophagus under the high altar, and four porphyry columns on it. the other columns

columns also are antique. In the second chapel on the right are paintings by Ant. Carracci.

S. Bibiana. The statue of that Saint, by Bernini; the chastest of his works, and without flutter. Her body is said to repose in the finest piece of oriental alabaster in Rome; it seems to have been a bath. The fresco paintings, by Pietro da Cortona and his scholar Ciampelli have little merit.

S. Carlo à catenari, by Rosato Rosati, the front by Soria. The procession of S. Carlo Borromeo in the plague of Milan, at the high altar, is by Pietro da Cortona. S. Carlo, a fresco, behind it, by Guido. The tribuna, by Lanfranco. The annunciation, in the first chapel on the right, is also by him. The cardinal virtues in the angles of the cupola, by Domenichino. The death of S. Anne, by Andrea Sacchi.

S. Carlo al Corso is by Lunghi. The cupola is one of the best in Rome, but the front is miserable. At the high altar is a picture by Carlo Maratti, of the virgin and child, S. Carlo and S. Ambrogio. There is also a mosaic, from a picture of his, in the church of S. Maria del popolo.

S. Cæcilia in Trastevere, rich in agates and marbles. At the high altar are four columns of *nero e bianco antico*. The executioner cutting off S. Cecilia's head, is by Guido. Annibale Carracci has painted the virgin Mary in a small round. The elegant cumbent statue of S. Cecilia, is by Stefano Maderni.

S. Clemente, one of the first churches in Rome. Some granite columns in front: behind a small, but handsome court, with an arcade of granite columns, and bad ionic capitals. Within three ailes, with granite columns of all kinds. As at S. Lorenzo, so here, a place raised in the body of the church for a pulpit and desk; and inclosed by a marble rail curiously wrought. Hence you go up several steps to the choir; that is, a deep recess ending in the segment of a circle, and the cove above it in old mosaic. The high altar is supported by four porphyry columns; the pavement is all of saracen mosaic. In the chapel of the passion is the history of S. Catherine, painted by Masaccio. The tomb of Cardinal Roverella is an ancient sarcophagus of white marble.

S. Costanza, see *S: Agnese fuori*.

S. Crisogono or *Grisogono* in trastevere, has twenty-two granite columns of different sizes from the naumachia of Augustus, and the baths of Severus; two very large porphyry

phyry columns, and four of oriental alabaster. Guercino has painted the ascension of S. Crisogono in the middle of the cieling.

S. Eusebio. The cieling finely painted in fresco, by Mengs, with the apotheosis of the titular saint.

S. Francesco a Ripa. Christ dead, with the virgin and magdalen lamenting over him, and S. Francis with two little angels; by Annibale Carracci.

Il Gesu, built from designs of Vignola, and finished by Giacomo della Porta. The altar of S. Ignatius is rich and elegant beyond description: the quantities of lapis lazuli, porphyry, gilt bronze, and the most precious marbles, which are used about it, are prodigious; and yet they are put together so as not to offend the eye. The pillars that support it are entirely of lapis lazuli fluted with gilt bronze. Among the statues, that of religion, by Le Gros, has great merit. The statue of S. Ignatius, bigger than life is of massive silver.

S. Giovanni Battista de' Fiorentini, terminates the *strada Giulia,* and was built from the designs of Giacomo della Porta: the front is by Galilei, and is elegant, with two orders of corinthian three-quarter columns, all of Tivertine stone: within it is old, but repaired: the doors have very chaste entablatures. The high altar was designed by Pietro da Cortona, but finished after his death by Ciro Ferri. The painting of S. Jerom is by Santi di Tito—that of the saints Cosmo and Damiano, is by Salvator Rosa—S. Francis is also by Santi di Tito: the frescos by Niccolò Pomerancia.

S. Giovanni Evangelista de Bolognesi. S. John the evangelist, and S. Petronius bishop of Bologna, with the virgin and Christ above, and below a charming group of little boys, playing with the mitre; by Domenichino: little inferior to his famous S. Jerom.

S. S. Giovanni e Paolo is an ancient church, divided into three ailes by thirty granite columns: there are two lions of porphyry at the gate, and under the altar of S. Saturninus, a fine urn of porphyry. Here are mosaic pavements of the 11th or 12th century.

S. Girolamo della carità. S. Jerom dying, and receiving the communion; by Domenichino: esteemed one of the four first pictures in Rome.

S. Giuseppe: a bad front, small and handsome within. The nativity, by Carlo Maratti.—Under this church is an ancient Roman

man prison, built of very large stones of Piperino; now called the prison of S. Peter, who is said to have been imprisoned here: it has a fine spring, which they tell you issued forth miraculously to enable the apostle to baptize the gaolers and forty-seven other persons. A staircase now leads down to it from the church; and there is a hole into a dungeon under the other, where Jugurtha ended his days: though this is now thirty feet below the surface, it does not follow that it was anciently under ground, the soil of the city having been so much raised.

S. Giuseppe a capo le case. The virgin and the angel waking Joseph, by Andrea Sacchi; at the high altar, S. Theresa, by Lanfranco.

S. Gregorio magno, on monte Celio. S. Gregory between two angels, and little angels hovering above, by Annibale Caracci! In the chapel of S. Andrea adjoining, are the two trial pieces in fresco of his scholars Guido and Domenichino. That of Guido is on the left, and represents S. Andrew going to martyrdom. Domenichino has painted the flagellation of the same Saint.—In the chapel of S. Silvia, Guido has painted a concert of angels on the cieling. The titular Saint

Saint is painted by John Parker, an Englishman.

S. Ignazio is a very magnificent church, and a handsome piece of architecture within. Domenichino, among other artists, gave plans for it, and they selected what seemed best. The front is by Algardi. The two altars in the cross are rich: the bas-relief (in the Lancelotti chapel) of S. Luigi Gonzaga, is one of Le Gros's best works. The cieling of the nave is by the famous Jesuit Pozzi: it represents the apotheosis of S. Ignatius; and from his head issue rays, illuminating the four parts of the world. With all its faults it produces a great effect, owing to the justness of the perspective.

S. Isidore. Two chapels painted entirely by Carlo Maratti. S. Isidore at the high altar is by Andrea Sacchi. The virgin and child in the chapel next to this is by Carlo Maratti, and one of his best compositions.

S. Lorenzo in Lucina. Over the high altar, a crucifix, by Guido, esteemed the best in Rome. A dying nun, by Benefiali. Nicola Poussin is buried here.

S. Luigi de' Francesi is handsomely fitted up with different marbles, and gilt stucco. The front is by Giacomo della Porta. At the

the high altar is an excellent assumption, by the elder Bassan. In the first chapel on the right, S. Andrew and S. John Baptist, by Lanfranco. In the second, a copy by Guido, of Raffaelle's famous picture of S. Cecilia at Bologna. The story of S. Cecilia is painted on the walls by Domenichino. S. Matthew, and the sides of the chapel next the high altar, are by Caravaggio.—In the Sacristy is a large picture, by John Miel; and a small holy family, by Corregio.

S. Marco, adjoining to the palace of the same name, in which the Venetian ambassador resides, contains the following paintings among others. The frescos of the middle aile, by Francesco Mola and others. The picture of the first altar, by Palma, and the sides by Tintoretto. The third, by Carlo Maratti—the adoration of the Magi, a much-admired picture. S. Mark, in the chapel of the sacrament, is by Pietro Perugino; the other paintings, as also the tribuna, by Borgognone; but the Evangelist in the middle, by Romanelli. The pictures of the two altars beyond the Sacristy are by Mola. The third by Ciro Ferri: but S. John and S. Mark by Pietro Perugino, and the paintings on the sides by Carlo Maratti. In the
chapel

chapel of the holy virgin, the nativity of the virgin, by Giov. Franc. Bolognese. The annunciation, by Alberti. The flight into Egypt, and the assumption, by Alessandro Bolognese.

S. Maria degli Angeli is the noblest church in Rome next to S. Peter's, made out of Diocletian's *thermæ* by Michelangelo. It was the room in which the youth performed the exercises in bad weather. The roof and eight granite columns, with their capitals and entablature, are ancient; the columns at least forty feet high, and seem to stand in the same place they anciently did. the four angular ones are corinthian, and the others composite. The church is nearly in form of a greek cross. Benedict XIV. fitted it up under the direction of Vanvitelli, and removed hither some pictures from S. Peter's, which were displaced to make room for the mosaics. —S. Jerom, by Muziani. The fall of Simon Magus, by Pompeio Battoni. The baptism of Christ, by Carlo Maratti. The martyrdom of S. Sebastian, by Domenichino. S. Basil, or the greek mass, by Subleyras. S. Peter raising Tabitha, by Baglioni.

Bianchini traced a meridian line upon the pavement.

On

On each side of the entrance, where anciently was an hypocaust, are the tombs of Carlo Maratti and Salvator Rosa.

S. Maria dell' anima. In the sacristy, a picture by Giulio Romano, wherein S. John presents S. Rocco to the virgin and Christ; S. Mark is below with the lion; angels above: architecture and small figures in the back ground. The cieling by Romanelli. There are paintings by Salviati and others in the church: and two monuments with boy angels chiffelled by Fiamingo.

S. Maria in Araceli is situated on very high ground near the Capitol, doubtless on the spot where stood the temple of Jupiter Capitolinus. The ascent to it is by eighty marble steps, all ancient. The granite columns which support the nave are common; but there are two of white marble, in the lower part of the church, which probably were within the ancient temple. Here are many ancient monuments, and a great number of chapels, adorned with marbles, sculptures, and paintings. At the high altar is one of S. Luke's virgins, as they are called; and opposite to it, in the choir, is a picture by Raffaelle, which some say is only a copy. In

one

one of the chapels are the conversion and death of S. Margaret, by Benefiah.

S. Maria in Campitelli is remarkable for a cross of alabaster over the high altar, appearing of the colour of fire. It was cut out of a column found in the ruins of Livia's portico.

Concezione d' Maria Vergine de' Cappucini, in Piazza Barberini.—In this church are some good ancient ionic columns. Over the door is Giotto's carton for the mosaic at S. Peter's. The conception at the high altar, and the nativity of Christ, both by Lanfranco. S. Antonio raising a dead body; the virgin with a bishop, and four others, not very good, by Andrea Sacchi. S. Francis supported by an Angel, by Domenichino. But the two best pictures are, the archangel Michael, by Guido; and Saul restored to sight, by Pietro da Cortona.

S. Maria di Loreto. A beautiful statue of S. Susanna, by Fiammingo.

S. Maria Maddalena, in the Corso. The Magdalen penitent, by Guercino.

S. Maria ad martyres, commonly called *la Rotonda.* See *Pantheon* among the Antiquities.

S. Maria sopra Minerva, so called from it being

being built where there was a temple dedicated to Minerva by Pompey. The altar picture in the Aldobrandini chapel is the last work of Baroccio. In a small chapel is a crucifix painted by Giotto, on wood. But the statue of Christ holding his cross, by Michelangelo Buonarroti is the greatest object of curiosity here.

S. Maria di monte santo, on the Piazza del Popolo: the first chapel on the right is entirely painted by Salvator Rosa. In two other chapels, the holy family, and S. Francis with S. Roch praying to the virgin, both by Carlo Maratti. In the Sacristy, the virgin with the infant Jesus, by Baciccio, and other paintings by him and Chiari.

S. Maria in Navicella, so called from an antique ship in marble, in the area before it, has eighteen curious columns of granite, and two of porphyry. The frieze is painted by Giulio Romano and Perino del Vaga.

S. Maria dell' orto built from designs of Giulio Romano; the front by Martino Lunghi. Paintings—the Visitation, by Federigo Zuccheri. The nativity, by Taddeo Zuccheri. The annunciation, fresco, by the same, &c.

S. Maria della Pace, so called from its being

ing erected by Sixtus V. upon peace being restored to Italy in 1482. Here are frescos of the prophets and sibyls, by Raffaelle, almost effaced.

S. Maria del Popolo. The most remarkable thing here is a statue of Jonas standing on the fish, executed by Lorenzetto from a design by Raffaelle; who himself, as they say, attended every stroke of the chisel. The three other statues, one by Lorenzetto, and two by Bernini, are far inferior. The chapel in which they are was made by Baltazare di Perugia, from a plan of Raffaelle's: the altar picture by Sebastiano del Piombo. In the first chapel on the right is a præsepe or nativity, by Pinturicchio. In the second, the conception of the virgin, with four saints, by Carlo Maratti. S. Augustin, with the virgin, in the third, is by Pinturicchio. The assumption of the virgin, in the chapel next the high altar, on the other side, is partly by Annibale Carracci, and partly by Albani and the martyrdom of S. Peter, as also the conversion of S. Paul, are by Caravaggio.

S. Maria in scala cœli is an octagon, by Vignola. Under it is an opening to the catacombs, and just by is the place where S. Paul is supposed to have been martyred. Here

Here they have built a pretty little church, called *alle tre Fontane*, because within it are three fountains which sprung up, say they, where the head of the saint took so many bounds, after it was cut off. These fountains are adorned with six columns of numidian marble, and a bust of S. Paul on each. There is a picture of the martyrdom of S. Peter, by Guido and some mosaics in the tribuna.

S. Maria in Trastevere has twenty-three or twenty-four columns of granite of different sizes. The mosaics of the tribuna are of the 12th century, but have been repaired by Cavallini. On the last pilaster to the left is a piece of ancient mosaic; and underneath, a bas relief in marble, by Buonarroti. The assumption of the virgin on the cieling, is by Domenichino. There is a picture of S. John Baptist by Antonio Carracci, and some other paintings. Lanfranco and Ciro Ferri are buried here.

S. Maria in vallicella, a handsome shell; the dome finely executed, and well lighted; painted by Luca Giordano; the vault of the nave by Pietro da Cortona. Of the pictures the principal are, the entombing of Christ, by Michel' Angelo da Caravaggio. The virgin,

virgin, Christ, S. Carlo, S. Ignazio, and Angels, by Carlo Maratti. S. Filippo Neri, by Guido. Three pictures at the high altar, by Rubens. The presentation of the virgin, and the visitation, both by Baroccio. The Annunciation, by Passignani.—In the Sacristy, the statue of S. Filippo Neri, and his bust over the door, are by Algardi, and the cieling is by Pietro da Cortona.

The Convent has a considerable Library, with many manuscripts.

S. Maria in via lata, designed by Pietro da Cortona.

S. Maria della Vittoria, built at the expence of the catholic powers, to show the triumph of popery in the death of Gustavus Adolphus. Maderni was the architect; the front is by Giov. Battista Soria, and the inside is by Bernini. The architecture is better than in most of the churches; but within it is overcharged with rich marbles, lapis lazuli, &c. without taste.—Paintings are, the virgin, Christ, and S. Francis, by Domenichino. The Trinity, by Guercino, &c. The most remarkable thing in this church is S. Teresa in extasy, with an angel; marble group by Bernini.

S. Martino S. Luca, belonging to the ac-

...emy of painters, is built after the designs of Pietro da Cortona.

In the apartments of the academy of S. Luke, adjoining to the church, is a collection of pictures.*

SS. Martino e Silvestro a i monti, said to be built on the ruins of Titus's baths. It is

full

---

* The principal of these are—

In the first room.

Bertha spinning. Three old bearded heads, by Francesco Mola.

Repose of the holy family, by Baroccio.

A pietà, by Giuseppe Chiari

Six landscapes, by Orizonte

Appearance of the angels to the shepherds, by Giacomo Bassano.

Two landscapes, in one of them a view of Ti..., by Salvator Rosa

Mad cat's heads, by the same.

Christ with the two disciples at Emmaus.

The magdalen anointing the feet of Jesus. Both Benedetto Luti

S. Luke painting the virgin and Christ, by Rafaele. This was in the church, and is much damaged; a copy is put there in its room.

Ercolo..., by Guido.

Three

full of ancient granite and cipolline columns, but the greatest curiosities here are many landscapes, slight but in a good taste, all by Gaspar Pouffin, except two next the altar of S. Maria

Three marines; by Vernet.
Two ruins of Rome, by Paolo Panini.
A man with a dog and goats, by Rosa di Tivoli.

In the second room.

Cupid with a bird, by Guido.
Two landscapes, by Pouffin.
Render to Cæsar, &c.; by Tiziano the same as in the Pitti palace at Florence.
S. Jerom, by Salvator Rosa.
Cattle, with figures and ruins, by Berghem.
The miracle of the bloody host, commonly called the miracle of Bolsena, by Trevisani.
A head, by Guercino.

In the third room.

A fine large cattle-piece, with a landscape and ruined buildings; by Berghem.
A little boy's head, in a round; by Tiziano.
Samson pulling down the temple of Dagon, by Solimene.
Ruins of Rome, by Panini.
Susanna and the elders, by Paolo Veronese.
Hope, by Angelica Kauffman.
A woman's

S. Maria Maddalena de' Pazzi, which were painted by Giov. Franc. Grimaldi da Bologna. Nicola Pouſſin painted the figures in ſome, and Pietro Teſta in others.

S. Nicolò in carcere, ſo called becauſe it was the priſon, wherein paſſed the celebrated ſcene, called the Roman charity. It has nothing ancient except the two columns in

A woman's head with flowers, by Cignani.
A marine, by Vernet.
A drawing, by Salvator Roſa.
The flagellation of Chriſt—and Chriſt carrying his croſs, both by Trevilani.

This Academy was founded in the ſixteenth century, by Muziano, its reputation was raiſed in the ſuit, by Pietro da Cortona, and it received a conſiderable encouragement in the preſent, by the prizes inſtituted by Clement XI. On the 18th of September theſe prizes are diſtributed in the large hall of the Capitol, on which occaſion it is richly hung and illuminated. Many Cardinals, and other perſons of conſideration, are preſent. the Arcadians have their places in the front row, and the members of the Academy in the ſecond. Some pieces of muſic are performed, an oration is delivered, ſonnets are repeated by the Arcadians, and the prizes, which are ſilver medals, are diſtributed by the Car-

K   front,

front, and a sarcophagus of black porphyry, with two heads of Egyptian women on it in relievo.

S. Onofrio, at the extremity of the Janiculum, has some good paintings.

Three histories of S. Jerom, and other pieces, by Domenichino.

Our Lady of Loretto, by Annibale Carracci.

Barclay, Tasso, and Alessandro Guido, are buried in this church; and there is the portrait of the second in mosaic.

S. Pietro in carcere; see S. Giuseppe.

S. Pietro in Montorio is a small old church, which would not deserve notice, were it not for the Transfiguration, by Raffaelle, generally allowed to be the first easel painting in the world. Over the first altar on the right is the scourging of our Lord, by Sebastiano del Piombo. The situation of the church, and convent of Franciscans, to which it belongs, is airy and good, on the top of the Janiculum.

In the court of the convent is the round doric temple of Bramante, built of Tivertine stone, and surrounded by a portico of sixteen columns of oriental granite, with mar-

ble

the bases and capitals. S. Peter, they say, suffered martyrdom here.

S. Pietro in vincoli. The monument of Pope Julius II. by Michelangelo. In the upper part, the Pope is leaning on a sarcophagus, between two of the cardinal virtues: in the lower part is the famous statue of Moses, between the other two cardinal virtues.

The paintings are—S. Peter delivered out of prison; Domenichino.

S. John, S. Augustin, S. Margaret, S. Peter delivered out of prison, and the portrait of Cardinal Margotti; all by Guercino.

An ancient painting by Pollaiolo, with his tomb and bust.

The tomb also of Giulio Clovio, the miniature painter or illuminator, is here.

S. Prassede, an ancient church, in which are four antique columns of white marble, fluted. Before the chief altar is a *ciborio* supported by four porphyry columns, joined to pilasters of giallo-antico. In one of the chapels is a column, brought by one of the Colonna family from the holy land in 1223, pretended to be that to which our Saviour was tied for flagellation. There are also some

curious

curious pillars of black and white granite, of Serpentino nero antico, and oriental alabaster.

In *S. Romualdo* is the famous picture by Andrea Sacchi, of S. Romualdo sitting, with other Camaldules standing. This is esteemed one of the four first paintings in Rome.

S. Sabina, on the top of the Aventine hill, was built about the fourth century, on the ruins of the temple of Juno, of which twenty-four fluted corinthian columns still exist, and support the roof. The upper part of the church is incrusted with marble; there is much verd-antique, porphyry and serpentine; and the inside of the arches is covered with small pieces of white marble, well joined by little cramps of iron. On the outside of the church are two large columns of black Egyptian granite; four wreathed columns, &c.

A black stone of a spheroid form is preserved here, with a formal inscription, telling you how the Devil threw it at S. Dominic one night to frighten him from his prayers. It is of basalt, and is nothing but an ancient weight.

On one of the altars there is a picture by

Sasso-Ferrata, of the virgin and Christ with saints and angels. There are also paintings by Federigo and Taddeo Zuccheri.

This church, and that of S. Alessio or Alexis, and the Priory of Malta, are finely situated for a view of Rome in its whole extent.

The church of *La Sapienza* is in a singular style of architecture, by Borromini. On the outside it is a deep concave, with a wretched cupola; within a sort of octagon, with a sugar-loaf dome. At the altar is a picture of S. Ivo, advocate of the poor, by Pietro da Cortona; the bottom by Ciro Ferri.

S. Silvestro a monte Cavallo. Four famous *tondi* in fresco, by Domenichino. The subjects—1. Judith and Holofernes. 2. Ahasuerus and Esther. 3. David dancing before the ark. 4. Solomon on his throne, with Bathsheba.

S. John the evangelist and Mary Magdalen, by Algardi.

Descent of the Holy Ghost; by Giacomo Palma.

In the chapel of the Magdalen, paintings by Polidoro da Caravaggio and Cav. d'Arpino.

Near the great door is the monument of Cardinal Bentivoglio.

The Convent is handsome, has pleasant gardens and a fine library.

S. Tomaso, dedicated not to the incredulous apostle, but the turbulent archbishop of Canterbury. This fifth church was originally dedicated to the Trinity by Offa in 630, and that he built an hospital for English pilgrims adjoining to it. Saint Thomas a Becket having lived here when he was at Rome, the Trinity was turned out, and the church was dedicated to him. The hospital also was converted into a college by Gregory XIII, and Cardinal Norfolk rebuilt it in 1575.

God the father, with Christ dead in his bosom, is painted over the high altar, by Durand Aleriti.

Pomerancia has painted several English martyrs in fresco.

In the Hall are portraits of martyrs in the time of Henry VIII. and Elizabeth.

Trinità de' monti, on the Pincian hill, with the Convent of French Minims adjoining, is finely situated near the Villa Medici. The ascent to it is by a prodigious flight of steps, from the Piazza di Spagna.

In

In this church is the famous descent from the cross, by Daniele di Volterra; and the only picture by him on a large scale. It is in fresco, and much damaged.

Trinità de' pellegrini. A capital picture of the Trinity, by Guido. God stands in heaven, supporting Christ on the cross; and below are two angels adoring it.

PALACES.

The CAPITOL, now called *il Campo doglio*, is in a high situation; and the ascent to it is by a noble flight of steps. At the foot of them are two fine Egyptian lionesses in basalt, from the baths of Agrippa. In the area before the building are colossal statues of Caius and Lucius, nephews of Augustus. The trophies of Marius, as they are called, but more probably of Trajan. Two statues, called the sons of Constantine. A roman mile-stone, found one mile from the old *porta Capena*; a proof that they reckoned from the gates, and not from the forum. The pillar which answers to this is modern. In the middle of the area is the fine equestrian statue of Marcus Aurelius, bigger than life, of corinthian brass, anciently gilt.

The building consists of a centre and two wings, forming three sides of this area; all of stucco, and making a pretty appearance. The architect Michelangelo Buonarroti. The Senator of Rome inhabits the centre, and the ascent to it is truly noble. The right wing contains the famous Museum and on the left is the palace of the Conservators, a cabinet of pictures, &c. The ancient Capitol fronted towards the arch of Severus; the foundations *(Capitolii immobile saxum)* are still visible, in that part which is opposite to the temple of Jupiter Capitolinus; but much more so on the other side, towards the temple of Concord. I shall not undertake to determine whether a man would break his neck, by a fall from the Tarpeian rock the height is now 58 or 60 feet perpendicular, and the ground below is probably raised 20 feet.

Going up to the central building is a fountain, with a statue of *Roma triumphans* in porphyry, brought from Cori, one of the oldest towns of Latium; and on each side, the rivers Nile and Tiber, in greek marble. In the apartments above, there is a room painted in fresco by Cavalier d'Arpino; in six pieces, representing the first great events of the Roman history. The next room is painted by

Tommaso Laureti: and here are busts of Julius Cæsar, Hadrian, Caracalla, &c. On two columns of verd-antique, the head of Severus and another. The wolf, with Romulus and Remus, in white marble. In the antichamber next to this, the frieze is painted in fresco by Volterrano: here is the famous wolf in bronze, supposed to be that which was struck with lightning at the death of Julius Cæsar; the shepherd Cneius Martius extracting a thorn from his foot, and one of the Camilli, statues in bronze; the bust of Lucius Junius Brutus, son of Marcus. In the fourth room are the Fasti Consulares; over the door the head of Mithridates in bassorilievo, a Vestal and Diana. In the fifth room are several busts—Sappho, Socrates, &c. A painting of the holy family, by Giulio Romano. In the Stanza dell' Ercole, Annibale Carracci has painted in fresco the exploits of Scipio in the frieze. Here are statues and busts of Appius Claudius, Cicero, Virgil, Galba. Statue of Hercules in bronze. Busts of a Bacchant, and Alexander the great. Pallas, Lucretia, Messalina. In another room, fresco by Pietro Perugino. Statues of Silence, Cybele, and Ceres. Busts of L. Cornelius, and Hadrian.

Hence you come to the building erected by Benedict XIV. for the pictures which he purchased of the Sacchetti and Pio families. They are in two large rooms, and few of them are capital.

In the court on the left hand, where the Conservators' palace is, the most remarkable things are, the feet and one hand of a mutilated colossal statue of Apollo, supposed to have been 41 feet high; the great toe measures 37 inches round. A lion tearing a horse, repaired by Michelangelo. A fine bas-relief of a weeping province, supposed Dacia, on the pedestal of the colossal figure of Roma triumphans.

Two captive Bulgarians, in pietra di paragone.

Colossal head of Commodus, in bronze.

Colossal head of Domitian, in greek marble.

Statue of a Bacchant, seems modern.

At the foot of the staircase, by which also you go to the picture-gallery, is the famous rostral column, said to be erected in the forum in honour of Duilius, who gained the first naval victory over the Carthaginians. It is so perfect, that one cannot but doubt its antiquity, considering that it stood in the open air.

air. The pedestal, on which is the inscription, is certainly antique, and much worn.

On the opposite side is the Museum, the best in Rome for busts, inscriptions, and sarcophagi; with several fine statues.

At the end of the court, opposite to the gate, lies Marforio, which is a cumbent statue of the Rhine. Two terms in form of satyrs, are on the sides; and two others, a man and a woman. A curious bas-relief of three ancient fasces, and another of Saturn and Rhea. Over the doors, heads of Philosophers. Under the portico, two large Egyptian idols, one of red granite, the other of basalt. A large sarcophagus, of Alexander Severus, and his mother Julia Mammæa, with good bas-reliefs on it. A colossal statue of Pyrrhus, king of Epirus; and some other statues. A column of oriental alabaster.

In a room at the foot of the staircase a fine collection of Egyptian deities in basalt, and granite, found in Hadrian's villa.

On the staircase is a curious plan of ancient Rome, on twenty-one pieces of marble. It was the pavement of the temple of Romulus and Remus in the via sacra, and is as old as the time of Alexander Severus. Bas-reliefs of the history of Marcus Aurelius; and a

curious

curious one of Curtius, leaping into the gulph. The elder Faustina and Juno, statues.

The apartment above consists of six rooms, and a gallery.

The Vase room, so called from a fine vase of white marble, with an antique round altar for a pedestal. The walls are covered with inscriptions. Here are five sarcophagi. The mask of a satyr. Three statues, of a muse, cupid, and an attendant at the baths.

Hercules room. A large Apollo with his lyre, leaning on a griffon. Psyche. Agrippina sitting. The hunter Polytimus, with a staff and hare. Cupid and Psyche embracing. Antinous, fine features without expression; the legs, hands, and one arm, modern. A Menade, or old drunken priestess of Bacchus, holding a flask, and her head thrown back. Three busts. A female term. Two piping Fauns. Hercules, a term. Mars and Venus. Hercules burning the hydra's heads. Three boys, with a goose, mask, and serpent.

Sala grande. Above thirty antique statues, and a great number of busts. The dying Gladiator. countenance vulgar, as it was; expression fine; body admirable. one arm restored

restored by Michelangelo.—Falling Gladiator. the body and head only antique. Two Centaur, in paragon marble, very excellent: the cupids are gone, and are in the Borghese. A tall Osiris, in white marble. Clemency. Venus. Leda. Faun. Apollo. Amazon, very excellent. Diana. Muse. Priestess, with a vase. Juno. Faun, with a lion's skin and flute. Marius, a consular figure standing, with the fierce, penetrating countenance he is said to have had. Augustus. Ceres. Young Antinous. Hadrian naked, in the character of Mars. Apollo. Julia Pia, as a vestal. An Egyptian priestess, with the sistrum and lotus. Ptolemy. Marcus Aurelius. A *pleureuse,* or weeper at a funeral, with a lacrymatory. Pallas. Hygieia. Muse. Harpocrates.—A colossal statue of Innocent X. sitting; in bronze, by Algardi.

Stanza di Filosofi. Statues of Zeno, a gladiator, &c.

Busts. Metrodorus and Epicurus, as a Janus. Asclepiades. Plato. Hiero. Pindar. Leodamas. Lycias. Pythodoris. Archimedes. Virgil. Diogenes. Aristomachus. Pythagoras. Lucius Apuleius. Theophrastus. Aristotle. Agatho Erythræus. Heraclitus. Alcibiades. Carneades. Socrates.

Aristides. Hippocrates. Seneca. Dionysius of Utica. Marcus Aurelius; and many unknown; 103 in all.

Two statues, a son and daughter of Niobe.

Over the door, a bas-relief of the death of Meleager; and in the room several others.

Stanza di Imperadori. Statue of Flora, found in the Villa Adriani: a pretty figure, with good drapery, but not equal to the Farnese. Venus issuing from the bath, the best statue of her in Rome; the nose, right hand, and two fingers of the left, modern. Statue of Hercules Aventinus, an overgrown boy, in basalt. Eighty-three busts of Emperors, Empresses, &c. A fine bust of Jupiter. Several bassorilievos.

Gallery. The walls covered with inscriptions. Statues of Jupiter and Æsculapius, in *marmo bigio*. Sylla sitting, on an altar dedicated to Hercules. Jupiter is on a round altar, with figures of Apollo, &c. Agrippina sitting. Ceres also sitting, on an altar with festoons and instruments of sacrifice. Busts of Trajan; Scipio Africanus; a Muse; Juno, colossal, Antoninus Pius; Marcus Agrippa, &c. A small urn with bacchanals; and other urns, vases, altars, &c.

Miscellaneous room. Ancient inscriptions on

on the walls. The chief things here, for there are many, are a Faun holding up a bunch of grapes; at his feet a goat upon a basket, in *rosso antico*. Diana triformis in bronze. A small statue of an old Satyr.—Busts of Ariadne; Alexander the great; Jupiter Ammon; Domitius Oenobarbus; Sylvanus; Bacchus. Gabriel Faerno, by Michelangelo.—A beautiful bronze vase, found in the port of Antium.—Pigeons on a vase, a most beautiful ancient mosaic.

The VATICAN is a vast palace[*], and very irregular, having been built at many different times. I shall not pretend to describe any thing but what highly merits the attention of a stranger.

One of the Courts has *loggie*, or open galleries, and three orders—doric, ionic, and corinthian: the architect Bramante. The upper *loggia* is painted with the sacred history from the creation, on the cieling; and

[*] There are 13,000 rooms in it, according to Bonanni, but in this account he must include the cellars, &c. Venuti makes them 11,500. Keysler says there are 12,524 rooms, 11,246 chambers, and 22 courts. Richard gives it only 4422 rooms.

on the walls with arabesques, in a wonderful fine taste, by Raffaelle's scholars*, from designs of their master's. These frescos being on walls exposed to the open air, have suffered considerably, and most of the historical subjects have been more or less repaired.—Some of the best are—the Creation; the Angel driving Adam and Eve out of paradise; Lot and the three angels; Lot and his daughters going from Sodom; Joseph explaining Pharaoh's dreams; finding of Moses; Moses striking the rock; and the judgment of Solomon.

From this *loggia* you enter an apartment of four rooms, called *le stanze di Raffaelle*, wherein are the first works in fresco painting which the world can boast †. They are much injured by time, damp and smoke.

---

* Giulio Romano, Perino del Vaga, Francesco Penni, surnamed il Fattore, and Giovanni di Udino. The accounts of what Raffaelle himself executed are various. Richardson says, only the figure of Eve, whereas De La Lande attributes the six first histories to him, with the baptism and the last supper.

† They are described at large by Bellori, and others.

In

In the hall of Constantine are four large pieces—1. Constantine's vision. 2. His victory over Maxentius. 3. His baptism, by Pope Silvester. 4 The donation of Rome to the same Pope. The two first of these are by Giulio Romano; the two last, by Giov. Francesco Penni; from designs of their master Raffaelle. The second is incomparably the best.

In this room, at one end of the battle, is a most admirable figure of Justice, by Raffaelle's own hand; as is also that of Mercy.

In the next room are four large pieces. 1. Incendio di Borgo, or the fire in the suburbs of Rome, extinguished by Leo IV. This has been retouched. 2. The victory of the same Pope over the Saracens at Ostia. 3. The justification of Pope Leo III 4. The coronation of Charlemagne, a collection of fine portraits. The cieling is by Pietro Perugino.

In the third room, the four principal pictures are—1. Heliodorus driven out of the temple by angels under Onias: dated 1514. Raffaelle has introduced an episode of Pope Julius II. brought into the temple. 2. Attila coming to destroy Rome, restrained by S. Leo the great. dated 1514. Leo X. is here represented under the character of Leo I. 3. The miracle of Bolsena: dated 1512. 4. S Peter delivered out of prison by the angel: most singular picture for effect. It has three lights—from the angel—from the moon— and from the moon and torch: the angel all effulgence.

In the cieling of this room, among bot little stories and grotesque ornaments, don. by painters who worked here before Raffa elle, are four scripture stories, corresponding with the larger works. 1. God appearing to Moses in the burning bush. 2. Noah re turning thanks for being preserved from the deluge. 3. The sacrifice of Abraham. 4. Jacob's dream.

In the last room, called *la camera de la Segnatura*, are also four principal pictures—1. The dispute of the doctors concerning the Eucharist. 2. The school of Athens; for composition, and variety and justness of ex pression unrivalled. 3. Mount Parnassus, a picture full of beauties. 4. Justinian giving the digests to Trebonian; and Gregory IX. under the figure of Julius II. giving the de cretals to an advocate.

Besides these, the four cardinal virtues are painted over the windows: and on the ciel ing

ing are four rounds, the subjects of which correspond with the four principal pictures. 1. The temptation of Adam. 2. A woman looking on a globe. 3. The judgement of Solomon. 4. The story of Marsyas. To represent Theology, Philosophy, Jurisprudence, and Poetry.

The surbases of the rooms, and some windows, are painted in chiaro-oscuro, by Policore Caravaggio; as great a master in his way as Raffaelle was in his.

Bernini's great staircase leads to the *Sala regia*, painted with large histories. The entry of Gregory XI. into Rome from Avignon, by Vasari, is the most esteemed*. This hall

---

* The others are—

Charlemagne restoring the patrimony to the church, by Taddeo Zucchero.

Gregory IX. excommunicating the emperor Frederic II. by Giorgio Vasari.

Pepin, king of France, regaining Ravenna to the Roman see, by beating Astolfo king of the Lombards, by the same.

Peter, king of Aragon, coming to Rome to do homage to Innocent III. by Livio Agresti.

Otho I. restoring to the church the provinces he had seized, by Marco da Siena.

Gregory

hall is a kind of vestibule to the Sistine and Pauline chapels.

The *Sistine Chapel* is chiefly remarkable for the last judgement, by Michelangelo Buonarroti, which fills the east end: there is great confusion in this immense work, but some detached parts of it are very fine. The cieling is also painted by him, and has some things of great merit; no man can see the Eternal disentangling the chaos, which is near the upper end of the room, without awe and astonishment.

On the walls are six histories on each side from the old testament, by Pietro Perugino and other old painters.

In the *Pauline Chapel* are also two large pictures, by Michelangelo, the crucifixion

Gregory II forcing Luitprand to confirm a former donation to the church, by Orazio Sammachini.

The Emperor Barbarossa at the feet of Pope Alexander III by Salviati.

The victory over the Turks at Lepanto, by Vasari.

Gregory VII absolving the Emperor Henry IV by Taddeo and Federigo Zuccheri.

Massacre of the Huguenots, by Vasari.

of S. Peter, and the conversion of the gentiles; these are said to be his last works. The cieling is by Federigo Zuccheri; and the fall of Simon Magus, with other histories, are by Lorenzino Sabatini da Bologna.

The Vatican *Library* is in form of a T. In the vestibule are some landscapes by Paul Brill. The principal gallery is upwards of 200 feet long, and about 52 feet wide. The collection of books consists of the ancient library of the Popes; that of the dukes of Urbino, of Heidelberg, and of queen Cristina. Clement XI. enriched it with syriac and arabic manuscripts; and Benedict XIV. gave the manuscripts of Ottoboni, and Marchese Alessandro Capponi. This library is not so remarkable for printed books as for manuscripts; of the former there are perhaps about 30,000 volumes; of the latter upwards of 40,000. Being all in close presses, they are wholly concealed from the eye; these presses are low, and painted on the outside.

Besides the books, there is a fine column of oriental alabaster; a noble collection of etruscan vases, a *museum christianum*, consisting of antiques, mostly relative to christianity, medals, and other curiosities. There
are

are also some little pictures of high antiquity—an original portrait of Charlemagne on stucco. Eight little pieces, among which one by Cimabue of a virgin and Christ; and another by Giotto, which is a scripture history in three compartments. Many old greek paintings antecedent to the times of those masters who are generally reputed the restorers, if not the inventors of the art; but who evidently copied the greeks, and improved upon them. Among others here is S. Theodore, *in Musivo XI. Seculo*. These are in cabinets, in one of the side galleries at the end of which is an elegant little room fitted up with the finest marbles, and a beautiful cieling, by Mengs; and beyond this another room, on the cieling of which are three actions of Samson, by Guido.

The *Belvedere* communicates with the Vatican by an open gallery. Here is that noble repository of antique sculpture, called the Clementine Museum; and the present Pope has fitted up a set of apartments, worthy them and him, for their better reception*.

In

---

* I am not able to do this collection justice. It was in great confusion when I was at Rome, on account

In the niches of a portico surrounding a small open court, is the famous Apollo Belvedere, and the no less famous Laocoon; the former incomparably the finest single figure, and the latter the noblest group in the world. Apollo is supposed to have just discharged his arrow at the Python: his attitude is beautiful, natural, and unaffected; his countenance composed and elegant; the workmanship of every part exquisite: he is longer from the middle downwards than nature; but this deviation from the proportion of the human figure adds clearly to his dignity; and upon the whole he has an unspeakable sublimity, that inspires admiration, awe, and reverence. The foot upon which he rests has been broken, and the hands have been restored.

In the Laocoon there is not a feature or muscle which does not show the deepest anguish. The father's flesh is all contracted in consequence of the poison, and his very toes are visibly affected by it. The youngest son is falling down in the agonies of death: the other is not yet hurt, and is looking towards his father, wishing to help him, and at the

count of the improvements which the Pope was then making.

same

are also some little pictures of high antiquity—an original portrait of Charlemagne on stucco. Eight little pieces, among which one by Cimabue of a virgin and Christ; and another by Giotto, which is a scripture history in three compartments. Many old greek paintings antecedent to the times of those masters who are generally reputed the restorers, if not the inventors of the art; but who evidently copied the greeks, and improved upon them. Among others here is S. Theodore, *in Musivo XI. Seculo*. These are in cabinets, in one of the side galleries at the end of which is an elegant little room fitted up with the finest marbles, and a beautiful cieling, by Mengs: and beyond this another room, on the cieling of which are three actions of Samson, by Guido.

The *Belvedere* communicates with the Vatican by an open gallery. Here is that noble repository of antique sculpture, called the Clementine Museum; and the present Pope has fitted up a set of apartments, worthy them and him, for their better reception*.

In

---

* I am not able to do this collection justice. It was in great confusion when I was at Rome, on account

In the niches of a portico surrounding a small open court, is the famous Apollo Belvedere, and the no less famous Laocoon; the former incomparably the finest single figure, and the latter the noblest group in the world. Apollo is supposed to have just discharged his arrow at the Python. his attitude is beautiful, natural, and unaffected, his countenance composed and elegant; the workmanship of every part exquisite: he is longer from the middle downwards than nature; but this deviation from the proportion of the human figure adds clearly to his dignity; and upon the whole he has an unspeakable sublimity, that inspires admiration, awe, and reverence. The foot upon which he rests has been broken, and the hands have been restored.

In the Laocoon there is not a feature or muscle which does not show the deepest anguish. The father's flesh is all contracted in consequence of the poison, and his very toes are visibly affected by it. The youngest son is falling down in the agonies of death: the other is not yet hurt, and is looking towards his father, wishing to help him, and at the same time wanting help himself. Two arms of the sons which are lifted up, are ill restored by Comaccini. Michelangelo attempted to restore an arm of the father in marble; but desisted in despair to do it justice. Bernini put on one in *terra cotta*. Pliny mentions this group, and says it was the joint work of three Rhodian artists, Agesander, Polydore, and Athenodorus. None of the ancients have made mention of the Apollo.

In the other niches are a Venus with Cupid. Hercules Commodus, or Commodus in the character of Hercules. Antinous, as it is called; though some rather think it to be a Meleager. The Emperor Lucius Verus. Bacchus with a Faun. Ganymede with the eagle. Here also is the famous *Torso*, or trunk of an antique Hercules, commonly called Michelangelo's study *.

MONTE

---

* The other principal things in this collection, for I pretend not to give them all, are—the rivers Nile and Tiber, two cumbent colossal figures, with their proper attributes:

Another Meleager

Hercules young and old.

Cleopatra

MONTE CAVALLO, the Pope's summer palace, on the Quirinal hill, has its name from two colossal statues, with each a horse which they formerly held by the bridle. They

Cleopatra dying under this the sarcophagus of the giants.

Apollo darting at a lizard.

Genius, beautiful character, legs and arms broken off and lost

Diana with a dog, shooting.

A Faun, Seneca, Venus, Narcissus, Apollo, and the Muses.

A Hero in a singular habit

A Discobolus, a drunken Faun

An Amazon, a Satyr and Nymph.

The effeminate Plato, as it is called.

An old man with a fire-pot, such as is still used in Rome by the common people.

Paris, Silenus, Venus marina with the dolphin.

A Faun in rosso antico.

Mercury, Neptune, Jupiter.

BUSTS.—Jupiter Serapis; Oceanus.
Pluto in basalt, Cato, Portia, &c &c.

ANIMALS —A sow and pigs, a goat.
Two fine dogs.
An ass's head in basalt, and another in rosso an-

A sheep

They bear the names of Phidias and Praxiteles; but whoever was the sculptor, they are certainly grecian, and much the most pleasing colossal statues in Rome. That which is ascribed to Phidias is the best. The horses have great spirit, but their necks are too thick, and their heads too little. The bridles are lost.

The building is round a large court, which is surrounded by a portico. A wide double staircase conducts to the great hall.

A sheep hanging over a pedestal.

A cow in basalt.

Grayhounds playing.

VASES and COLUMNS.—A vase of oriental alabaster, a vase of basalt, a fine porphyry column, in which there is a mixture of the different sorts.

Four columns of giallo antico.

Two of verde antico.

And many fine ones of the different sorts of granite.

The ancient Mosaics with which some of the rooms are paved, are very beautiful. In the garden of the Belvedere is the large Pine of bronze, which Dante mentions in his *canto inferno*. It was on the mausoleum of Hadrian.

PICTURES.

The martyrdom of S. Erasmus, by Nic. Poussin.

S. Gr

The garden is almoſt a mile round: there are ſome ſtatues in it, a grotto, and a Caſino, called the Coffee-houſe, in which are five pictures by Pompeio Battoni, two landſcapes by Orizonte, and two large views of Rome by Paolo Pannini.

S. Gregory turning the earth of the coliſæum into
ood, by Andrea Sacchi.

A chapel painted in freſco, by Guido—and the annunciation at the high altar, in oil, by him.

S. Petronilla, by Guercino.

S. Sebaſtian, with S. Catherine, and four other ſaints, by Tiziano.

S. George, by Pordenone.

S. Peter crucified with his head downwards, by Guido.

Ecce homo, and David with Saul: both by Guercino.

Transfiguration, by Cantarini with the gene-*alogy* of Raffaelle's family.

Two holy families, by Baroccio.

A dead Chriſt, by Calabreſe.

Martyrdom of SS. Proceſſus and Martinianus, by Valentin.

Other Palaces.*

Palace of the *French Academy* in the Corso, purchased by Louis XIV. and furnished with casts of all the famous statues &c. It is a pompous building, but in too bad a style to criticise.

The *Albani* palace fronts to the strada Felice and Pia, at the piazza de' quattro Fontane; so that it is in one of the finest situations in Rome. It has a considerable library, and many pictures.

There is also a collection of drawings by the Carraccis, Polidore, Lanfranco, Spagnoletto, Cignani, &c.

The *Altieri* palace is one of the largest in Rome. It is plain on the outside, and a remarkably good piece of brick work. The

---

* The palaces of Rome line the streets and squares, which thus owe their greatest ornament to these vast edifices. The architecture is good in very few, but in many the prodigious extent, united to a magnificence of decoration, is striking. Such are the Barberini, Borghese, Bracciano, Altieri, and Colonna palaces. In the interior distribution, magnificence is the leading feature, to which convenience often gives place.

archi

architecture of the court is by Antonio Rossi. The staircase is grand. The chapel is painted by Borgognone. The library of Clement X. is in this palace, rich in manuscripts, medals, &c. The princess's apartments consist of seven noble rooms, well furnished. In the bed chamber are two of Claude Lorrain's landscapes, both fine, but in that wherein Æneas is landing in the Tiber, the water is not good; the other, which represents the temple of Vesta at Tivoli, and a view of the Campagna, is deservedly esteemed his *chef-d'-œuvre*. In this room is a dead Christ, two angels and the virgin lamenting; a small, admirable piece, by Annibale Carracci.

The *Barberini* palace is on the extremity of the Quirinal hill. It is very large, and is said to have 4000 rooms in it. Bernini built it for Urban VIII.; and the two stories, where are the doric, and the ionic columns over them, are well executed; the rustic, and the doric ornaments about it, are very good. The upper part of the front was finished by Borromini. The great hall is a most noble room for size and height, the ceiling is near 50 feet high, and is coved: the paintings on it by Pietro da Cortona are his master-piece; and perhaps there is no performance

formance of this sort superior to it, both for colouring and composition. In a room adjoining is a cieling by Andrea Sacchi; it represents the divine wisdom. There is also another cieling by Chiari, representing Plato in the cradle, and the bees playing about him.

Many pictures have been sold out of this collection, and yet enow remain to form a considerable cabinet.

Many *Statues* and *Busts*, far from capital; the former chiefly colossal.

The drunken faun asleep, an admirable greek statue; the legs and arms by Bernini.

A Juno, remarkable for the drapery.

A sick satyr lying on his back, by Bernini in the hall.

Busts of Marius, Sylla, and Scipio Africanus, of Cardinal Barberini, by Bernini.

A bas-relief of the death of Meleager.

The library is in the upper story, 197 steps leading up to it: they pretend that there are 60,000 volumes of printed books, and 9000 manuscripts. The great room is 100 feet long, 34 broad, and 20 high, with a coved cieling. There is a cabinet of medals, antique gems, bronzes, &c. The family jewel are

are kept in a large cabinet, and form a kind of *regalia*.

In the *Bolognetti* palace, fronting the piazza di S. Marco, the apartment, commonly shown consists of seven rooms, all about 28 feet by 24; the gallery is only 24 by 14, and 20 feet high: there is not a tolerable statue in it.

The celebrated *Borghese* palace is very bad architecture, both within and without. a vast extent of front, without any break, order, or elegance. It is all of brick stuccoed. The great court has double porticos, supported by 100 granite columns, and an ugly building over them, that looks too heavy for what holds it up.

It is said that there are 1700 pictures in the apartments; but they are mostly in bad lights, in bad frames, and some of the best worm eaten. It is the first collection in Rome for the old masters; and having been made all at once, there are no modern pictures, and only one, which is by Pietro da Cortona, since Guido. There are six or seven undoubted Raffaelle's, and ten or twelve Tiziano's; but no good landscapes, and not more than four in the whole[*].

[*] There is a printed catalogue of the whole collection.

The front of the palace of the *Cancelleria* is by Sangallo, and very well upon the whole; though the pilasters are too high for their diameters. The orders are doric, and two composites, with a good entablature. The church is part of the front, with three ailes, and lofty; but plain, without any ornament.

The *Colonna* palace, fronting to the square of the twelve apostles, is of great extent; and the apartments are magnificent, and handsomely fitted up. They are full of pictures by the best masters. The gallery is one of the finest and richest in Europe, and has some very capital paintings; as, the prodigal son, the entombing of Christ, and the Magdalene dead, by Guercino. A large landscape, by Nicola Poussin. Cephalus and Procris, and Ganimede with the eagle, by Tiziano, &c.

The upper apartment has been lately fitted up, in a neat rather than a splendid manner; and there are a few good pictures in it.

The gardens, on the side of the Quirinal hill, are in a bad taste.

The *Corsini* is a noble palace, without architecture; 22 windows in front, a fine suite of rooms and a large garden, part of which is on the Janiculum, and commands one of the noblest views in Rome. The library is
well

well difposed and public. It confifts of four rooms, 24 feet fquare, and 16 high, in one of which is a large collection of prints and drawings, three others for new books, and a gallery about 70 by 20. There is alfo a gallery of pictures by the beft mafters.

The *Coftaguti* palace is remarkable only for four cielings painted in frefco, by Domenichino, Guercino, Albano, and Romanelli.

The *Farnefe* palace, belonging to the king of the two Sicilies, is the moft fuperb in Rome. It was built by Michelangelo, except the fouth front, which is by Giacomo della Porta. In the court are three orders, doric, ionic, corinthian, with open arcades round it: here is the famous Farnefian Hercules; and a Flora, remarkable for her drapery: and in a little court, the prodigious group called the *Toro*.

In the apartments of this now deferted palace are fome good ftatues and bufts. But the great ornament of it is the gallery painted in frefco by Annibale Carracci.

In the *Farnefina*, or little Farnefe palace, Raffaelle and his fcholars painted in frefco the ftory of Pfyche, with the affembly and banquet of the gods. The gallery in which thefe frefcos are, was formerly open, and the colours were much hurt by being exposed to the air. Carlo Maratti repaired them. Here also are some statues and busts.

The *Ghigi* palace fronts both to the Corso and the piazza Colonna: it was begun by Giacomo della Porta, continued by Maderni, and finished by Felice della Greca. There is a good library, and a large collection of pictures, but few good ones.

The *Giustiniani* is a vast palace, with a suite of melancholy, though well proportioned rooms. The collection makes a great figure in print, but the statues and bas-reliefs are chiefly of the lower ages.

The *Mattei* palace is large, and has four stories. Here is a profusion of bad statues and bas-reliefs, with abundance of inscriptions. There is a curious head of Cicero; an indifferent cieling by Domenichino; and a good painting of Dædalus and Icarus, by Andrea Sacchi.

The palace of Prince *Odescalchi*, duke of Bracciano, is the least exceptionable of any modern building in Rome. The pictures which were once here are in France; the statues in Spain; and the gems, &c. dispersed all over Europe.

The *Pamfili* palace is large and magnificencent, the architecture by Borromini; the front towards the corso by Valvasori. It may give some idea of the extent of this palace, to know that upwards of 4000 persons were entertained in it, when Prince Doria, the present possessor, received the archduke and archdutchess of Austria, in the year 1780.

The pictures are numerous, but many of them indifferent. This palace abounds particularly in landscapes.

In the other *Pamfili* palace, in the Piazza Navona, besides the great hall, there is a gallery near 100 feet long, the cieling painted by Pietro da Cortona, and a suite of nine handsome rooms. The library is open to the public.

There are no less than eighteen palaces belonging to this family, seven of which are in Rome.

The *Rondonini* palace in the corso, though not so large and magnificent as some, has apartments as comfortable as any in Rome. It has a collection of statues, busts, pictures, &c.; particularly an antique head of Medusa, much admired.

The *Rospigliosi* palace, on the Quirinal hill, possesses one of the finest frescos in the world

—the Aurora of Guido. It is the cieling of a pavilion in the garden.

In the *Santa Croce* palace are ten good rooms, besides the great hall, elegantly furnished; and there are some good pictures in it. As the Assumption, by Guido. A battle, by Salvator Rosa; and Job on the dunghill, by him. Magdalen, by Guercino, &c.

The *Spada* palace, by piazza Farnese, is remarkable for an antique colossal statue, of Pompey, as supposed. There is a room painted by Giulio Romano, and his scholars; besides many easel paintings.

The architecture of the *Caffarelli*, now the *Steffani* palace, is curious, as being from a design of the famous painter Raffaelle d'Urbino.

Palazzo Strozzi is very large; remarkable principally for a cabinet of medals, among which are twelve in gold of the first twelve Cæsars, of cameos, intaglios, and some paintings.

The *Verospi* palace in the corso, otherwise inconsiderable, is visited for a gallery at the back of the court, formerly an open loggia; the cieling of which is painted by Albano. There is a remarkable harpsichord here, so contrived, that by playing on one, you make three

three others play at the same time. Over it, is a large and good landscape, by Gaspar Poussin. In the court, is a good statue of Jupiter sitting, with his thunderbolt.

The Roman nobility are well bred; the midling rank are addicted to the polite arts, and particularly to poetry; the populace are daring and ferocious. Rome abounds in *improvisatori*, poets who will compose and repeat verses extempore on any subject. The studies of the belles-lettres and antiquities are more followed at Rome than the Sciences.

La Sapienza is the principal of the Colleges, and as it were the center of the University. The building was begun by Leo X. There are eight professors of theology, six of civil and canon law, eight of medicine, five of philosophy, one of belles lettres, and four of the eastern and greek languages.

The college of *la Propaganda* was founded by Gregory XV. There are several professors belonging to it, who give lectures in theology, philosophy, the belles lettres, and the oriental languages, to the young ecclesiastics who are designed for foreign missions. The building is in a shocking style, by Borromini.

The *Roman* college is a vast, heavy edifice, built

built by Gregory XIII. from a design of Ammanati's. This is dedicated to the education of youth; as are also the Clementine and Nazarene colleges. Kircher's Museum is in the Roman college, and contains, among many other things, a fine set of precious stones. It was much increased by Bonanni, who published a large account of it. Cardinal Zelada also has a handsome cabinet of natural history.

For the encouragement of learning, there are also many public *Libraries* in Rome. That of the Vatican is universally known. The other principal ones are in the Altieri, Albani, Barberini, Borghese, Corsini, Ghigi, Imperiali, and Pamfili palaces; at the Sapienza, Propaganda, and Roman colleges; in the convents of S. Agostino, Gesu, S. Maria sopra Minerva, augmented by the library of cardinal Casanata, S. Silvestro, &c. Most religious houses of note have considerable libraries, which are easily accessible.

Rome is certainly not a place of amusement for the gay and dissipated: no public spectacles being allowed, except during the time of the carnival, which lasts from the seventh of january to ash-wednesday. Then indeed they are attended with an ardour unknown

known in capitals where the inhabitants are under no such restraint. Seven or eight Theatres are open; the principal of which are the *Argentina, Aliberti, Tordinone,* and *Capianica*. the two first are appropriated to serious operas, the third to plays, and the last to burlettas. No women are permitted to appear upon the stage, but castrati play the female parts. During the carnival there are also festinos or balls, masquerades, and horse races.

But though public diversions are not usually allowed, except in carnival time; yet the frequency and pomp of religious functions, in some degree make a stranger amends. Among these, that of the holy week takes the lead. On palm sunday there is a procession of the Pope and Cardinals to the chapel of Monte Cavallo, in order to bless the palms. On monday the famous *miserere* of Allegri is rehearsed by select voices. On wednesday the *tenebræ* are performed at five o'clock in the afternoon in the Sistine chapel, and conclude with the *Miserere* which is repeated on good friday in all its solemnity. On thursday, the Pope, after assisting at high mass, pronounces his benediction from the front of S. Peter's, and then washes the feet of of twelve poor priests, and serves them at table. On easter sunday, high mass is again celebrated by the Pope, and he gives the benediction a second time: in the evening, the cupola, front, and colonnade of the church, are superbly illuminated. There is another grand benediction on Ascension day. On *Corpus Christi* day is a magnificent procession; and on this occasion nineteen pieces of tapestry from the cartons of Raffaelle are displayed in the cloister leading up to the Vatican. On S. Peter's day, june the 29th, there is a grand musical performance, in the large winter or canonical chapel of S. Peter's; besides oratorios and other music in Chiesa nuova, S. Girolamo, S. Apollinario, S. Cecilia, and other churches. In the evening the cupola of S. Peter's is illuminated, and grand fireworks are played off from the castle of S. Angelo. At this time also is the ceremony of presenting the horse to the Pope, from the king of the Two Sicilies.

Besides these constant functions, the 8th of september, being the nativity of the virgin, is celebrated once in ten or twelve years. Soon after the election of a new Pope, his holiness goes in grand procession to the church
of

of S. Giovanni in Laterano. This is called the *possesso*, and is equivalent to the coronation at Westminster, or the consecration at Rheims. And lastly, once in twenty-five years is the jubilee; which will not be celebrated till the year 1800.

Out of carnival time, except when any functions are going forward, the gay and idle have no resource but parading in the corso, and in the *conversazioni* or assemblies.

A stranger will form no high idea of the beauty of the Roman women, from the specimens he sees in the fashionable circles; but he will be often struck with the fine character of countenance he sees in the streets; and perceive a resemblance between living features and those of the antique busts and statues.

The common people are in a ferment during all the time of the Lottery, which is drawn eight times a year. Such is the rage for it, that the quantity of bread baked in the city is at these seasons considerably less than usual. In short, it is the locust which consumes what the caterpillar had left.

The troops which do duty at the pontifical palace, &c. are a regiment of foot of 1200 men, a troop of chasseurs of 200, a hundred cuiraffiers, and 200 Swifs foot, armed with cuiraffes. The infantry is a medley of deferters from all nations: the cavalry have been moftly domeftics to cardinals or noblemen. The whole corps is cafhiered at every new pontificate.

Befides thefe troops, there is a militia, for every quarter of the city, under their own officers, who are citizens.

Rome has fome manufactures of filk, but the material is bad, and when wrought it is neither fightly nor ferviceable. The only articles of exportation are vitriol, mufical ftrings, beads, artificial flowers, perfumed powders, pomatums, and effences, gloves, combs, fans, and fuch trifles. Medals, ftatues, bufts, paintings, and *ftudii* of marbles, make an article of commerce. Holland, Ireland, and Swifferland, fupply the city with linen; and England with woollen and cotton goods. There is very little cafh in Rome; fo that payments are moftly made in paper. There are feveral confiderable banking houfes, which keep the courfe of exchange very high.

Provifions are plentiful and good; their *vitella mongana* particularly excellent, as is alfo their fwine's flefh; the worft meat is mutton

mutton: they have *capretti* or kid, and the venison of wild deer or *capreole*, but very lean. porcupine is also sometimes sold in the markets. Poultry and wild fowl are fine and plentiful. They eat all sorts of small birds, down to the wren; and several birds which we never touch, as hawks, jays, magpies, and woodpeckers. They have a good variety of fish, both of the fresh waters, and of the sea.

The air of Rome is reckoned good for asthmatic people in winter. The climate is mild, the frosts slight, and the snow generally melting as it falls. There are sometimes thick, stinking fogs, but they are not very frequent, and generally disperse before noon. In summer some parts of the city are supposed to be unwholesome, nor will the most indigent person sleep on a ground floor during this season. The country about Rome is mostly flat, and burnt, being covered with volcanic ashes; the hills are calcareous.

The Villas of the Roman nobility in and near the city are many of them very magnificent. Of the first there is the *Aldobrandini*, on the top of the Quirinal hill, remarkable for a fine antique fresco representing a marriage:

riage: it is in a pavilion in the garden; and was found in the baths of Titus.

Villa *Lanti* is in a lofty situation on the Janiculum, and has a fine command of the city. The house is by Giulio Romano.

Villa *Ludovisi* on the Pincian hill, is a mile and half in compass, and commands a fine prospect. The gardens are peopled with busts and statues. In a *casino*, on the staircase, is a fine colossal head of Juno, grecian sculpture. In the apartment, Pyrrhus, a good bas-relief. Mars reposing: good proportion and attitude. Another Mars; the head fine. Papirius and his mother: the best group in Rome next to the Laocoon. Pætus and Arria, another fine group, but far inferior to the last.

In a summer-house, a fine cieling, by Guercino; the subject, Aurora in her car. In the room over this, another cieling by the same hand—Fame founding her trumpet. There is also a landscape, by Guercino, and another by Domenichino. A satyr, by Michelangelo.

Villa *Mattei* on monte Celio, is the pleasantest of any situation within the walls. Here are statues, busts, urns, &c. in vast abundance: the most remarkable are, a small statue

statue in a confular habit, called Cicero; perhaps Cato of Utica. A large head of Jupiter Serapis, with the modius, of bafalt. Bufts of Brutus and Portia, in a group. Head of Alexander; the fineft coloffal head in Rome. An excellent eagle. Statue of Livia Drufilla. Satyr drawing a thorn out of Silenus's foot. Equeftrian ftatue of Antoninus Pius. Two Meleagers. A flayed horfe, in bronze, by Giovanni Bologna. A beautiful table of green porphyry. Buft of Plotina. Some very ancient bas-reliefs.

Villa Medici, finely fituated on the Pincian hill, is a large fpot of ground, but flat; always open to the public. In one of the rooms, the ftory of Hero and Leander is painted on the cieling in oil, by Guercino. The gallery is full of marbles, bufts, and ftatues; but the beft have been carried to Florence. The back front of the houfe is full of bufts and bas-reliefs; and there are fome ftatues of porphyry, and excellent bas-reliefs in the garden.

Villa Negroni is a fine fpot of ground, with walks fhaded by cypreffes and other trees of long ftanding. There are two excellent ftatues fitting in curule chairs, called Marius and Sylla.

Out

Out of the city the principal villas are—

Villa *Albani*, in a fine situation, commanding Tivoli and the Sabina; and unquestionably the most elegant and neatest villa in Italy. There are twelve rooms fitted up in the finest taste; and the gallery is the sum of elegance; the cieling painted by Mengs: the finest thing here is an alto relievo of Antinous, over a chimney, the size of life.

Villa *Borghese* is the first of them all, whether we consider the situation, or the rarities it contains. It is very near the city; takes in a view of the chief part of Rome, and of all the country as far as Frescati and Tivoli, and has extensive gardens, with a park three miles round, full of inequalities, and woods of evergreen oaks, and pines.

The house is noble, with eight excellent rooms on a floor; the outside charged with ancient bas-reliefs. The inside has lately been fitted up in a superb manner by the present prince. Almost all sorts of marbles and hard stones are to be found in the columns and tables. In statues, it is perhaps second only to the Capitol. The most remarkable are, the fighting Gladiator. Silenus and the young faun. Seneca, as it is called, in black marble rather a servant of the baths. A

Camillus.

Camillus. The hermaphrodite. The Centaur, with Cupid behind him. Two young piping Fauns. Ceres. An Egyptian fortune teller. A young Nero.—Busts of Lucius Verus! Alexander. Faustina the younger Venus. Several fine bas-reliefs: a remarkable alto-relievo of Curtius: a vase with bacchanals; another supported by the graces two Cornucopias, &c.

Villa *Madama* belongs to the king of Naples, and is deserted. The situation is delicious, and it commands a fine prospect of the city, with the bend of the river quite from ponte molle. Two of the fronts were designed by Raffaelle, a third by Giulio Romano the portico of the garden front is one of the noblest pieces of architecture about Rome. Giulio's front is chaste. Two rooms are painted by him in arabesque most elegantly.

Villa *Olgiati* was inhabited by Raffaelle, who has left three frescos on the cieling and sides of one of the rooms—two of Alexander's marriage with Roxana; and the third, a group of men shooting at a shield held by a arm the whole room is ornamented with arabesques.

Villa *Pamfili*, called also *Belrespiro*, is in a charming

charming situation, without the gate of S
Pancrazio. The whole is seven miles in
compass, and has some fine broken ground
but is so subdivided and frittered down, as to
produce no effect. The house is built by Al
gardi, and makes a pretty appearance, though
void of architectural merit. There are some
good stuccos in it by him; but no good pic
tures, and little fine sculpture. The best
Seneca, or the attendant at the baths. Clo
dius in woman's apparel. Bacchus in rosso
antico. Some bas-reliefs.

Ample descriptions of this, and the Bor
ghese villa, are printed, each in a folio vo
lume.

Two excursions from Rome are indispen
sable:—to Frescati, Albano, &c. and Tivoli.

FRESCATI is twelve miles from Rome
Some ruins of ancient Tusculum are to be
seen in the upper part of it. It is now
adorned with several magnificent villas of the
Roman nobility. Taverna and Mondragone
belonging to the Prince Borghese. Aldo
brandini. Conti. Bracciano. Falconieri, &c.
The situations of these are in general fine
with happy inequalities; but we meet with
nothing but bad water-works, olives, stone
pines, and clipped hedges. The apartment

of the houses are calculated for the hot season, when the Romans resort much to Frescati, where abundance of lodgings are to be let for that purpose.

GROTTA FERRATA is supposed to be the site of Cicero's Tusculan villa. It is low with respect to Frescati, yet it is on a good eminence, with a tolerable plain, a stream by it, and a full view of the Campagna. In the abbey is a chapel painted in fresco by Domenichino.

At CASTEL GANDOLFO the Pope has a house or castle, wherein to pass the autumnal season or *villeggiatura*. It is a plain, strong-looking, old-fashioned house; with nothing remarkable in it. The town is built on the border of the lake, called now *lago Castello*; and has fine views of the sea, over the city and campagna of Rome. Here are the gardens of the villa Barberini, in which are the ruins of the ancient villa of Domitian.

Two charming shaded roads lead to AL-BANO, along the side of the lake. Many of the Roman nobility and gentry have country houses for the *villeggiatura* in this place. Near the gate towards Riccia (anciently Aricia) is a large ruined mausoleum, terminating in several pyramids, commonly called

M the

the tomb of the Curiatii. Some suppose it to have been erected in honour of Pompey.

The Lake of ALBANO, or *Lago Castello*, is the crater of a worn-out volcano, and seven or eight miles in circuit. There are several remains of temples on its banks, but they are not considerable. A canal or drain, called the *Emissario*, is dug through the mountain, two miles in length, four feet wide, and about six feet high, arched and lined with lava. This is to discharge the water of the lake, which used sometimes to run over and drown the country. It is commonly said that it was made by the Romans during the siege of Veii, in obedience to an oracle.

The quarries of black compact lava, called *silex*, are near Albano. It is used in and about Rome for paving, and for restoring antique basaltine statues.

The other beautiful lake of NEMI is also a crater of an extinct volcano. It was anciently called *speculum Dianæ* and *lacus Aricinus*. Riccia is near this lake; as is also Genfano, called so corruptly from *Cynthianum*, and placed opposite to the town of Nemi. From the garden of the Capuchins, just above the lake, is the most delicious prospect

prospect imaginable. All the eminences about both these lakes are shaded with forest trees: the water and wood set off each other, and combine to form a landscape, which is at the same time delightful, and unusual in Italy.

TIVOLI is about eighteen miles from Rome. The situation is high, but the town itself is a wretched place, made more disagreeable by a number of forges. The cathedral is built upon the ruins of a temple of Hercules. The ancient name of the place was *Tibur*. The principal beauty of Tivoli arises from the river Anio, now called the *Teverone*, which falling headlong about fifty feet down the rock, forms a noble cascade, and several lesser ones, called *le cascadelle*. The latter are extremely picturesque; as is also a deep ravine in the hill, called *la grotta di Nettuno*, into which the great cascade falls. To enrich the view, here are some fine remains of ancient buildings, as the villa of Mæcenas, and particularly the little round temple of the Sibyl, as it is commonly called, but rather of Vesta; one of the most elegant remains of Grecian architecture.

The naturalist will here take pleasure in observing the continual formation of new Tiburtine stone from the deposit of water descending from the calcareous Apennines.

Villa Istense is a curious specimen of gardens in the old taste, with terraces, clipt trees, scroll-work and water-works.

Villa Adriani, between Tivoli and Rome, may serve to give some idea of Roman magnificence. Immense ruins spread over a prodigious tract of ground. Here was an amphitheatre, theatre and circus, temples, baths, an hippodrome, vast barracks for the soldiers, and great rooms, with mouldering walls only now remaining, so encumbered with thorns, that it is difficult to get at them. Many of the finest pieces of ancient sculpture that adorn modern Rome, were found buried in this astonishing villa of the emperor Hadrian.

On the road from hence to Rome there is a lake, with small floating islands on it, formed of grafs, reeds, &c. on which men push themselves about for the amusement of strangers.

A small brook that runs from the lake forms incrustations, some of which, from their resemblance to sugar-plums, are called *Confetti di Tivoli*.

SECTION

SECTION VIII.

Journey from Rome to Naples, and description of that city and its environs.

ON leaving Rome by the *porta latina*, you will find many ancient sepulchres by the road side. You afterwards discover an old roman aqueduct, which still brings water to modern Rome; and you pass under it at *Torre a mezza via*. Hence, leaving Laricem on the right, the road passes by Marino, near *lago Castello*, to *la Faiola*, and so to *Veletri*. This town is in a good situation, and not ill built; it has several public fountains, and in the square is a statue in bronze of Urban VIII. cast by Bernini. The *Ginnetti* palace is a noble structure; the front to the street very large, and the staircase wonderfully elegant. The mountain of Veletri is volcanic, and so is all the country from Rome. Near the little town of *Cori* are many ruins of two temples, and some very ancient walls of curious construction. Between Sermoneta (anciently *Sulmena*) and Cafe nuove, but out of the road, are remains of an ancient temple of Saturn, at Sezze; anciently *Setia*, or *Setinum*. The road from Veletri to the foot of the mountain of Piperno is good; but the ascent of the mountain itself is very rough, and stony, and the descent very steep. The town of *Piperno* is wretched, ill-built, and has no remarkable edifice. Having passed the mountain, you get into a narrow valley, with bad roads, and thence into a forest of cork-trees, before you arrive at Terracina.

If instead of crossing the mountain, you go over the Pontine marshes; you quit the old road about three miles from Sermoneta, and come to Terracina, by a much shorter and easier cut. The present Pope having drained the marshes, and made a road of fifty feet wide, twenty-five miles in length across them*.

---

* I have not heard that the post is established this way, or that they have yet conquered the mai ... so far as to venture to build posthouses. Travellers may however go by *vetturino*, or by the post, if they apply to the postmaster at Rome, who will order relays upon the road, for which double the common price of horses must be paid.

At

At *Terracina* are ruins of a palace of Theodoric, and some remains of the Appian way. The cathedral is on the site of an ancient temple; and under the portico, which is supported by beautiful marble columns, there is a large vase of white marble, adorned with relievos*. The air here is mild, and the views picturesque. The Pope has a garrison; and also a guard at the barrier separating the two states, five miles beyond this town; and a mile still farther is a guard belonging to the king of Naples.

The situation of *Fondi* is delightful, but stagnant waters render the air putrid; and it is ill-peopled. The town is a square, divided by two streets at right angles: that which runs from east to west, has the ancient pavement still entire. The walls are curious; the lower part of them being older than the roman times. The king of Naples has a garrison in the castle. In the neighbourhood is a cave, where Sejanus concealed Tiberius.

Between *Itri* (Mamurra) and *Mola di*

---

* The ancient *Anxur* was on the top of the hill, under which the high road passes the ruins of it deserve attention.

Gaeta, to the right of the road, is a tower, called the tomb of Cicero.

Mola di Gaeta, anciently so celebrated for its wines, is a handsome, well-built village, beautifully situated*. The quay before the inn is very pleasant, the bay expanding in front, the city of Gaeta seeming to rise out of it, and orange groves hanging over the water. Here the baggage of travellers is always examined.

At the city of *Gaeta*, in the cathedral, the font is a curious antique vase. The bones of the constable of Bourbon, which were exposed to view in the castle, have been inhumed in the present reign.

You next pass the river *Garigliano* (anciently Liris,) and arrive at *S. Agata*: the inn is delightfully situated among hills, in the midst of gardens.

When you arrive at *Capua*, a neat little city, fortified in the modern way, and the only place that covers the approach to Naples; the formality of sending your passport

---

* The hill where *Formiæ* stood is now covered with excellent vineyards. That Cicero had one of his finest villas here is well known, and it was near it that he was assassinated.

to the governor, and waiting his permission to proceed, will give you time to view the cathedral, with two pieces of sculpture in it, by Bernini. Here you cross the Volturno by a bridge. The whole country from Mola is one of the richest in Europe, and nothing can be finer than the road from thence to Naples. All along the way side are bays, myrtles, laurustinuses, pomegranates, figs, lentiscuses, evergreen cytisuses, flowering with many herbaceous plants in the middle of winter.

NAPLES.

Naples is one of the most agreeable places in the world to reside at. The climate is mild, the situation admirable, the city gay and populous, the environs beautiful and interesting. In respect to population, Naples is reckoned the third city in Europe, the number of inhabitants being about 350,000. It is about nine english miles in circuit. The quarter of Santa Lucia is the best built, and most inhabited, by the nobility and ambassadors, for the conveniency, beauty, and wholesomeness of its situation. One of the great beauties of Naples is the

Chiaja, a charming dry walk, along the sea shore, above a mile in length; with the fine bay full in view, the island of Capri in front, on the right the coast of Pausilipo, and on the left Vesuvius, with Portici and its environs. The principal street, *strada Toledo*, is about 1170 yards long, wide, straight, and well built. In the heart of the city, the streets are narrow, and because the houses are high, they are gloomy and close. The pavement of all is a dark lava. The squares are in general small and irregular, many of them have an ugly ornament in the middle, which they call an *aguglia*: it is a kind of short obelisk, loaded with decorations, and ending in a gilt virgin. The fountains are in the same bad taste. The principal squares, or *Largo*, for that is their name here, are *il largo del Castello*, where the barbarous show of the *cocugna* used to be exhibited. *Largo dello Spirito Santo*, built by Vanvitelli in 1758. That by the *Studii*; and the market of the *Carmini*, remarkable for the catastrophe of Conradine and Massaniello.

The walls are no longer of any real defence, and the gates are never shut. To repel an enemy by sea, there is to the west *Castel dell' Uovo*, towards the east are some batteries,

batteries, the bastions of the arsenal, and *Castel nuovo*. A block-house and batteries defend the mouth of the harbour; and at the eastern extremity of the city is *torrione del Carmine*. The castle of S. Elmo commands Naples in every direction, but is calculated to awe the citizens, not to defend them from foreign invaders. The triumphal arch, erected in honour of Ferdinand of Aragon, at Castel nuovo, is all that merits attention in point of Architecture.

The dock-yard and magazines are spacious. The harbour is rather too confined: it is entirely the work of art. A lofty pharos points out the entrance of the harbour; but the hill behind rising very high, the lights are easily confounded with those of the city.

Architecture is by no means in a good taste at Naples. Of 300 churches and upwards, there is not one, with a front or portico which has any merit: many of them indeed present nothing but a bare wall. They endeavour to make amends by abundance of interior decoration: there is a profusion of gilding and painting in them; but their painters have been corrupted by the national taste for brilliancy and extravagance.

The most remarkable of the Churches are the following:

The *Duomo*, or Cathedral, dedicated to S. Gennaro, and built by Nicolo Pisani. The body of the patron saint is kept in a chapel under the choir; and the chapel in which the famous blood is preserved, is very magnificent: the cupola is painted by Lanfranco, the angles only by Domenichino. From the vast treasure contained in it, this chapel is called *il Tesoro*.

S. Anna de' Lombardi. Virgin and child presenting a rosary to S. Domenico. S. Gennaro kissing the hand of Jesus; both by Lanfranco: and several other pictures by him, Caravaggio, Passino, and Luca Giordano.

The church of the *Annonziata* has been lately built at a great expence, from designs of Vanvitelli.

At *S. Anier's Abbate*, they show an ancient painting in oil, which they pretend to be by Antonio di Fiore about 1362, and therefore prior to John van Eyck.

S. Agostin. The cieling, &c. by Lanfranco. Adoration of the shepherds, Joseph's dream, Birth of the virgin, and the presentation in the temple: all by Luca Giordano. The great chapel in the left transept, is decorated

corated with five pictures in mosaic, from Guido; and with a beautiful concert of children, by Fiamingo.

In the church of the *Afcenfion*, on the China, are two pictures by Luca Giordano—the victory of S. Michael over the rebel angels; and S. Anne prefenting the virgin to God.

The church of *S. Martin*, belonging to the *Carthufians*, is richly adorned with precious ftones, ftucco, gilding, and the choiceft marbles. The roof is painted by Lanfranco. The defcent from the crofs, and the twelve prophets, are finely painted by Spagnoletto; and they reckon above an hundred pieces by him, in the church and convent.—In the choir, is the nativity, by Guido; faid to be left unfinifhed at his death; and four other pictures. S. Martin in one of the chapels, is by Annibale Carracci. In the chapel of S. John Baptift, the altar-piece is by Carlo Maratti. The facrifty is a fine one; the cieling by Giordano a dead Chrift, with S. John, the virgin and magdalene, one of Spagnoletto's beft pictures. There are many other pieces in the church, and about the convent, by Giordano, Calabrefe, Domenichino, Caravaggio, Guido, Lanfranco, Carracci, &c. and many curious ones in the prior's apartments.

Thefe

There is a noble view from this fine and rich convent, over the whole city, the bay, and the country round.

S. Chiara is a rich convent of noble ladies. The church is decorated in so airy a style, that it has more the elegance of a ball-room, than the solemnity of a temple. The cieling is painted by Sebastian Conca. Nothing of Giotto's is now remaining.

S. Domenico grande is another very considerable convent. In the church is a virgin and child, the angel Raphael, Tobias, and S. Jerom, by Raffaelle. The annunciation, by Tiziano. Two pictures by Guido. The flagellation, by Caravaggi, &c. The sacristy is handsome, and Solimene has painted a glory in the cieling.

The church of *S. Filippo Neri* is highly decorated with marbles and paintings. The whole history of the Saint is represented by Solimene. Other pieces are, Christ driving the buyers and sellers out of the temple. S. Teresa with her carmelites, at the foot of a great crucifix; both by Luca Giordano. S. Francis, with the virgin, &c. in the clouds, by Guido. S. Alexis expiring, by Pietro da Cortona. In the sacristy, pictures by Guido, Domenichino, and Palma.

G. su

Gesu nuovo. Heliodorus driven out of the temple, a great fresco, by Solimene. Three pictures, by Spagnoletto, in the chapel of S. Ignazio; and in that of the Trinity, a picture, by Guercino. The sacristy, besides a rich treasure, has two pictures by Raffaelle, one by Ann. Carracci, &c.

L'Incoronata. Some remains of frescos, by Giotto. The portrait of Q. Joan, and her coronation, by him, in the chapel of the crucifix.

S. Maria del Carmine is the best sample of ecclesiastical architecture in Naples. Large columns of antique granite divide the nave from the side ailes in a most majestic manner. The best of the paintings, is an assumption, by Solimene, who also painted the chapel of the crucifix. The Convent is large and fine; and their library rich, both in printed books and manuscripts.

S. Maria la nuova. Adoration of the magi, by Luca Giordano, &c.

In the church of the convent of *Monte Oliveto*; the purification, in the choir, by Vasari, who painted the sacristy. The assumption, by Pinturicchio. In the chapel of S. Christopher, a picture by Solimene, &c.

S. Paolo maggiore, was once a temple of Castor

Castor and Pollux: part of the portico is still remaining; the rest was overturned by an earthquake in 1688. Some of Solimene's best pictures are in this church; and there are some allegorical figures by him, in the sacristy. In the cloister of the convent are some remains of an ancient theatre.

The nunnery of *S. Trinità*, is one of the finest and richest in Naples. In the church, is S. Jerom; and, the virgin with Joseph and saints; both by Spagnoletto. The picture of the Rosary, and the shutters of the organ, are by Palma vecchio.

The civil architecture of Naples is in no better a style than the ecclesiastical. Their buildings are heavy, and crowded with gigantic prominencies. They are five or six stories high, with flat roofs, covered with puzzolana terras. There are few such magnificent buildings as we see so frequently in Rome; the city however, in general is more equally built and there are few hovels by the side of palaces.

The *King's Palace* was begun in 1600 by the Count di Lemos, from designs of Fontana. It has a handsome front, decorated with three orders, doric, ionic, and corinthian, a magnificent staircase and apartments

suitable

suitable to the inhabitants. The pictures in it are but few.

The present king of Spain built another palace at *Capo di monte*, but discouraged by the difficulty of access and procuring water, he left it unfinished.

Twenty-four rooms of this neglected palace are filled with the collection that was removed from Parma, consisting of an invaluable set of pictures, a library, a fine cabinet of medals, and a great number of cameos and intaglios, particularly an onyx *tazza*, eight inches in diameter. The pictures are either standing about on the floors, or at best hung up without taste or order; the library still continues packed up as it came from Parma in 1730; and every thing is in the greatest confusion. There are many fine pieces in this collection by Parmegiano, Correggio, Annibale Carracci, &c. A whole room full of Carraccis. The famous Danae, twenty-four portraits, &c. by Tiziano. Thirty-two pictures in one room by Schidone. In another room thirty pieces by the Bassans. Three holy families by Raffaelle. Leo X. between two cardinals, inferior to that at Florence; and said to be the copy with which Andrea del Sarto deceived Giulio Romano.

Holy

Holy family by Andrea del Sarto. A head by Leonardo da Vinci. S. George and the dragon by Rubens, &c. &c.

The ancient palace of the sovereigns, near the Capuan gate, is now occupied by the courts of law; the cellars are transformed into dungeons for malefactors; and one room is set apart for the drawing of the lottery.

The palaces of the nobility are large, with long suites of apartments, and a great gallery for the reception of company. The principal are the Madaloni; Orsini; Francavilla, the apartments of which are handsomely furnished, and the garden reckoned one of the best at Naples: della Torre; della Rocca: the Gravina palace, however, is the only one which is in a good style of architecture.

In the palace of the prince di Tarsia is a library, open to the public three days in the week. In the chapel of the palace of San Severo, belonging to the duke of Sangro, are two curious modern statues, one representing modesty, the head covered with a veil, through which the features are clearly discernible; the other, a man caught in a net, from which he is endeavouring to disengage himself. the first is by Corradino, the second by Queirolo of Genoa.

Genoa. Giuseppe Sammartino has imitated the former in a dead Christ, covered all over with a veil.

I Studii Publici are the buildings of the university, made from designs of Fontana: the front is adorned with antique statues found at Cuma. Professors read lectures here in theology, medicine, politics, law, mathematics, physics, history, the humanities, and languages.

The principal *Libraries* are the King's; that of the Seggio, or S. Angelo á Nido; S. Filippo Neri; the prince of Tarsia; the convents of Monte Oliveto, S. Giovanni di Carbonara, &c.

There are near forty *Hospitals* and *Conservatories* at Naples, and yet no where more beggars and idle people in the streets. The *Albergo de' poveri* is an extensive hospital, being intended as a refuge for the poor from all parts of the kingdom. That of the *Annonziata*, by the *porta Nolana*, is one of the finest establishments here: it is very rich, and relieves not only the sick, but madmen, penitent prostitutes, and foundlings: it has also funds for portioning poor girls; and houses in the country, where the sick are sent, for bathing, or better air.

The

The great *Theatre of S. Carlo*, adjoining to the royal palace, is vast, noble, and elegant. The form is a truncated ellipse, like the other italian theatres. There are six ranges of boxes, thirty in each row, except the three lowest, out of which the king's box is taken: this, as usual, is in front of the stage. In the pit are fifteen rows of seats, thirty in a row, separated by broad rests for the elbow: they are mostly let for the season; and turn up, and are locked in the absence of the proprietor. The price of admission into the house is three carlini, about thirteen-pence half-penny. The stage is of an immense size; the scenes, dresses, and decorations, are magnificent. On public nights, such as the king's and queen's name-day, &c. the house is superbly illuminated: in the front of each box is placed a large mirror, before which two large wax tapers are set; these, with the lights within the boxes, and on the stage, make a prodigious splendor. The size of the theatre, and the noise of the audience, are such, that neither voices nor instruments can be heard distinctly: but the Italians consider the opera so much as a place of rendezvous and visiting, that they seldom attend to the performance, except when a favourite air is singing.

finging. It is common not only to receive company in the boxes; but to take ices and other refreshments, to sup, and to play at cards. The opera generally begins on the fifth of november, and lasts till september.

Besides the great Theatre, there is *Teatro de Fiorentini*, about the size of our little theatre in the haymarket, only much loftier and *Teatro nuovo*, less, and, notwithstanding its name, older than the last. In both these, burlettas or comic operas are performed, without dances. There is a neat little playhouse, in which they act comedies. All the theatres are open on saturday and sunday evenings, and each of them once besides.

There are three *Conservatorii*, in this city, for the education of boys in the profession of music. These furnish a band for the church of the Franciscans, morning and evening, during eight days in october. The octaves indeed, or eight days following the festival of the patron saint of every church, are a continual solemnity, at which the finest voices and best hands attend both morning and evening; and the churches at Naples are so numerous, that the octaves make one continued entertainment throughout the year. At the festival of Corpus Christi, the richest churches

engross

engross the whole opera—voices, instruments, machines, and decorations.

The *Carnival* begins on S. Charles's day, and continues till lent. All this time the city is very gay with the customary amusements of operas, balls, masquerades, &c., terminating with horse-races in the strada Toledo; and sometimes with a royal masquerade procession of the Grand Signior to Mecca, which is a most magnificent spectacle. The barbarous *Cocagna*, in which a prodigious number of calves, sheep, hogs, lambs, and poultry, were assembled, every sunday, to be torn in pieces by the populace, is now discontinued.

The nobility and gentry drive every afternoon along the Chiaja in habit of gala: with their splendid carriages; volantis and other servants in rich liveries; and beautiful horses finely caparisoned; they make a gay and brilliant appearance.

The common people of Naples are very devout, or rather superstitious. Next to S. Gennaro, their patron saint, the Madonnas which are frequent in the streets, seem most to attract their attention. On christmas eve they play off fireworks the whole night. But one of the greatest singularities of Naples the *Presepe*, which is a representation of the birth of our Saviour with all its concomitant circumstances, in small figures. It is exposed on the flat top of the house; and by means of mofs, paper, cork, and branches of trees, forms a historical landscape. Some of these *presepes* are pretty enough; they contrive to make the sky and distant country a part of it, and the optical illusions are really wonderful.

Naples, with respect to its municipal police, is divided into six *seggi* or wards, five of which are governed by a committee of nobles, the last belongs exclusively to the plebeians, who are distributed into twenty nine *ottine* or quarters, under the direction of an *eletto* or mayor, with his assistants. These wards meet in open porticos, which alternately have the honour of being the theatre, whereon the liquefaction of S. Gennaro's blood is exhibited in the month of may. In September the exhibition is in the cathedral.

This city has neither watchmen nor lamps; but of late years darkness has been dispelled in many streets, by the piety of father Rocco, a Dominican; who has persuaded the people to subscribe oil for lamps, to burn before images: he fixes them up in the most convenient ment places, and thus turns their devotion to public account.

Provisions are plentiful and cheap: poultry, game, and fish, are abundant; fruits and garden-stuff are to be had all winter in so favorable a climate. The wants of nature are so easily satisfied here, that the lower class of people work but little; their great pleasure is, to bask in the sun, and do nothing. Persons of a middle rank pass much of their time in coffee-houses, and other places of public resort; and few pursue their callings with any great degree of zeal and activity. The nobility are fond of splendor and show; as appears in the brilliancy of their equipages, the number of their attendants, the richness of their dress, and the grandeur of their titles. About a hundred of them have the title of Prince; a still greater number bear that of Duke. In the female sex, the passion for finery is said to be superior to all others, which seems scarcely credible in so genial a climate. That furious jealousy, for which the nation was so remarkable some generations ago, is pretty well eradicated here, as well as in the rest of Italy.

Education has been little attended to. Few people of rank would suffer their children

dren to frequent academies or public schools; but kept them at home, where, in this soft climate, they acquired habits of indolence and effeminacy. The pains and expence government has been at in establishing public seminaries; the patriotic efforts of the new academy of sciences and belles lettres; and the fashion which begins to prevail among the nobility of visiting foreign countries; will probably bring on a gradual improvement.

Many of the streets are more crouded than even those of London or Paris: the people doing little or nothing, and having no public walks or gardens to resort to. In the midst of all this idleness, fewer riots or outrages happen than might be expected. This is owing partly to the national character of the Italians, and partly to the common people here being universally sober. Their great luxury is iced water; and nothing would be so likely to raise a mutiny in Naples as a scarcity of ice. The king grants the monopoly of this commodity to certain persons, who are obliged to furnish the city all the year, at a certain price, which is about three farthings a pound. It all comes from the mountains about eighteen miles off, where pits or reservoirs

voirs are made to preserve it; and it is sent to the city only as it is wanted.

There is not perhaps a city in Europe, in which so few of the inhabitants contribute to the wealth of the community, by useful or productive labour, as Naples. The number of nobility, priests, monks, lawyers, musicians, footmen, and lazzaronis, surpasses all reasonable proportion. The religious are said to be about 10,000, the lawyers 8000, and the lazzaronis 40,000. Many of the last have neither house nor property: it is not however strictly true, that they pass their lives in the open air, and sleep all weathers in the street: in winter, though the cold might be supportable, yet they could not stand the heavy rains. In the rainy season, vagrants resort in crouds to the cave under Capo di monte.

The ENVIRONS of Naples are highly interesting to the classical scholar, the naturalist, and the antiquary. To the west are Puzzuoli and Baiæ; to the east Vesuvius, the subterraneous cities, and the museum at Portici.

The readiest mode of visiting these environs, is to hire a *calesso*, which is an open carriage

riage, resembling our one-horse chaises; and is to be had at a minute's warning in most of the streets. The common price is a carline an hour, or twelve carlines a day, and two to the man; but as there is no fixed price, a stranger must make a bargain.

In order to go to Puzzuoli, you must pass the beautiful suburb of Chiaja, and the grotto of Pausilipo. On the Chiaja are the two churches of Piedigrotta and la Mergellina. The first famous for an image of our Lady, to which, on the 8th of september, the king comes in solemn procession, with his whole court, and almost every inhabitant of Naples and its neighbourhood.

The church of *la Mergellina*, or *S. Maria del Parto*, was founded by the poet Sannazaro. His tomb, on the top of which is the bust of the poet, accompanied with two genii, is adorned with heathen gods and satyrs: to save appearances, the names of David and Judith are inscribed on the pedestals of the statues of Apollo and Minerva. The terrace before this church affords a comprehensive view of Naples on the side of the Chiaja.

Close to the sea-shore, at the extremity of the Chiaja, is a vast palace in ruins, commonly called queen Joan's palace; but probably built by the last princess of the Caraffa family, whose name was *Ogni Anna*. A little farther are the ruins of another, formerly belonging to the Roccella family, and of the same age.

The *grotto of Pausilipo* pierces through the promontory of that name, in a direct, but ascending, line, nearly from east to west; it is cut in the tufo stone, is arched, and receives light from the two mouths, and some diagonal apertures in the roof. In the most elevated part it is 89 feet high; in the lowest not above 24; in length it is 2316 feet, in breadth 22. The dust is very disagreeable, and the scantiness of light distressing. It reflects honour on the national character, that no one ever meets with an insult in such a long, dark passage. It was probably made by Lucullus; and from an expression of Seneca's we guess that it was passable only for foot passengers. Alphonsus I. widened it for carriages; and since his reign it has been considerably heightened and levelled.

The whole hill of Pausilipo is entirely covered with beautiful houses and gardens, the resort of the Neapolitans in summer; being protected from the hot south and west.

Abou

Above the eastern entrance of the grotto, on the very brink of a precipice, sixty feet above the road, is a ruinous vaulted building, called the *tomb of Virgil.* It is built in *mattoni,* or with bricks placed lozenge-wise; and within are several niches for urns, whence we may presume it was intended for a family tomb. The ruin is a very picturesque one; but as to the bay that grows upon the top, it is of a very modern date. Beautiful points of view offer themselves at every step in ascending to it. Farther on towards the north is the convent of the *Cumaldoli,* from which there is a most sublime sea view, and a most beautiful land one. Hence you may go through forests of chesnuts, opening sometimes to noble views, till you reach the glacis of the castle of S Elmo, where the whole city and suburbs will appear in one collective picture. The Carthusian convent adjoining to the castle is perhaps the best situated monastery in Europe.

But to return to the grotto of Pausilipo— As soon as you have got through it, you open to a view of the gulph of Baiæ; and passing through a fertile vale, you arrive at a lake, once the crater of a volcano, called *Lago d'Agnano.* It is about three miles in circuit.

On the verge of it, are the sweating stoves of San Germano; and the much-talked-of *Grotta del Cane*, where a mephitic vapour rises about ten inches from the ground, fatal to the animal whose organs of respiration are immersed in it. Experiments are usually tried upon dogs, who, after laying some time dead to all appearance, are recovered by being carried into the air, or thrown into the water.

The king's park at *Astruni* is another volcanic crater, about five miles in circuit; filled, not with water, but with noble timber trees, and wild boars.

Hence you go to the *Pisciarelli*, or spoutings of hot aluminous and sulphureous water. It is used medicinally, and the situation is retired and pleasant.

Crossing the hills from these springs, you arrive at the *Solfatara*, anciently *forum Vulcani*, and the only volcano of the *Campi Phlegraei* which now shows any signs of burning; the last eruption from it was in 1198. It is a plain, of an oval form, measuring above a mile one way, and near one third of a mile the other; environed by hills of moderate elevation. This plain has many holes from which issues a moist vapour smelling of hepar sulphuris, and in dark nights sometimes appearing luminous. It is all hollow underneath, sounding like a drum, when stamped upon, and if the ear be laid to the ground, a bubbling and hissing, like that of boiling water, may readily be distinguished. Notwithstanding this, vines and other fruit trees grow on the outer declivity; a variety of shrubs shoot up along the banks; and a wood of chesnut trees flourishes on a part of the area itself. They make alum here, by gathering the white clay from the surface, and heaping it round the holes from whence the steam issues strongest. This clay was a lava, and being penetrated by the hot steams of a sulphureous acid, has undergone this change.

Hence it is but about a mile to *Puzzuol*; to which you may also go directly from the *town*, by a good carriage road, along the sea-shore. In approaching the town, you will observe the great quarries of *Puzzolana*, which takes its name from this place.

Puzzuol stands on a small peninsula; and is a town of near 10,000 inhabitants. The cathedral was a temple sacred to Augustus: no more of the ancient temple remains, than some corinthian columns, with their capitals, and part of the entablature, of parian mar-

...re, and beautiful workmanship; in one of the side walls of the cathedral. In the square is the pedestal for a statue of Tiberius, with bas reliefs upon it. An ancient Amphitheatre still remains: the entrances, the dens for the wild beasts, and the arches which supported the seats, are still almost perfect; the building was of two stories only; the lower of lava, the upper of brick.

The temple of Serapis is still buried; what has been uncovered is the court and pronaos. The court is square, environed with cells for the priests, and baths for the votaries: in the center is a raised circular platform, with vessels for fire, an altar, rings to which the victims were fastened, and other appendages of sacrifice, entire, and in their proper places. Sixteen columns of african marble that upheld its roof, and the statues, were removed to the new palace of Caserta; the pedestals only of the statues remaining. Three columns of the pronaos are standing; they are of cipolline marble, and about ten feet above their bases, are full of holes eaten in them by the file-fish or pholas.

The mole of the harbour of Puzzuoli, vulgarly called Caligula's bridge, is a stupendous work: it was repaired by Antoninus Pius and since that in 1575. There are now fourteen piles remaining, well built of brick and piperino, connected by half-ruined arches.

From Puzzuoli you go to *Monte Barbaro*, anciently *mons Gaurus*, undoubtedly of volcanic origin, though in times beyond the records of history. Near this is *Monte Nuovo*, which was thrown up in forty-eight hours, to the height of 400 fathoms, and 3000 paces in circuit, in the month of September 1538. The crater of this is about a quarter of a mile in depth. The famous Lucrine lake was reduced by this eruption to a little dirty pool.

The *lake of Avernus*, so celebrated by the poets, was once the crater of a volcano. Its form is nearly circular, and it is about 600 yards in diameter. The banks that surround it are steep, and when they were covered with the thick woods which Agrippa levelled, must have given it a very gloomy aspect, and might possibly stop the mephitic exhalations, and render it unwholesome. The *cave of the Sibyl*, as it is commonly called, is to the eastward of the lake: it is about three yards wide, near five high, and 220 or 230 yards to the end: here is a narrow way, descending to two small cells, where there are baths. From the largest of these they say there is a corridore or passage, ending in an outlet, now made up with bricks; and that there is a third cell, with a bad winding staircase, leading from it to the top of the mountain, but now stopped up with dirt.

The *temple of Apollo*, as they name it; though others rather think it was dedicated to Mercury, or Neptune, or the Infernal gods; stands near the lake to the right. It is a large building of brick, the marble casing and decorations having been carried off round within and octagonal without: there are seven great niches, over each of which is a large window: the roof was vaulted, but is now fallen in.

Leaving the lake of Avernus on the left, you come to a large brick arch, called *Arco Felice*, thrown across a chasm in a ridge that bounds the plain where Cuma stood, to the eastward: it is supposed, but without any probability, to have been a gate of the city of Cuma. The height is seventy feet, and the opening twenty feet four inches wide. From this high ground you have a view of the place where Cuma stood, and of the flat shore of *Patria*; where are some heaps of stones, the ruins of *Liternum*, whither Scipio Africanus retired. Tradition says his ashes were deposited here; and the word *patria*, still remaining fixed to the wall of a watch-tower, is thought to be part of his epitaph—*ingrata patria, neque enim ossa mea habebis*. Certainly no memorial of this illustrious person has been found in the sepulchre of the Scipios lately discovered at Rome. The rocky hill, where stood the citadel of Cuma, is hollowed into many spacious caverns; but you will look in vain for the grotto of the Cumæan Sibyl. that sanctuary was destroyed in the gothic wars.

Returning hence by the Lucrine lake, you find by the sea side, the natural hot stoves and baths called *Sudatorii de' Tritoli*, or Nero's baths, consisting of passages and rooms, cut out of the mountain, and full of hot steam, issuing from the hot baths below. These are much frequented, and there are sometimes 500 patients from the hospital of the annunciation at Naples.

You will now proceed to take a view of several ruined buildings, near the shore of the gulph of Baiæ. The temples of Venus—Diana and Mercury, and the sepulchre of Agrippina: names given without authority. Hence you arrive at the *mercato del Sabbato*, a street or double row of *columbaria*, or small hollows

hollows in the bank, wherein urns, containing the ashes of the dead, were deposited. The plain, which descends gradually towards the sea, has been dignified with the title of the Elysian fields. This whole coast of the gulph of Baiæ, so celebrated by the roman poets, and so filled with the villas of their great men, is now become mostly a barren and unwholesome waste.

A little beyond the mercato del sabbato is the *Piscina mirabile*, a great reservoir of water, conjectured to have been made by Lucullus, to supply his villa, which was hereabouts, or by Agrippa, for the fleet, when it lay at Misenum, which is more probable. It is now dry, and you may descend into it by forty steps: the arched roof is supported by forty eight pillars in four rows: they are covered with a tartar or selenites deposited by the water.

All hereabouts are ruins of ancient brick or tufo buildings. The most considerable of them is that called *Cento Cam relle*; the destination of which no one has been able to ascertain. Some think it was a reservoir of water, others that it was a prison, others again that it was the lower story of some great building.

Just below this is *Mare morto*: they pretend that dead bodies were carried over this lake from Misenum to the Elysian fields. It is separated from the open sea by a narrow channel, closed up in such a manner, that the fish can enter the lake, but cannot escape again; so that the fishery here is very valuable. A slip of sand divides it from the channel of Procida; and at the extremity rises the promontory of Miseno; at the foot of which are remains of a theatre, and other ruins of the ancient town. Here were the villas of Marius, Lucullus, and the Emperors: a few fishing huts, with a lonely public house, have succeeded them. It is hazardous to pass the night on this shore, before the equinoctial rains have fallen.

Walking across the isthmus, between cape Procida and the Baian hills, you will come to like *Fusaro*, otherwise called *Lago della Colucca*. This also is valuable for its fisheries; and the flocks of water-fowl which blacken its surface. Near the canal by which it discharges itself into the sea, they show you the ruins of the tomb of Caius Marius.

The whole country from Puzzuoli, along the gulph of Baiæ to Capo Miseno, is nothing but craters and other remains of volcanos.

Avernus,

Avernus, Solfatara and Monte Nuovo give a complete idea of extinct volcanos. Avernus is filled with water; Solfatara is hot, and smoaks with sulphureous and aluminous steams: Monte nuovo is still hot in places, its crater is very deep, quite dry, and scarcely smoking at all.

In fine weather, nothing can be more delightful than to coast the gulph of Baiæ. This you may do, by hiring a boat either at Naples or Puzzuoli. If at the first, soon after you have doubled the cape of Pausilipo, you will see the ruins of many ancient buildings, among others, those commonly called the Schools of Virgil, which were probably part of a villa of Lucullus. Hence you will come to picturesque quarries of puzzolani, and leaving the island of Nisida on the left, you will arrive at Puzzuoli; where you may disembark, and survey the lakes, craters, &c. already described. The lazaretto is at Nisida.

Continuing your route from Puzzuoli, along the gulph, you will observe prodigious foundations of buildings, at the bottom of the sea, into which we know the opulent Romans extended their sumptuous edifices, in and about Baiæ. You may coast it by Bauli till you come to the promontory of Misenum; surveying the several ruins before mentioned, the Elysian fields, &c. as you go along. Thus may you view the whole of this interesting country with little fatigue, and with the enjoyment of a most delightful voyage, in the finest bay, and the most delicious climate that can be desired.

Having now seen every thing to the westward of Naples*, you will proceed to the opposite side, which is no less interesting, on account of Vesuvius, Herculaneum, Pompeii, and the museum at Portici.

In order to survey mount VESUVIUS, you go either to Portici or Resina, little more than four miles from the extremity of Naples; and there you may hire mules and guides. When you have rode as far as you can, you will proceed on foot, the guides assisting you in the ascent, by fastening a girdle round you, and pulling you along; unless you prefer trusting to your own strength aided by a good staff; which you

* Unless you extend your voyage to the islands of Procita and Ischia, which lie off the cape of Misenum, and are well worth the trouble of a visit.

will

will find much better. The cone of the mountain is covered with loose ashes and cinders; it is therefore very fatiguing to ascend it, for you sink up to the knees, and go two steps backwards for every three that you set the way to get forwards is not to be in a hurry, but to go on gently, and often to take breath. After all, you will find it great labour, without much instruction or amusement, for in general you will not be able to discern much of the crater; however favourable circumstances may perhaps allow you a peep into the fiery gulph; or at least if the weather should be fine, the view of the surrounding country may pay you for your trouble. To a naturalist, a survey and scrutiny of the several streams of lava that have flowed from this volcano, will be much more to the purpose. Some of these streams are six or seven miles in length, and have lost themselves in the sea; whilst others, arrested in their course, have accumulated in the vallies. There are shops, both at Portici and Naples, where specimens of all the varieties of lava, and of the other substances, which are thrown out in the eruptions, both rough and polished, may be seen and purchased. It will take an hour and half to go from Portici to the foot of the cone; little more than an hour to ascend it; and about half that time to come down again.

Vesuvius is computed to measure 24 miles round at its base, and to be 3694 feet perpendicular height above the level of the sea. It is accompanied by two other mountains, called *Somma* and *Ottayano*; which probably made one mountain with Vesuvius. The space of valley between them is called *Atrio d Cavallo*, and forms an area three miles long, and about 370 toises wide: this is loaded with accumulated lava, and other volcanic substances*.

It is at Portici, in a wing of the royal palace, that the superb Museum of antiques, found at Herculaneum and Pompeii, is deposited. To view this, it is necessary to have permission from the king himself; and this is obtained by means of the ambassador. Only one company is admitted at the same time;

---

* It seems unnecessary to say more on a subject, on which so much has been said, and so well, by Sir William Hamilton. See his letters in the Philosophical Transactions, which are also printed in a little volume by themselves.

and nobody is suffered to make sketches, or observations in writing.

Many statues have been found; and above 150 are engraved in the Antiquities published at the expence of his Sicilian majesty; they are mostly of bronze, and the greatest share of merit is allowed to a Mercury sitting, the size of life; a Jupiter, larger than life, wrestlers, a drunken and sleeping Faun, and in the glass cases, are abundance of *lares* and panthers, small statues in the same metal. There are however two fine equestrian statues in marble, of the two Balbi, father and son, a statue of one, the wife of the elder, and mother of the younger Balbus, and some others of inferior note. The *busts* fill several rooms, and many of them are of the best greek workmanship—Plato, Scipio, and Seneca, are among the finest. Few rare medals have been found; the most curious is a gold one of Augustus, struck in Sicily, in the 15th year of his reign, some of Vitellius, a triumph of Titus, and one of Vespasian with *Judæa capta*. But this museum possesses not only statues and busts, intaglios and cameos, medals, altars and inscriptions, which make the whole boast of others, but an entire assortment of ancient domestic utensils, such as tripods

tripods of elegant form, and exquisite workmanship, lamps in endless variety, candelabres or stands for lamps of the most elegant shapes, silver strainers nicely worked, vases and basins of ample dimensions, scales for weighing, with variety of weights, mirrors of polished metal, elegant cups and saucers in silver, shells and marks for pastry, spoons, but nothing like forks, utensils for the baths, as brushes, strigils, phials for oils and perfumes, tesseræ or ivory tickets for the theatre, dies for playing, some of them loaded; all the apparatus for writing, as styles, tables, &c.; a kitchen completely fitted up with bronze pots and pans, some lined with silver, kettles, cisterns for heating water, and every utensil for culinary purposes; a lady's toilet, fully furnished, with combs, thimbles, rings, paint, ear-rings, bracelets, pins for the hair, &c. here is also a complete set of the chirurgical instruments in use among the ancients; many instruments of music, such as flutes, sistrums, lyres, cymbals, and crotali; thuribles, censers, pateras, and other appurtenances of sacrifice; a fine *lectisternium*, or couch, consecrated to the gods; a curule chair of bronze found in the theatre at Herculaneum, helmets, shields, and all sorts of

arm

arms; screws, locks, keys, latches, bolts hinges, and nails. Almost every thing of iron was destroyed by rust; a gridiron was one of the most perfect utensils discovered of that metal various utensils in glass; and coloured glass so hard, clear, and well stained as to appear like precious stones; many of which that are genuine have appeared, set in gold very clumsily for rings, as amethysts, emeralds, onyxes, cornelians, &c. but no diamonds; abundance of intaglios and cameos, little bottles, &c. of crystal; nets, balls of thread, gold lace, colours for painting, the measure of a roman foot: instruments of husbandry, little bells which they hung about the necks of their cattle, letters in metal for marking, &c. Various sorts of eatables, retaining their form, though burnt to a cinder; as corn, flour, bread, of which there is a loaf nine inches in diameter and four in height; a pye or tourte about a foot in diameter in its pan; wheat, peas, almonds, dates, beans, nuts, figs, grapes, eggs, fish, oil, and wine The floors of the rooms which contain these venerable relics of antiquity, reserved in the bowels of the earth, safe from the ravages of time and barbarians, during seventeen centuries

turies, are paved with most beautiful antique mosaics.

The learned thought that they had made a more valuable acquisition than statues and pictures, when near 800 volumes of manuscripts were found: but the difficulty of unrolling these calcined volumes, of pasting the fragments, and decyphering the letters, has proved such an obstacle, that very little progress has been made in the work. The method of proceeding, invented by Padre Antonio Piaggi, is dropped, and the manuscripts be neglected. One volume, which was completely unrolled, was found to be a greek treatise on the bad effects of music in a republic.

The *paintings* are to be seen in another part of the palace. There are near 700, most of them small, and representing single female figures, centaurs, &c. on dark grounds; heads or winged genii in a variety of amusements or employments; arabesques, animals, fruits, vases, shells, whimsical buildings, &c. Some of them however are large historical pieces; two of the most remarkable are Theseus with the Minotaur dead at his feet; and the finding of Telephus, with two figures of and Hercules. The composition and design

design of these pictures, it must be confessed, are in general very indifferent, not to say any thing of colouring, which may have suffered: the small pieces of fruit, animals, arabesques, and fancy subjects, are the best. They are mostly painted *a tempera*, or in distemper, as we call it; and in order to preserve them, they have been sawn from the walls, framed with iron, backed with slate, and glazed.

The royal palace is spacious, and well situated, open on one side to the sea, on the other to a large garden, and wilderness of evergreen oaks, with the mountain in the back ground.

Resina is most immediately over the city of *Herculaneum*, Portici however is over some parts of it; a circumstance the modern inhabitants little dreamed of, till the accidental discoveries at the beginning of this century. So far back as the year 1689 some inscriptions and other things were found, which gave a suspicion that Herculaneum and Pompeii, which were known from Pliny's account to have been overwhelmed in the eruption of the year 79, were hereabouts; but the works which were carried on by the prince d'Elbeuf in the year 1718, put the matter out of all doub doubt. The first intelligence we received in England of these discoveries was in the year 1752; and the first excavations which were made by order of his Sicilian majesty, were in the year 1738. The city of Herculaneum was found not to have been overwhelmed by a stream of lava, but buried in ashes, &c. hardened into a tufo; six streams however of lava have since flowed over it: the pavements also, both of this city and Pompeii, are of lava, and strata of volcanic substances are found under both the streets were seen to be straight, with raised footways on each side the insides of the rooms were generally painted *à tempera*. The principal buildings discovered at Herculaneum were the *Forum* or *Chalcidicum*, a court 228 feet long, and 132 broad, surrounded with a peristile of 42 columns. The statues of the Balbi, and many others, were found here. This building communicated by means of a portico with two temples; one of them 150 feet in length, by 60 in breadth; the other only 60 by 42. The *Theatre* has 21 rows of seats disposed in a semicircle of 160 feet diameter, the stage is a rectangle of 72 feet by 30, with architectural decorations, and marble columns in the proscenium. The theatre is kept disembarrassed of rubbish, and there is a commodious descent to it: all the rest is filled in again, and no excavations are now going forward at Herculaneum.

POMPEII is twelve or thirteen miles from Naples, in the same road; passing through the two villages of *Torre del Greco*, and *Tor del Annonziata*. The lava has mo e than once reached the former: the latter is very near the ancient *Pompeii*. They begun to dig here in the year 1755, and this town being so distant from Vesuvius, it was covered in some parts twenty, but in general only from twelve to fifteen feet; and that chiefly with the lightest materials, ashes and pumice stones. This induced the king to dig here rather than at Herculaneum, which is buried very deep, and in materials much more difficult to penetrate.

You enter the place by the barracks for the garrison: a portico runs round a square court, supported by stone pillars, stuccoed and painted: the soldiers amused themselves with drawing figures, and writing their names upon the plaster. Near the wall, in this angle, lie fragments of an old Doric temple, of much higher antiquity than the rest of the town. One opening displays some

houses

houses, part of a street, and a temple of Isis. The architecture of this is slight, the walls are covered with ornaments in stucco, executed in a coarse manner: the inscriptions and paintings have been cut out of this, and other buildings, and removed to Portici for greater safety, but they have left disagreeable vacancies, that disfigure the walls. The *penetrale* of the temple, is a small pavilion, raised upon steps, under which is a vault, supposed to have served the purposes of ocular imposition. The statue of the goddess was fled from her pedestal; but a variety of instruments and utensils for the sacred ceremonies were found here; and also some skeletons of her priests. One cannot but wish that they had left the temple as they found it: with all its furniture and paintings. Hence you go through vineyards, to where they have laid open part of a principal street, one of the city gates, a length of wall, some tombs, and a road without the gate. The walls are built with large pieces of lava in regular courses, and the streets are paved with the same material. Carriage wheels have worn traces in the pavement, from which we may observe, that the distance between the wheels in the Roman carriages was four feet:

and this street being ten feet wide, there was just room for two of them to pass each other: there is a foot-way raised high on each side, three feet in breadth.

In the street, some of the houses advance before, while others retire behind the line: the materials of which they are constructed are limestone and calcareous concretions from the Apennines; lava, tufo, and pumice. The shops have stone seats before them, and over their doors sometimes emblems of their trade in relievo. The houses are small, and built round courts, from which all the apartments are lighted; in the center of the court is a grate to carry off the water. The walls of the rooms are stuccoed, and painted in a pretty light taste, with festoons and garlands, masks, animals, fruits, landscapes, and capricious architecture, on brown, orange, and other strong-coloured grounds. The rooms are small, many of them without any light but through the door: the windows were mostly closed with wooden shutters; some few had glass, which was very thick, and far from transparent, others had selenites or isinglass split into thin plates.

On each side of the highway, leading towards the sea are tombs. That of the Tarentian family is uncovered: it confifts of a fquare court, on the walls of which are placed the fkulls of animals facrificed in funeral ceremonies, and large mafks with weeping countenances and hollow eyes: the pile on which the bodies were confumed, ftands in the center of the court, near a tower, where the urns were placed in niches.

The greateft curiofity out of the town, is a fuburban villa, exactly in the fame ftate, except that the roof is beaten in, as it was on the day of the eruption. It confifts of four levels; namely, the cellars, a ground-floor with its portico or cloifter; and as it was on a fteep declivity, a court above, in which was the ftreet door, and over that a floor for bedchambers. Like the houfes in the eaft, it prefents nothing to the road but a bare wall; the windows being all towards the garden. From the town you enter by a court, furrounded with ftuccoed columns, adjoining is a triangular area, diftributed into alcoves and clofets for baths. From this floor a terrace projects on each fide, round a large fquare: and under it is a broad gallery, and covered apartments, for fummer refidence. on each fide, under the terraces, runs a portico, meeting oppofite the houfe in a hall, that probably opened into the vineyard or pleasure-grounds. Here was found the skeleton of the master, with the house key, and a purse of gold. The cellars still contain several amphoras, ranged along the walls; and the bones of many wretches, who fled hither for shelter. The cielings and walls of the rooms in this villa were adorned with a variety of painting: and in the window of a bedchamber, some panes of glass are still remaining.

STABIA is near *Castell' a mare*; it was swallowed up at the same time with the two others, and was the smallest of the three, indeed it seems rather to have been a string of country houses than a town. It was first discovered about the year 1750. An earthquake seems to have damaged the houses before they were covered, and the hot ashes had consumed every thing combustible few excavations therefore were made here, and these were filled in again.

You are now on your way to Pæstum, or Pesto, anciently Possidonia. You go by Nocera to Salerno, where you may hire a boat for Pesto, thirty miles distant. This was a colony of Dorians; and few cities have left such noble monuments of their architecture. There are superb ruins of several temples

temples, which are of the same kind of doric as those in Sicily.

Another excursion from Naples is to Caserta, sixteen miles distant. Here the late king, who is now king of Spain, erected a prodigious palace, from designs by Vanvitelli. The two principal fronts are 787 feet in length, and contain five stories of thirty-seven windows each: the two other sides are 616 feet long. Within are four courts; and in the center of the palace is a superb staircase, crowned by a circular hall, which affords a communication to every set of apartments. There is a profusion of the richest marbles every where. The chapel is incrusted with pannels of yellow marble: the paintings by Conca are bad; but there is a beautiful presentation, by Mengs. The theatre is a very fine one; antique columns of alabaster support the roof, and divide the house into forty-two boxes, richly decorated.

The gardens are very extensive, but resemble the formal insipid scenes of Le Notre; with wide sultry allies, and crouded rows of statues. The aqueduct for supplying the palace has three stories of arcades, of which the upper one is divided into forty-three arches: the work is plain but strong: from hence the water is carried in a channel to the cascade, and passes under Caserta vecchia. The last and present monarchs have expended large sums in embellishing the environs; the air however is infected by noxious vapours, arising from stagnant water in the ditches, that surround the rich meadows in this neighbourhood.

In fine weather it will be a pleasant voyage to the island of CAPRI, anciently *Capreæ*, eighteen miles south of Naples, at the entrance of the gulph. Tiberius spent ten years here in the most beastly debaucheries. Where the island is not rock, the soil is very rich; and every spot that will admit it, is industriously tilled. They catch annually from twelve to sixty thousand quails; and one year 160,000 were netted. The accommodations at the inn are very bad; the island however unites such a variety of beauties, the scenery is so charming, the climate so fine, the fruits so excellent, that it is well worth the attention of a traveller.

In Naples there are several *manufactories* of silk, velvets, velverets, handkerchiefs, and stockings; their sope is much esteemed, they also make liqueurs, essences, diavoloni, artificial flowers, and abundance of excellent macaroni

macaroni: the best musical strings are made here, from the intestines of lambs, seven or eight months old: there is a manufactory of tortoiseshell, which they inlay curiously with gold for snuff-boxes, and a variety of other articles, and they carry on a considerable commerce in polished marbles and lavas.

The weather is very uncertain, with much wind and wet during winter. Though consumptive people resort to Naples, yet this is a frequent disease here, and the climate is probably unfavourable to it, from the want of movement in the bay, the height of the hills behind the city, and the sudden transitions from heat to cold *.

* There is a little *Guida de' Forastieri* for the city, and another for the environs: indifferent enough. Sir William Hamilton has done much for the volcanic history of the neighbourhood, and I have had frequent obligations to Mr Swinburne's excellent travels, in the foregoing account. The best history of Naples is by Giannone.

SECTION IX.

Return to Rome, and journey from thence to Florence.

BEFORE you quit Naples, you must have a passport, and order for post-horses, which you will obtain by application to the British ambassador. It will also be convenient, to write to your banker or correspondent at Rome, for a *lascia-passare* to meet you at the gate of that city, to avoid your being obliged to drive to the *dogana* or custom-house, in order to have your baggage searched.

It will be worth your while to return by *monte Cassino*, to see the noble convent of Benedictines. The road, which is bad in winter, passes by Capua, Toricello, Cujanello, San-Vittore, and San Germano; and the convent is about sixty miles from Naples. It is situated on a high mountain, and the hosp of the abbey will furnish you with mules for the ascent. The community consists of near eighty religious, all of noble birth; the Abbot is chosen for six years, and by his office is

first

first Baron of the kingdom of Naples. The convent looks down on thirty-six villages, which, with the adjacent lands, belong to it; besides various possessions in Calabria, &c. Every traveller has a claim to bed and board for three days, in proportion to his rank. The monks are at liberty to go any where within the limits of Italy.

You pass through three courts before you arrive at the Church, than which nothing can be more rich and splendid; or in a worse taste, both as to the architecture and incrustation. the paintings are by Lanfranco, Luca Giordano, Solimene, and Conca. In the convent are paintings by Raffaelle, Annibale Carracci, and other great masters, and some of Luca Giordano and Solimene's best performances.

If you give up this deviation, and are not fond of a sea voyage, you will return by the road you came: or if you did not make an excursion from Naples on purpose, you may take the royal palace of Caserta in your way. Hence you may visit the ruins of ancient Capua, and so return into the direct road to Rome.

Ancient Capua is two miles and an half from the modern town. The principal ruin here

here is an amphitheatre; the lower order tuscan, with a doric over it: the architecture appears clumsy in its present imperfect state it was built of brick, faced with stone or marble; but the facing is all carried off there were four entrances to it. There is also a double arcade, supposed to have been a gate.

The country from Naples to Mola is generally flat; beyond this, the road ascends the calcareous Apennines. They stretch to Terracina, which has a harbour well situated in a fine gulph, sheltered by high mountains against the north winds; and the country about abounds in corn, vines, pomegranates lemons, &c. If you go by Piperno, buffaloes will drag you up the mountain; and you will see many of these animals feeding in the swamps of the Pontine marshes. From Piperno you have a long, rough, and stony descent, till you come within a few miles of Sermoneta, where the country begins to be flat, with the marshes on the left, and the Apennines on the right. A sulphureous smell arising from several hot springs near the road, is very offensive, especially in hot weather, when the mephitic air off the marshes renders this part of the country unwholesome

some, and even dangerous for travellers. The innkeeper and his family at Sermoneta, bear testimony to this by their yellow looks.

Beyond Sermoneta the Apennines run more to the right.

After descending the mountain of Veletri, the road goes by la Faiola and Marino then descends suddenly into the plain which extends to Rome.

Rome to Florence.

You will probably rest yourself at Rome, and see once more some of the fine things which struck you most, before you quit it finally for Florence. Your road will now be by Viterbo and Siena, and is more intresting to the naturalist, than pleasant to the traveller

From Rome to Ponte Molle, the road lies through a valley between the Pincian and Marian hills, which would not be unpleasing, were it not for the dismal prospect of bare hills, and plantations of reeds.

The country to Baccano is broken into faint inequalities; and the soil is generally good. there are few parts of Europe however that lie so miserably neglected; and

about

about Baccano they are poisoned by the stagnant waters of the lake. The road for several miles lies upon the ancient Cassian way, which is well preserved but in very few places the worst road imaginable is an old broken Roman causeway. Volcanic tufo hills continue to Monte Rosi; beyond that a lava torrent. Near Ronciglione a beautiful deep valley, with picturesque romantic views. The town is the best in this part of the papal territories, both with respect to situation and buildings, which are of tufo stuccoed. Between Ronciglione and the mountain of Viterbo, anciently *mons Ciminus*, you travel by the lake of Vico, a fine body of water, for three miles: it is encompassed by hills, clothed with beautiful woods. The mountain consists of various volcanic substances accumulated without order. That there is some richness in the soil of the mountain, is evident from the noble plantations of oaks chesnuts and beeches, with which it is covered.

Viterbo is a pretty town, situated in a plain at the foot of the mountain: several square lofty towers produce an agreeable effect at a distance. It is well built, the houses are in a good taste, there are some pretty fountains

and

and some fronts of churches in a good style of architecture. The streets are paved wholly with lava in pieces from four to eight feet in length: and the population is estimated at 10,000. The churches best worth seeing are the Cathedral, and those of Santa Rosa and S. Francesco: in the latter there is a dead Christ, &c. by Sebastiano del Prombo, painted from a design of Michelangelo's. Beyond Viterbo, to the left, is a lake of hot water, with a sulphureous smell. The country to Montefiascone has a melancholy face; time has not yet meliorated the volcanic matter by the rotting of vegetables.

Montefiascone stands upon a very proud eminence, commanding an immeasurable prospect, and appearing at a distance like a metropolis, as it was, in fact, in ancient times; but as we approach it, we discover it to be a poor mean town, which would scarcely be known, were it not for the muscat wines in its neighbourhood.

There are few spots in Italy which furnish more delicious and magnificent scenes than the environs of *Bolsena*, which stands upon the ruins of the ancient *Volsinium*, one of the chief cities of Etruria; but is now no more than a contemptible village; in which nothing

thing is to be seen but an antique sarcophagus in the church yard.

Near it there is a fine lake thirty miles in circumference, which was anciently the crater of a volcano; and opposite to this, close to the road, is a remarkable hill, covered with regular prismatic basaltine columns, most of them standing obliquely, and a considerable length out of the ground: they are generally hexagonal, and flat at both ends: this hill is noticed by Kircher*.

In the tufo hills near *S. Lorenzo delle grotte* are a great number of artificial caverns,

---

* At no very great distance from Bolsena is *Orvieto*. The Cathedral is a very fine gothic building, the front at least as beautiful as that of Siena, and very rich in sculpture and mosaic. Nicola Pisano had some hand in it as a sculptor, but not as an architect. It contains a great deal both of sculpture and painting within. Of the latter, a chapel painted by Signorelli, with the last judgement, is most remarkable, particularly because Michelangelo used to study it. Of the sculpture a Pieta, or dead Christ in the lap of the Virgin, is most admired. The wines of this place, Montefiascone and Montepulciano, are in great esteem.

The road is so rocky, that it will be necessary to make this excursion on horseback.

which were probably formed at first by digging *puzzolana*, and now serve as shelters for cattle, or implements of husbandry. The present Pope has benevolently caused the old town to be demolished, an account of the *mal aria* which reigns there, and has built a new one very handsomely at the top of the hill.

Acquapendente takes its name from an inconsiderable stream tumbling down a rock; there are many ruins on every side of the town, and abundance of tufo and cinders.

The soil all the way from Rome to this place is volcanic; from hence to Siena are mostly hills of marl. The mountain of *Radicofani* however is an isolate volcanic rock, surrounded in the valley with marl, but no ashes or puzzolana: on the other side of this valley is another volcanic mountain still higher, called *S. Fiore*. The town of *Radicofani* is on the top of the mountain, and has a small garrison, in the castle: the inn large, cold, and uncomfortable; not in the town, but below it. Hence to *S. Quirico* the road continues over marl hills: but near this place the hills consist of calcareous tufo, with sea shells enclosed. The houses of this village

village are built of *travertino*, a proof of neighbouring limestone*.

From S. Quirico to Siena there is a succession of marl hills, exhibiting a most dreary prospect.

Siena, in the midst of hills, of the most pleasing shapes, excellently cultivated, is perhaps the most desirable place in Italy for a stranger to pass some time in; the climate being moderate, living reasonable, society good, and the language spoken in the greatest purity. It is also within a moderate distance both of Rome and Florence: the houses are built of brick, and the streets are paved with it.

---

* A few miles from S. Quirico a narrow road leads to *Chiusi* through the middle of desolated hills of clay and marl. *Chiusi* was anciently called *Clusium*, the metropolis of Porsena, but is now a miserable town, containing about a thousand inhabitants, and dignified with the title of a Bishoprick, of not more than 150 pounds a year. Not far on the right are the *Bagni di S. Filippo*, the waters of which deposit a fine calcareous tufo, which is precipitated or moulds from medals, bas-reliefs, &c. and make most beautiful impressions.

The population of Siena amounts to sixteen or seventeen thousand, and it is near five miles in circuit. The city still retains a shadow at least of those rights which it enjoyed, whilst an independent state, before it formed a part of the dutchy of Tuscany.

Siena is particularly agreeable in the hot season on account of its lofty situation and salubrious air. It has produced many famous painters, architects, and poets; the nobility are as distinguished as any in Italy, and have a *Cassino*, or Assembly of both sexes.

The Duomo, or Cathedral, is a fine gothic building of black and white marble. The great portal was begun in 1284, after the designs of Giovanni da Pisa, and finished in 1333 by Agostino and Agnolo, Sienese architects. The front is prodigiously loaded with ornaments. All the work of the inside is most highly finished, as the carving in wood of the choir; the sculpture in marble of the pulpit, and especially the historical engraving of the pavement, representing in chiaro-oscuro the most remarkable stories of the Old and New Testament.

In the Chigi Chapel are two statues by Bernini, S. Jerom, and the Magdalen; also eight columns of verd-antique. The *Benitier* is handsome; as is likewise the pulpit: and the bas-reliefs, especially of the staircase, are admirable. The two pictures by Carlo Maratti have suffered.

At the end of the church. Esther before Ahasuerus. Children of Israel gathering manna, companions by Salimbeni. The Ascension in six pictures, by Beccafumi.—Altar in fifteen pieces, by Duccio Buoninsegna. Virgin, Child, S. Peter, and S. Paul, by Raffaelle Vanni.

In a round chapel. Statue of S. John Baptist, by Donatello—several paintings by Pinturicchio, Sori, and Trevisano.

Ancient octagon marble pulpit, by Nic. and Giov. da Pisa, with basso-relievos, in 1207.

Baptistery under the choir cieling in fresco, by Ambrogio Lorenzetti. And before the entrance into the choir are four large frescos, by Ventura di Arcangiolo Salimbeni. In the chapel of S. John are several good statues, the best of which is S. John, by Donatello.

In the left transept is a vaulted room, called the Library. There remain now no other books besides forty large folio volumes of church music in manuscript on velum, finely illuminated, by a Benedictine Monk of Monte

Monte Cassino. The Spaniards carried off all the rest. In the middle of this room, on a pedestal, stands a group of the Graces in white marble; it is mutilated, and the middle Grace is without a head. This was once reckoned the finest antique in the world.

The greatest curiosity in this library is a set of ten large pictures in fresco, in fine preservation and freshness of colouring, by Pinturicchio the subject is the life of Pope Pius II*.

The church of the *Augustins* is a very handsome modern building, by Vanvitelli.

The paintings are—the Adoration of the Shepherds, by Romanelli. An Assumption, of a bishop and saint, praying to the Virgin in the clouds, by Carlo Maratti. Opposite to this a piece by Pietro Perugino, of Christ on the cross, with several saints kneeling at the foot of it.

The church of the *Dominicans* is remarkable for a very ancient picture on wood, representing the Virgin with the infant Jesus in

---

* It is said Raffaelle gave the designs for some of them, and even assisted Pinturicchio a little in the execution. Vasari says he made either the sketches, or the cartoons, for them all.

her

her arms, by *Guido Senese*. It is dated 1221, and is in the Venturini chapel. Though so ancient, it is still in good preservation. In the same chapel are two pictures, on the side. Vasari mentions a Madonna painted by the same Guido, in the *Oratorio della campagna di S. Bernardino*, pictures in the *Capitolo*, or chapter-house of the Augustins, by *Ambrogio Sanese*; and a Madonna over the door of the Duomo, by *Simone Memmi*.

In the church of *S. Quirico*, is a flight into Egypt, and an Ecce Homo, by Francesco Vanni. A descent from the cross, by Alessandro Casiolani. Crowning Christ with thorns, Ventura Salimbeni. Nailing him to the cross, by Sori.

In *S. Martino* the circumcision, by Guido.—In *S. Maria in Provenzano*, a holy family, by Andrea del Sarto. At *S. Francesco*, the pope blessing a cardinal, by Calabrese, S. Martina, by Pietro da Cortona. At *San-Spirito* and *Santa-Catherina*, many pieces, by Sienese painters.

Il Carmine. Annunciation, by Fr. Vanni. Fall of the angels, by Dom. Beccafumi. Virgin, child, and saints, by Bernardo Fungari. 1512.

S. Agostino

S *Ag fimo*. Chrift on the crofs, furrounded by faints and angels, by Pietro Perugino.

Adoration of the Magi Sodoma.

Chrift bearing his crofs, by Aleff. Cafolani and Ventura Salimbeni.

Virgin, Chrift, and faints, by Carlo Maratti.

Camaldules out of the city. Chrift on the crofs, furrounded by faints and angels, the moft capital work of Fr. Vanni.

The Univerfity has feveral learned profeffors. The library and mufeum are common to this, and the Academia Fifico-critica, which has publifhed four volumes in quarto, under the title of *Atti dell' Accademia di Siena*. There are four or five other academies in this city.

In the hofpital of *S. Maria della Scala*, in the chapel, is a fine large frefco of the pool of Bethefda, by Sebaftian Conca.

The *Palazzo Publico*, or Guildhall, is in a place or open area, in form of a fhell. There are many ancient frefcos in it. thofe in the *Sala della pace* by Ambrogio Lorenzetto, are worn out, and feem never to have been good for any thing. This is the cafe alfo with one in Sala di Configlio, by *Simone di Lorenzo* and *Simone Mimmi*. The frefcos in

the

the chapel and anti-chapel, by Taddeo Bartoli, are damaged, and not extraordinary. There is a painting at the altar, by Sodoma, of the Holy family with S. Antony. In the *Sala di Bala*, the Life of Pope Alexander III. is painted in fresco by old masters*. In the

---

* This life of Alexander III. is extremely curious. It consists of sixteen pieces, four large and twelve smaller, arched at top—they are valuable, not only as specimens of the style of painting in Italy at a very early period, but because they give us the arms, weapons, ships, manner of fighting, and in short the whole costume of the age in which they were painted, more completely than they would be obtained from any thing else now existing in the world. It is not well made out who was the author of these pictures—from their style he was evidently of the school of Giotto. They are painted in Chiaro oscuro (if I mistake not) in imitation of relievos, and perhaps may be the "storia di verde terra," which Vasari says Ambrogio Lorenzetti painted in this palace, though he speaks of eight only, and here are sixteen. Pecci says, I know not upon what authority, that they were begun by Martino di Bartolomeo da Siena, and finished afterward by Spinello di Luca and his sons, painters of Arezzo in 1407.—I never heard of this Martino

Sala del Confiftorio, the cieling painted by Beccafumi, is well executed, and yet in good preservation. The subjects of these frescos are some Greek and Roman histories, with ornaments between them. In this room is the judgement of Solomon, by Luca Giordano; the Assumption of the Virgin, by Vanni; and many portraits.

The Theatre is a part of this palace; it was burnt down in 1742 and 1751, and has been rebuilt in a handsome manner, with four rows of boxes, and twenty-one in each row.

The territory of Siena comprehends eight towns, and two hundred boroughs, villages, &c. It has been described by two celebrated naturalists, Micheli and Targioni. Their marbles are well known.

The Maremma of Siena formerly so fruitful and populous, now lies waste and unpeopled *.

The

---

* *Volterra* is not a great way from Siena. Since the removal of Riccarelli's famous flaughter of the innocents to Florence, it does not possess a great deal to attract the attention of a connoisseur. Its situation however, the singularity of the country about

The whole road from Siena to Florence is one of the most charming in Tuscany; the country being finely varied with hills, cloathed with olive-trees, vines, cypresses, firs, oaks, beeches, &c. The great number of country houses, old castles and villages, make it extremely picturesque. The road is all good, but continually ascending and descending, and paved all the way.

There is another road from Rome to Florence by Perugia, which will be interesting to such as wish to study the ancient Roman school of painting, and particularly the works of Pietro Perugino, the master of Raffaelle. Ombria, the best cultivated part of the Apennines will be passed through, and the lake of Perugia will be seen. In taking this road, you must return as far as Foligno on the way by which you came from Bologna, and there going to the left, you find it two posts to PERUGIA, or near twenty-one miles. This is a considerable city, built on the top of a mountain; and has several handsome churches, and elegant fountains.

about it, and the views it presents, are very striking. Most of the churches abound with the works of the old Tuscan painters.

In the Cathedral is, the Marriage of the Virgin, by Pietro Perugino. The descent from the cross, by Barroccio. Virgin, child, &c. by Luca Signorelli.

S. Maria nuova. Virgin, Christ, Saints, and Angels.—Virgin, Christ, S. Paul, the Hermit, and S. Francis.—A Nativity, with God the Father over it, in a semicircle—and three small pieces. all by Pietro Perugino. Virgin, Christ, and four Saints, by Sinibaldo Perugino. A Transfiguration, seemingly by Raffaelle.

S. Agostino. Adoration of the Magi, and five small pictures under it.—God the Father and Cherubims. Burial of Christ, &c. fourteen pictures, by Pietro Perugino, in the choir. In the Sacristy, sixteen small pictures by him; and the marriage of S. Catherine, by Raffaelle.

S. Francesco. Christ with four saints. The Resurrection: both by Pietro Perugino. Assumption of the Virgin; and dead Christ, with eight figures: both by Raffaelle.

S. Pietro, belonging to the Benedictines, is a beautiful structure, supported by marble pillars, with a fine choir. In this church is the Ascension, one of Pietro Perugino's best pieces. A dead Christ, with four figures.

God the Father, two pictures, with a single Angel in each; and two Prophets in small rounds: all by him.—The marriage of Cana—Elijah—and S. Benedict: by Vasari.—In the Sacristy: eleven small pictures, by Pietro Perugino—and two by Raffaelle.

S. Severo. Saints by Perugino and Raffaelle, four circular pieces, by Pietro Perugino.

Monte Morofini. Adoration of the shepherds and its companion*: by Pietro Perugino.

S. Francesco fuori, a convent of Recollets. The Crucifixion: and Assumption of the Virgin †, by Pietro Perugino.—In the Sacristy: Virgin, Child, and Saints, by Pietro Perugino.—In a little Chapel, Adoration of the shepherds, by him.

---

* These are two fresco paintings or fragments saved out of the walls of the old church when was taken down. K

† These pictures are painted on the two sides of the same board.

N. B. The Christ and Cross are sculptures wood; and the only figures by P. Perugino in the former, are the Virgin, Magdalen, S. Francis, a male saint, and two angels. K.

S. A

S. Michele's church was an ancient Temple of Vesta.

S. Anna. Virgin, Christ, S. Anne, &c.

S. Girolamo. Virgin, Christ, and Saints.

S Ercolano. Virgin, Christ, and three Saints.

S. Dominico. Virgin, Christ, and Saints, in the clouds. all these by Pietro Perugino. In this church are also several other pieces by painters of his time.

S. Antonio Abate. Holy family, angels, and shepherds; by P Perugino.

S. Giuliana. S. John in the island of Patmos, by P. Perugino. Not one of his good pictures.—Virgin and child, and saints; by Domin. Paridis.

Palazzo Publico. Virgin, Christ, and four saints, by Pietro Perugino—and in the Chapel, Christ standing in the sepulchre: by the same.

Il Collegio del Cambio. Painted all over by Pietro Perugino.—In the Chapel, nine large pieces on the wall, and eleven on the cieling, by him.

Governor's House. Presentation; and Adoration of the Magi: by the same. small pictures.

Foncella, which is the next stage, is on

the banks of the lake of Perugia, anciently called *Thrasymene*, and famous for the defeat of the Consul Flaminius, by Hannibal *. It is above thirty miles in circumference, abounds with excellent fish, and has three islands in it; on a peninsula, is a town called *Castiglione*; in which it is said there is a handsome palace, and some good painting.

Above Camoccia, on a hill, planted with vines and fruit-trees, is CORTONA, belonging to the Dukedom of Tuscany; a town remarkable for its antiquity and academy the semicircular plain at the bottom is one of the finest in Italy.

The Cathedral is a very old building, remarkable only for a fine picture of the Nativity, by Pietro Berettini, commonly known by the name of Pietro di Cortona.

There is another picture by him, in the church of *Santa Chiara*. It is semicircular, and the subject is, the virgin and child, with S. Francis and S. Clare. And a third in the church of *S. Agostino*, which is also a virgin and child, with S. John, S. Jerom, S. Augus-

---

* M. Dutens has given the exact field of battle in a little plain between Tuoro, and a hill called to this day *Sanguinetta*.

tine, and another saint.—In *S. Michele* is a descent of the Holy Ghost, by Andrea del Sarto. And in several of the churches—as *Campagnia di Gesu, S. Margareta, S. Francesca, la S. S. Trinità,* &c. are many old pictures by Luca Signorelli: as there are in *S. Domenico* by Giovanni Angelica.

At the Academy of Antiquaries, is a library and museum, but scarcely worth the attention of a stranger.

AREZZO is in a charming situation, overlooking a small plain. Petrarch was born there in 1304. It is a very ancient town, and was much fallen to decay, when Cosmo d' Medicis took it under his protection; since which it has gradually recovered itself.

The Cathedral was built in 1300 by Margaritone, from a design of Giacomo Tedesco: the great altar is by Giorgio Pisano and his pupils: the windows are handsomely painted: at the entrance are two pillars of porphyry: and in the square before it, is a statue of the great duke Ferdinand.

In the *Badia,* or Olivetan abbey of *S. Flora,* is a noble picture in the refectory, of the marriage of Esther and Ahasuerus, by Giorgio Vasari: by whom also are two pieces, of S. Roch curing the plague; and S. Roch in the defart—the latter excellent; in the church of S. Rocco and in the Pieve several pictures by him. In the church of S. Francesco are old frescos by Pietro del Borgo the cieling of the choir is by Lorenzo di Bicci: and there is a crucifixion, by Margaritone.—In S. Margarita, and S. Girolamo, are pictures by Luca Signorelli. In S. Agostino, the circumcision, by Domenico Pecori. In S. Angelo, a famous old fresco, of Michael and the Devil, &c. by Spinello. There are many pictures here, by the old Tuscan masters, in most of the churches; of which it would be tedious to give a catalogue.

SECTION X.

Account of Florence.

FLORENCE, in Italian *Firenze*, is not without pretence to its common title of *la bella*, being finely situated upon the river Arno, and its buildings generally in a good taste. It is about three thousand yards in length, and six miles in circuit. The streets are clean, and well paved with very large flag-stones; but mostly narrow and winding. There are no less than 150 churches in this city, and the population is estimated at 80,000. The environs are delightful; the plain in which the city stands being surrounded by charming hills, well cultivated and adorned. But though Florence be thus in a kind of basin, the warmth of the south and south-east winds is so well tempered by cooler ones, that persons may often sleep abroad without danger. The autumn here is generally wet; and this city is a bad residence in winter, on account of the south-east or *sirocco*, and north, which blow often on the same day; and subject the inhabitants to inflammations in the breast and lungs. Florence therefore is best in summer, when the atmosphere about it is esteemed very salubrious.

The Arno divides the city into two unequal parts; it is about 140 yards wide, and navigable for small vessels. In the midst of summer it often wants water; and in winter it frequently overflows its banks. There are four stone bridges over it: that called *il ponte della Trinità*, was built by Ammanati, and is very elegant: the arches are cycloidal.

The Cathedral church, called *Santa Maria del Fiore*, was begun in the year 1296, from designs of Arnolfo di Lapo, disciple of Cimabue. It is all incrusted with black and white marble in compartments. The octagon cupola, by Brunellesco, is a very fine one. The marble pavement of the nave is by Francesco da San Gallo; that of the choir after designs of Michelangelo's [*]; and the rest by Giuliano di Baccio d'Agnolo. The cupola is painted by Federigo Zuccheri and Giorgio Vasari; and the bas-reliefs of the choir are by Baccio Bandinelli and Giovanni dell'Opera. The crucifix at the end of the choir is by Benedetto da Majano; and God the Father, and Christ supported by an Angel, large statues on the altar, are by Bandinelli. Behind the altar, is an unfinished pieta, by Michelangelo. Over the principal door, within, is the coronation of our Lady, a mosaic, by Gaddo Gaddi; and another, of the annunciation, over a door next *via de' Servi*, by Ghirlandaio. The tomb of Giotto is by one of the side doors; the epitaph by Politian.

[*] When we speak of Michelangelo simply, we always mean Michelangelo Buonarroti, as by Guido, we always mean Guido Reni.

Next to it is the tomb of Brunellesco the architect: the epitaph by Aretino. On the other side is a portrait of Dante. Over one of the doors is a statue of the virgin larger than life, with two angels, by Giovanni da Pisa. There are statues of the four evangelists, larger than life, by Donatello; and eight of the Apostles, by several hands. The door of the Sacristy is bronze, with bas-reliefs, by Lorenzo Ghiberti: and the boys within are by Donatello.

Near the cathedral, is the *Campanile*, or steeple; a tower, built after the designs of Giotto, of black, white and red marble, mixt in compartments. It is about 273 feet high, and 47 square. On each side are niches, with four statues, those over the door, and on the side next the square are by Donatello.

The *Baptistery* is an octagon, the diameter of which is near 92 feet. It is wholly incrusted with polished marble; and has three bronze gates: one by Andrea Pisano, put up in 1330; the two others, by Lorenzo Ghiberti, erected in the following century. Michelangelo, speaking of the last, used to say that they were fit to be the doors of paradise. The columns before the principal gate are of phury. over it are three marble statues, repre-

representing the baptism of Christ, begun by Sansovino, and finished by Vincenzio Danti; by whom also are three bronze statues, representing the beheading of S. John Baptist, over another gate. Over the third is S. John disputing with a pharisee and doctor of the law, by Giovanfrancesco Rustici. Within are sixteen large granite columns—the statue of John Baptist, with angels, by Girolamo Ticciati—the bas-reliefs and statue, on the tomb of Baldassar Cossa, or Pope John XII.—and also a Magdalen, by Donatello. The roof is in mosaic, by Andrea Tafi, disciple of Cimabue.

The church of *San Lorenzo* is by Brunellesco. Two pulpits supported by marble columns have bas-reliefs in bronze, by Donatello. This church is adorned with many paintings; as the marriage of the virgin by Rosso. A chiaro-oscuro of the virgin and S. Anne, by Bartolommeo, in which he has introduced his own portrait. A strange subject, of God on the cross, explaining to Adam and Eve the mystery of the redemption, by Andrea del Sarto, &c. &c.

The old Sacristy is by Brunellesco: the bas-reliefs, and the statues of S. Laurence, S. Stephen

Stephen, S. Cosimo, and S. Damiano, are by Donatello.

The architecture of the new Sacristy, or chapel of the Princes, is by Michelangelo; as is also the sculpture. 1. The tomb of Giuliano de Medici, with a statue of him, and two figures of day and night. 2. The tomb of Lorenzo de' Medici, with his statue, and two figures of morning and evening twilight. 3. Our Lady with Christ in her arms.

The *Chapel* of the *Medicis*, behind the choir, is an octagon, richly incrusted with jasper, oriental agate, chalcedony, lapis lazuli, &c. There are six superb tombs in it: four of egyptian granite, and two of oriental granite; from designs of Michelangelo. If this chapel were completed, it would be one of the finest things in Italy*.

The *Mediceo-Laurenziana Library* joins to the church. The gallery in which the books and manuscripts are arranged, is about 150 feet long, 35 feet wide, and 28 high. This was built by Michelangelo; the staircase, windows, and principal door, are much ad-

* The person who shows this chapel has specimens and *studii* of marbles, &c. to dispose of

mired: the very desks were executed from drawings, and under the immediate direction of this great architect. The manuscripts are said to amount to 14,800.

The architecture of the church of *San Spirito* is by Brunellesco. It is of the corinthian order: the columns are of pietra serena, which is a variety of macigno. The high altar is very fine, of gabbro and polvera di prato, green and black, or red and black spotted with white. There are many pictures by old masters in this church, as the virgin and three saints, by Giotto; in the choir on the right hand next to this, the virgin, Christ, and two saints; by Boticelli Christ bearing his cross, with many figures, and S. Veronica with the holy handkerchief by Ghirlandaio; the virgin, Christ, S. Thomas, S. Peter, and two angels, dated 1482. Vasari mentions several pieces, by Fra Filippo Lippi, and others. Here is also a statue of Christ holding his cross, by Taddeo Landini after Michelangelo.

The church of *Santa Maria Novella* was built in 1279: from the airyness of its plan Michelangelo used to call it *la Sposa*. The paintings of the choir are by Ghirlandaio: seven of them represent the life of the virgin

gin; and as many the life of S. John Baptist: in these pieces are portraits of the times. In the sacristy is an ancient piece, looked upon to be the chef d'œuvre of Cimabue. There are many other ancient paintings both in the church and cloisters of the convent.

In the front of the house built near this church by Viviani, the last disciple of Galileo, is a bronze bust of this celebrated astronomer, and scrolls between the windows, marking the epochas of his discoveries.

The church of the *Annunciation*, belonging to the Servites is built by Michelozzi. In the chapel on the left at entrance is a miraculous picture, in which they tell you that the virgin was painted by angels: in the same chapel is a head of Christ, by Andrea del Sarto. In another of the chapels is a group in marble of Christ dead, supported by God the Father; by Baccio Bandinelli. In a third, decorated at the expence, and after the designs of Giovanni di Bologna, this artist lies interred. There is also the tomb and bust of Bandinelli. The assumption of the virgin in the middle of the roof is by Volterrano, who also painted the cupola and tribuna. There are many frescos of miracles, by Ulivelli.

In

In the inner cloister of the convent is the chapel of the academy of drawing, with the picture of the high altar, by Agnolo Bronzino, 1571; and two fresco by Vasari and Santi di Tito. But the principal curiosity here is a most excellent fresco by Andrea del Sarto, is one of the cloisters, over a door; well known by the name of *Madonna del Sacco*. In a little cloister, which serves as a vestibule to the church, is a bust in marble of Andrea del Sarto, with more frescos by him and others, now almost worn out. This convent is large; the monks near 200 in number; and their library ample.

Santa Croce, built in 1294 from the designs of Arnolfo, is a church of the *Frati Minori Conventuali*. Over the principal door is a statue in bronze of S. Louis, by Donatello. The paintings are many—a descent from the cross, by Salviati: the crucifixion, by Santi di Tito: the appearance of Christ to S. Thomas—the descent of the Holy Ghost —and Christ carrying his cross; all three by Vasari: the entry of Christ into Jerusalem, and a dead Christ; by Cigoli. Frescos by Volterrano, in the Nicolini chapel. Several pieces by Santi di Tito, Bronzino, and others. The coronation of the virgin—cappella della concezione

concezione—a cieling—and in the facrifty, twenty-fix fmall pieces of the life of Chrift and S. Francis; all by Giotto. The altar piece, and pictures on the wall of the facrifty —the finding of the crofs, on the wall of the choir: by Taddeo Gaddi. A crucifix, by Cimabue; and another by Margheritone. In the church and convent other pictures by Cimabue and Giotto.

Here is the maufoleum of Michelangelo Buonarroti, great in the three arts of painting, fculpture, and architecture. Above is his buft, with three crowns, and the motto— *tergeminis tollit honoribus* under the farcophagus are three ftatues of the three fifter arts in which he fo fuperiorly excelled: that of painting is the beft: in the decoration of the monument is introduced a fmall picture by his own hand of Chrift dead, with the holy women at the fepulchre. Over againft Michelangelo refts the illuftrious, the injured Galileo. Viviani's executors found great difficulty in obtaining leave to erect this maufoleum, and to remove Galileo's bones into it, in the year 1737, almoft a century after his death. The dialogue, in which lay his principal crime, ftill continues profcribed in the *Index expurgatorius*, reviled by Benedict XIV.

in 1758, along with the works of Bacon, Copernicus, Kepler, Descartes, and Foscarini. Here also are the tombs of Leonardo Aretino, and Micheli the famous naturalist.

In the church of *S. Marco*, belonging to the Dominicans, are several pictures by Fra Bartolommeo, Paffignani, Santi di Tito, Jacopo da Empoli, &c. The chapel of Antonino is by Averardo and Antonio Salviati: the works in marble by Giovanni di Bologna, six marble statues, by Francavilla, his scholar; and six baffirelievi in bronze, by Domenico Portigiani, another of his scholars, and from his master's drawings. The cupola is painted by Aleffandro Allori, by whom also there is a picture of Christ, S. Rosa, &c. ten figures large as life. There are many paintings about the Convent by Florentine artists and a large, curious library, open to the public.

The Grand Duke's stables and manege are near this convent: and his Menagerie is on the square. There is also a Giardino de' simplici or Botanic garden; and a Botanical Academy.

The church of the *Carmelites* was burnt in 1771, and the works of Giotto destroyed. The Corsini chapel, and the Brancacci, in

which

which are Mafaccio's frefcos, were faved. In the chapel of the communion, Gherardo Starnina has painted the life of S. John. The pictures of Angiolo Gaddi in the choir were much fmoked.

Many other churches have curious and valuable pictures by the Tufcan mafters—as *S. Mar a Maddalena de' Pazzi, S. Pier maggiore, Ognissanti*, &c. &c.

Palazzo Pitti, which is the refidence of the Grand Duke, was begun from defigns of Brunelefco. The front is heavy; but the infide of the court is majeftic, and in a good ftyle, by Ammanati. It is full of fine pictures, mofaic work, marbles, &c. Many of the pictures are firft rate ones. As the famous holy family, called *Madonna della fedia*. portraits of Leo X. with two cardinals, and of Julius II., all by Raffaelle. Portrait of cardinal Bentivoglio, by Vandyck. Several fine Rubens's. Many excellent by Tiziano, Andrea del Sarto, Bartolommeo, Carlo Dolce, &c.

In the upper ftory of this palace, is a Library of about 35,000 volumes. The gardens called *Boboli* are extenfive, and have a great variety of ground.

Palazzo

Palazzo Vecchio, the old palace, is built after the designs of Arnolfo. There is a large room in it for public entertainments, 172 feet long, and 70 wide; in which the most celebrated actions of the republic are painted by Vasari, in fresco: in the corners are four great historical pictures, by Cigoli, Ligozzi, and Passignani. Other rooms on the same floor are painted by Vasari. In the *sala dell' udienza vecchia*, which is the upper story, the actions of Furius Camillus, &c. are painted in fresco, by Salviati. There is a conversation, by Rubens; and the chapel was painted by Ghirlandaio. Some modern statues and groups are in this palace, by Baccio Bandinelli, Michelangelo, and Vincenzio Rossi. But the *Guardarobas* attract the attention of the majority of strangers. Here are fifty-four large silver dishes or basins, finely worked, which are a tribute paid to the Grand Duke by the feudatory cities—Turkish arms—the crown with which Pius V. crowned Cosmo I.; his horse equipage—a rich *paliotto*, or covering for an altar; and many other curiosities. Here also are kept the original copy of Justinian's Pandects, and a curious manuscript of the gospel according to S. John. These cannot be seen
without

without a licenfe from the Mafter of the Wardrobes; and the manufcripts muft be particularly fpecified.

At the entrance of the palace is David triumphing over Goliath, by Michelangelo; and Hercules with Cacus, by Vincenzio Roffi, fcarcely inferior to that of his mafter Bandinelli, which is in the fquare.

Oppofite to the old palace is a *Loggia*, executed after the defigns of Orgagna. Under one of the arcades is a group in bronze, by Donatello, of Judith ftanding with her fabre raifed up over the throat of Holofernes, who lies down againft the pedeftal, round which is this infcription: *Publicæ Salutis Exemplum Civ. Pos.* Here alfo is Perfeus fhowing Medufa's head, in bronze, by Benvenuto Cellini: and the rape of a Sabine, a marble group, by Giovanni Bologna.

There is much good modern fculpture in other parts of Florence, and they reckon 160 public ftatues. The moft remarkable of thefe are—Hercules vanquifhing the centaur Neffus, by Giovanni Bologna, near the cathedral. In the Piazza del Gran Duca, a fountain with Neptune, eighteen feet high, in a conch drawn by four fea-horfes, and the tritons accompanying him; in marble, by Ammanati: and

and twelve figures in bronze of nymphs and tritons, surrounding the edge of the basin, by Giovanni Bologna. Here is also an equestrian statue in bronze of Cosmo I., by Giovanni Bologna.

In the Boboli gardens is a fountain at the end of the great walk, with Neptune larger than life, the Ganges, Nile, and Euphrates, at his feet, upon a basin of granite above twenty-two feet in diameter: this is by Giovanni Bologna. There is also Neptune in bronze, surrounded with sea monsters; by Lorenzi: and in a grotto are four unfinished statues, designed for the mausoleum of Pope Julius II. by Michelangelo.

Before the church of the Servites, or l' Annonziata, is a large square, with light and elegant porticos, by Brunelleico. In the middle is an equestrian statue of Ferdinand I, in bronze, by Giovanni Bologna. The fountains also are by him. Within the church itself is some good sculpture by the same hand.

Before the church of S. Lorenzo, in the square, is a pedestal, with bassirelievi, by Bandinelli. In several of the churches are statues and other sculpture, in a good taste.

Both palaces have a communication with
the

the famous *Gallery*, which is the principal object of every stranger's attention at Florence. It is indeed an inexhaustible fund of entertainment in antique sculpture and painting; open to the public from day-light till evening, except between the hours of one and three. Here strangers have the freest access; either walking about the open corridores at their leisure; or attended in the cabinets by the Cicerones, who look for a handsome gratuity at your departure †.

The Gallery has been newly arranged; has received considerable improvements; and the entrance to it has been entirely altered very lately, according to the original design of Giorgio Vasari. The ascent is now by a handsome well-lighted staircase. In the vestibule are placed busts of those princes of the house of Medicis who formed the gallery. Two antique wolf dogs guard the entrance to a second vestibule, which is an octagon. In this you enter the corridores, consisting of two narrow galleries, above 400 feet in length, connected by another gallery, about

---

† For a general account of the Gallery, see *Saggio Istorico della Real Galleria di Firenze*, in two volumes octavo, 1779.

130 feet

130 feet long; all only twenty-two feet in breadth. These corridores are furnished on either side with many antique, and some modern statues; busts of the Emperors, Empresses, and other famous personages of Rome; with a vast abundance of paintings and other curiosities. The cielings are painted with symbols of the arts and sciences, civil and military virtues, &c.; and with portraits of such persons as have most excelled in each.

The most remarkable of the *statues* are—

Agrippa sitting; and another lady, much finer, but the head modern.

Mercury. Flora. Bacchus leaning on a little Faun.

Four in bronze: the two best, a Minerva, and a man in the toga, haranguing.

Narcissus. Ganymede with the eagle. Jupiter.

Bacchus, by Sansovino; and another by Michelangelo.

A copy of the Laocoon, by Bandinelli.

An antique wild boar, in white marble.

Busts of all the Roman Emperors and Empresses, except six, are ranged along one side and are accompanied by other famous Romans. The most rare of these are Otho Pertinax, Didius Julianus, Herennius, Didia Clara,

Clara, Manlia Scantilla, Nerva, Annius Verus, and Antinous. The best are thought to be Caligula, Galba, Hadrian, Marcus Aurelius, Lucius Verus, Agrippina, Plautius, Commodus, Cicero, and Seneca.

Paintings of all the schools, to the number of 135, are hung up in these corridores. And from them you enter the several *Cabinets*.

A little room serving as a vestibule to the rest.

Statues, busts, and bas-reliefs. As Ganymede, a statue, restored by Benvenuto Cellini. Cupid and Psyche, a little greek group.

Cabinet of modern coins and medals.

In this room, besides the coins and medals, are some busts, bas-reliefs, and pictures.

Cabinet of Cupid.

So called from a small greek statue of Cupid set up on a table.

In this room, besides a few busts and an alabaster vase, are twenty-eight pictures; among which is an excellent one by Giacomo da Empoli, of S. Ivo sitting, reading petitions presented to him by widows and orphans.

Cabinet

Cabinet of Miniatures.

Here is a collection of 605 portraits in miniature, in seventy-two frames, sixty of which formed the portable cabinet of Cardinal Leopold di Medicis, the original collector: the other twelve were added in 1781. Few of these are now known, except Como I. Francis I. Como III. Henry IV. of France, Mary of Medicis, Vittoria della Rovere, Cardinal Richelieu, Erasmus, Aretin, and some others of less note.

In the middle of the room is a spiral column of oriental alabaster; on the top an antique statue of a child in a toga, supposed to be Britannicus or Nero. The cieling is painted with physical and mechanical instruments. In niches are twenty-one small statues, and twenty-three busts; besides several statues on the floor.

The most famous of all the cabinets is the *Tribune*, which is an octagon, terminating in a cupola, by which alone it is lighted; the floor is paved with the finest marbles in elegant compartments.

Statues.

The famous Venus of Medicis.
The *Lottatori* or wrestlers.

Florence. Gallery.

The *Arrotino*, employed in whetting a knife, and seeming to be in the attitude of listening.

The dancing Faun.

The little Apollo.

There are twenty-six pictures in the room, all choice ones. S. John Baptist, and three other pieces, by Raffaelle. The naked Venus, by Titiano. And some of the best performances of Michelangelo, Andrea del Sarto, Bartolommeo, Annibale Carracci, &c.

Cabinet of works in Terra cotta.

— porcelaine, &c.

Cabinet of Drawings.

Upwards of 220 large volumes of Drawings, Prints and loose drawings in the ti— eighty drawings hung up. Busts, &c.

Cabinet of Flemish Pictures.

In the first room, small busts of Vitellius and Trajan. A statue of Venus anadyomene. And 145 pictures, chiefly of the Flemish and Dutch School; among which many charming ones, by Mieris, Gerard Dow, Netscher, Vanderwerff, &c.

The second room, which is much larger

than any of the former, are two fine tables of florentine mosaic. The pictures in this room amount to 209, and are of all the schools, but particularly the Flemish.

Cabinet of precious stones, &c.

Four columns of verd-antique, and four of oriental alabaster. Six cabinets, with near 400 vases, cups, &c. of crystal, agate, jasper, &c. Eight small statues. Several busts in precious stones. Intaglios and cameos, ranged on tables in cases.

Cabinet of ancient Medals.

The medals are in twelve cabinets; the whole number is 14,730, of which 1112 are gold, and 3751 silver. There are also thirty-four pictures in this room.

Cabinet of the portraits of Painters.

This collection admits no portraits but such as are done by the artist himself. They are 329 in number, or thereabouts, and fill two rooms; in the first is an antique statue of Cupid—in the second, the famous urn of the villa Medici; the statue of cardinal Leopold, who made the collection, &c.

Florence Gallery.

... *of Inscriptions, and Busts in marble.*

... the greek and roman Inscriptions,
... are many urns, mile-stones, bas re-
..., &c.
Busts of Seneca, Demosthenes, Plato, Ho-
..., &c. Round the room are several an-
... on which busts are placed; on one
... m the famous colossal head of Alexan-
... another, the unfinished Brutus, by
... lo. Other busts are placed on
... ms. In the middle of the room is
... holding the centaur; and an an-
... Two other Torsos are by the
... the window.

Cabinet of the Hermaphrodite.

... The Hermaphrodite, from whence
... takes its name. Adonis, by Mi-
... Apollo. Venus cælestis and
... these two were in the tribune. B...
... forty-eight pictures. In the middle,
... table of florentine work, &c.

Cabinet of Niobe.

... some salon, fitted up by the present
... Duke, for Niobe and her fourteen
... es by different hands, but all

by

by greek artists. There are six pictures in this room.

Cabinet of ancient Pictures.

These are of the florentine school only—Cimabue, Gotto, Gaddi, Giovanni Angelica, &c. Here are also some statues and busts by Donatello, and other old Florentine sculptors.

Cabinet of Modern Bronzes.

Cabinet of Antique Bronzes.

Arranged in fourteen cases.

Tuscan Museum.

Urns, &c. in terra cotta—and some in alabaster.

Director's room.

Head of Oliver Cromwell, in plaster.
Head of a Faun, by Michelangelo.
The object-glass of Galileo's telescope, &c.

Corridore leading to the Palace.

Portraits of the Medicis family, on board[*].

---

[*] A catalogue of the whole gallery in three small volumes was printed in 1783, entitled—*Description de la Galerie Royale de Florence; par M. Franc. Zacchiroli Ferrarois.*

In the *Torrigiano* palace, adjoining to the Grand Duke's, or Palazzo Pitti, is the *Gabi-netto di Fisica*, or Museum of Natural History and Philosophy. It is necessary to have an order from the Grand Duke to see this collection, which consists of a series of most curious anatomical preparations in wax; quadrupeds, birds, fishes, shells, petrifactions, minerals, stones, materia medica, woods, &c.. a long gallery full of astronomical and physical machines; a room with a large electrical apparatus, and another in which are preserved the ancient machines of the Academy del Cimento.

Dr. Targioni also has a good cabinet of natural history, particularly of Tuscany*.

The Maghabecchi and Marucelli Libraries are each of them open to the public, on three

* ... a man of considerable learning, and has published several valuable works. There are many ... at Florence, as Abbate Felice Fon-..., S. Michelangelo Targioni, Sav. Ferd. Ma-... Antonio Durazzini, Ranieri Maffei, Abbate ... S. Fabrini, S. Nardini the famous ... Suora Maddalena Morelli, the celebrated ... commonly called the *Corilla*. Dr. ... D. Perelli, Di Guadagni, S. Bandini, ...

Q 3　　　　　different

Florence. Palaces. Theatres.

different days of the week. And besides the Medicæo-Laurenziana, several of the [...] are public Libraries.

The principal Palaces of the nobility, [...] Corsini, Capponi, [...] Strozzi, &c. The two first have considerable collections of pictures. Palazzo R[...] was built [...] by Cosmo the first, [...] of the house of Medicis; besides the [...] tures, there is a cabinet of antiques, [...], intaglios, medals, &c., and a [...] [...] manuscripts.

The house in which Michelangelo resided, is an object of curiosity to [...] have a pleasure in seeing the remains of extraordinary persons. There are [...] [...] seeing the principal labours of [...] [...] supposed to be by his own [...].

There are several [...] in [...] [...] during the Carnival, which [...] [...] after Christmas day, and [...] [...] [...] at other times also on [...] [...] except Lent and Advent. The principal is the Pergola, finished [...] and the new Opera house, first open[ed] [...]. This is very elegant, [...] stage is not so spacious as in the Per[gola]

Florence. Manufacture.

... ws of boxes, 106 in all, the pit
... ly hold 400. There is a little
... *Santa Maria ...a*, for burlettas;
... er, which is larger, wherein come-
... performed.

... city appears in its greatest brilliancy
... horse-races, which are at the end of
... The horses run, as usual in Italy,
... ..., from the west gate, at a place
... *P...*, to *Porta la Croce*, which is two
... the prize is a piece of velvet, of sixty
...

... manufactures of Florence are chiefly
... of satins, which are excellent. The
... manufactory, to which it owes the
... ... of its opulence and splendour,
... ...ely supplies the common people.
... velvet is fallen to nothing. At Doc-
... ..ee leagues from the city, is a manu-
... of Porcelaine. The Florentines have
... long famous for their Mosaic work,
... very different from the Roman,
... more expensive and less beautiful, it ...
... of the finer marbles, agates, jasper,
... ...ed into all sorts of stones, fawn than, and
... form of birds, flowers &c. ...
... the neighbourhood is excellent, and
they

they have a considerable trade for it, both in Italy and other countries.

In the environs, there is *Poggio*, or *Villa [Imperiale]*, only a mile and half out of town. This is the Grand Duke's favourite country residence; and he has laid out a considerable sum, in fitting up and furnishing it.

Poggio a Cajano is another seat, farther off. This contains a collection of beautiful cabinet pictures, by Italian and Flemish masters, and allegorical paintings of the history of the house of Medicis, by Andrea del Sarto, Franciabigio, Jacopo da Pontormo, and Alesandro Allori.

Six miles from Florence is another country house of the Grand Duke's, called *P[ratolino]*, where there are gardens and waterworks, and a statue of the Apennine [fifty] feet high. In the upper story of the house is a little Theatre, where, during the reign of the Medici, operas were constantly acted during the summer season.

The Grand Dutchy of Tuscany is [ ] miles in length from north to south, and eighty in breadth from east to west. Its population is estimated at a million; and there is supposed to have been an addition of 2,000 since the succession of Francis. It produ[ces] products are grain, silk, flax, oil, wine, and *agrumi*. It abounds in minerals, but the mines are not much worked, except in the island of Elba, remarkable for its fine iron ore. The salt-works are in good order, and they make some sulphur. It produces alabaster and chalcedony: lapis lazuli and borax at Massa, amethysts at Piombino; jasper at Barga, black slate, iron ore, marble, and cornelians, at Stazzena and Seravezza, mercury near Sevighani; silver, alum, honey, &c. The natural productions of Tuscany are largely treated of by the learned Dr. Giovanni Targioni Tozzetti, in his *Viaggi in la Toscana* *.

* The common Florence guide is entitled — *Antiquario, o sia Guida per osservar le cose notabili della Citta di Firenze*. There are many books which treat of the architecture, antiquities, and curiosities of Florence. The magnificent work, called *Musæum Florentinum*, is well known.

SECTION XI.

Excursion to Lucca, Pisa, Leghorn, &c. a journey to Venice.

IF you did not go by sea from Genoa to Leghorn, you must now make an excursion from Florence to that place, by Prato and Pistoia to Lucca, and from thence to Pisa. The church of S. Antonio at Pistoia will stop such as are curious in paintings of the old masters; there are also frescos by Puccio Capanna, in the churches of S. Francis and S. Dominic.

LUCCA is interesting, as being the capital of a little republic, which for its extent is the richest and best-peopled state of Italy. The territory is forty miles in length, and fifteen in breadth, containing about 450 square miles. The population is about 120,000, of which 20,000 in the capital. An air of cheerfulness and plenty appears among the people; and their scanty soil is improved to the utmost. The mountains are covered with vines, olives, chesnuts, and mul-

mulberries, their olives and oil are in great
esteem. Towards the sea much cattle is fed
in the meadows and marshes. No beggars or
idle people are to be seen in this republic; nor
has luxury yet corrupted the manners. The
coat of ceremony is black, and the Gonfaloniere is the only person who wears lace.
There are no titles, and nobody wears a sword.
The militia is 20,000; but 6000 only are in
constant pay.

The capital city has neither good streets,
nor handsome buildings. The *Pallazzo Publico*, or Town-hall, is partly by Ammanati,
and partly by Filippo Giuvara. There is
nothing else to be seen except some old pictures in the churches.

Round the ramparts is a pleasant walk of
about three miles in extent; and here the
company assemble after dinner, or in the
evening. The climate is temperate, and the
country round delightful, ornamented with
plenty of charming country houses.

The road from Lucca to Pisa is narrow and

*A full account of these may be had from a
book entitled—,*

Q 6

indifferent, though a flat country of corn fields, surrounded with poplars and vines.

Pisa, divided like Florence by the Arno, over which it has three bridges, is situated in a fine open country. A magnificent broad quay on each side the river, the cathedral, baptistery, leaning tower, convents, churches, &c. give it an air of grandeur, in defiance of poverty and desolation.

Though it is a large city, it has only about 15,000 inhabitants, and no commerce or manufactories. It is interesting however to a stranger, on account of the many learned men, and the good society which he will find here. The markets are well supplied with provisions and fruit at reasonable rates, and house-rent is extremely cheap. It is to be preferred as a winter residence to most cities in Italy, on account of the mildness of the air; but it is almost deserted in summer, by reason of the constant stagnation of vapours.

There are some remarkable buildings in Pisa: as the *Duomo*, the architect of which was Buschetto, a Greek, who began it, according to some accounts, in 1016, according to others in 1063. It has many fine columns of porphyry, granite, jasper, verd-antique, &c;

&c., taken from ancient buildings. The bronze gates are extremely curious, and were made by Bonanno*, those by Giovanni Bologna shut the two smaller entrances at the west end.

The *Baptistry* is a rotunda built after the designs of Diotisalvi, in the middle of the twelfth century. Within, it has eight columns of Sardinian granite; with another row over them supporting a cupola: in the middle stands a large octagon marble font.

The *Campanile*, or leaning tower, was finished in 1174. It is about one hundred and fifty feet high, and near fifteen feet out of the perpendicular †.

The *Campo Santo*, or burial place, is a court, surrounded by a portico of sixty arches, of a very light gothic, begun in 1278 from designs of Giovanni Pisano. The walls of the cloister are painted in fresco with sacred histories, by the first restorers of painting. the

---

* The history says that the old gates were destroyed by fire in 1595, and in 1601 were recast by Giovanni Bologna.

† Mr Dutens says one hundred and ninety feet high, and thirteen feet out of the perpendicular.

most

most important of them now remaining, are about thirty-three pieces of the history of the old testament, from the creation to Solomon, they fill the whole side opposite the entrance, and except the four first, were painted by Benozzo Gozzoli, who finished them in 1476. The works of the older masters, especially Orgagna's, seem to have been much hurt by repainting.

There are many good pictures, as usual in the churches, and in some of the palaces.

The *Sapienza*, or University, has an Observatory (*Torre della Specola*) furnished with good English instruments; a Botanic Garden, once very famous, but now much neglected; and a small Museum, which is modern, and consists of birds, fishes, shells, corals, and fossils, among others those of Gualtieri.

The hot baths are four miles out of town; they are handsome, commodious, and the price of lodgings and living is regulated at a moderate rate by government. They are esteemed beneficial in gouty cases, and diseases of the liver*.

LEGHORN

LEGHORN *(Livorno)* is only fourteen miles from Pisa. It is a free port, fortified on the land side with good bastions, and wide ditches filled with water: the garrison is 2000 men. The town is about two miles in circuit the general form is square: part of it has the convenience of canals, one of which is five miles in length, and joining the Arno, merchandize and passengers are thus conveyed to Pisa. The streets are straight; the chief street very broad; the squares spacious and handsome, but not regular. the great church magnificent. Cosmo and his two sons fortified the city, drained the marshes, established the freedom of the port, and formed two most commodious harbours, which however have not depth of water sufficient for men of war. There is nothing to be seen besides these, with the mole, lazaretto, coral manufactory, and statue of Ferdinand I. with the four slaves chained to the pedestal; the first by Giovanni dell' Opera, the slaves by Pietro Tacca Carrarese.

The inhabitants are about 45,000, of which about 15,000 are Jews, who have engrossed

cal cavaliere Pandolfo Titi.—At the end of his account of Leghorn

the

the coral manufactory, have a considerable trade, and possess the chief riches of the place.

The road from Florence to Bologna is very disagreeable; for as it crosses the Apennine in its greatest breadth, there is much ascending and descending: the country is dry and chearless, and there is nothing to be seen in the whole route, but the perpetual flames issuing from the ground at *Pietra Mala*, near Covigliaio. There is a fine view from the inn *alle Maschere*. It is a continued ascent from Caffagiolo to Covigliaio; and a continued descent, the two succeedings posts, till you come into the vale of Lombardy.

Bologna to Venice.

In going from Bologna to Venice, you pass by Cento to Ferrara and Padua. The country is flat, well cultivated, and enclosed: it bears vines, corn, mays, abundance of hemp, some mulberries, and has plenty of trees in rows. *Cento* is well known as the birth-place of Guercino some of his best works are in the churches here, and in the house of Sign. Chiarelli Pannini. A small pamphlet may be had on the spot, giving an ample account of them.

Ferrara.

FERRARA is a large city has been magnificent; but is now desolate. The tomb of Ariosto is at the Benedictines. The dutchy was formerly governed by its own Dukes, and the Ferrarese was for several generations one of the happiest and most flourishing spots in Italy. In 1597 it was annexed to the Ecclesiastical state, and has ever since been gradually falling into poverty and decay. There is now hardly any part of Italy more thinly inhabited, or less productive in proportion to the depth and richness of its soil. Swords are very commonly worn at Ferrara, and they furnish their neighbours with fencing masters. This city was famous formerly for a manufactory of sword blades.

You may also go from Bologna to Ferrara by water, and a *Procaccio* makes this voyage twice a week. If you are so disposed, you may hire a covered barge at Ferrara, and thus continue your route by water to Venice; passing by Chiozza and Palestrina, and entering the Lagunes by the haven of Malamocco. But unless you propose to return to Padua; or to make an excursion to it from Venice; you must go by land, passing through Rovigo.

In this case, at six miles from Ferrara you pass

pass the Po, and at six miles from Rovigo the *Canal Bianco*, in barques. The road is flat, narrow, and in winter, or after rain, very bad: it passes through cultivated ground, meadows, and marshes. Abundance of hemp is grown here. Three miles on the other side of Rovigo you cross the Adige: the road narrow and but indifferent: the country well cultivated.

PADUA is far from populous, considering its extent; not amounting at most to more than 38,000. The principal objects of curiosity at Padua are the churches of S. Antonio and S. Giustina. Il Salone. The buildings of the University by Palladio. The Botanic and Oeconomical Gardens. The Museum. And in the neighbourhood, the baths of Abano, Petrarch's villa and monument at Arqua. &c. The three gates also of Portello, Savonarola, and S. Giovanni; the church of S. Gaetano, by Scamozzi; Palazzo del Pecorá, and Palazzo del Capitano, merit observation. The Theatre is handsome and commodious. And in some of the other Churches, as the Cathedral, Santa Croce, S. Eremitani, the convent of la Maddalena, the Seminario, &c. are some good pictures, also in some Scuole, the public library, Palazzo del Podestà, &c.

The church of *S. Antonio* is a large gothic building, begun in 1255 by Nicola Pisano, and finished in 1307: it has six domes or cupolas, of which the two largest compose the nave: it is extremely rich, and so much ornamented, as to appear crouded with painting and sculpture. There are four immense organs in it; and even on common days forty performers are employed in the service. The best piece of painting is the martyrdom of S. Agatha, by Tiepolo. In the chapel of S. Antony, a crucifix in bronze, by Donatello. S. Antony raising a youth, and other bas-reliefs, by Campagna. In the chapel of S. Felix, the crucifixion, &c. by Giotto. Before the church is an equestrian statue of general Gattamelata, by Donatello. The Scuola near this church is all painted in fresco, with the life and miracles of S. Antonio; by Tiziano and others.

The church of *S. Giustina* was built by Andrea Riccio, a Paduan architect, after designs of Palladio. It is handsome, luminous, and esteemed by many artists one of the finest works in Italy. At the high altar is a good painting of the martyrdom of the

patron

patron saint, by Paolo Veronese. In the convent, which belongs to the Benedictines, and is very spacious, there is a fine library, in which are many of the scarce first-printed books; and several good pictures.

The hall of audience, or town-house, called *il Salone*, was begun in 1172 by Pietro Cozzo, but not finished till 1306. It is about 300 feet long, and near 100 wide*.

The *University* with the public schools, museum, &c. is one of the first objects of curiosity. The chemical laboratory, with a collection of minerals, has been lately established by the present professor of chemistry, Count Marco Carburi. The Anatomical theatre is curiously fitted up, to hold a mul-

---

* According to Ray it is 256 feet long, and 86 wide. Grosley makes the length to be 260, and the breadth 90, the latter being french measures, and the former english, do not differ very widely. De La Lande says it is 300 feet long, 100 wide, and 100 high. Giotto's paintings were restored in 1762 by Zannoni. Westminster Hall, which, like this, is said to be the largest room, unsupported by pillars, in Europe, is 270 feet in length, and 74 in breadth. It was built by William Rufus, but rebuilt, as it now is, by Richard II. in 1397.

titude of spectators in a little compass; but it is small and dark. Dr. Caldani, the present professor, has a fine collection of anatomical preparations in wax. Signor Vandelli, professor of surgery, has a collection of petrifactions from the Vicentine and Veronese moutains. The *Museum* of natural curiosities was collected by Antonio Vallisnieri. The *Botanic garden* is a very good one, and is arranged according to the system of Tournefort. Marsigli is the professor: he formerly spent three years in England, and is well acquainted with our literature. The *Oeconomical* garden, instituted for experiments in husbandry, is under the care of S. Giovanni Arduini: this excellent institution is in very good condition, under so active a naturalist. Padua has always had men of learning and eminence. It was the birth-place of Livy; Petrarch was a canon of the cathedral; Galileo lived here; and it lately possessed Tartini. Besides those already mentioned, Padua now possesses Padre Columbo, professor of mathematics; Abbate Sibilliati, professor of belles lettres; Marchese Orologio, who has a fine collection of the productions of the neighbouring volcanic hills; Guadagni, the famous singer; Padre Ant. Franc. Valleti,

leti, one of the best composers for the church in Italy; and several eminent musicians.

The *Theatre* is approached by two magnificent staircases. It has five rows of boxes, twenty-nine in each, with sliding shutters the pit has one hundred and fifty seats, which are turned up and padlocked. Between the grand staircase and the theatre there is a room for play, called *Camera di Ridotto*. There is a serious opera in this theatre during the fair of S. Antony in the month of June: at that time Padua is very gay, and full of company, from Venice and the neighbouring towns.

There is a cloth manufactory in the city for home consumption: but the excessive number of beggars with which the place swarms, is a strong indication, that trade and manufactures are by no means in a flourishing condition.

In the environs of Padua, the Euganean mountains will attract the notice of the naturalist: they are extinct volcanos, and full of all the productions of subterraneous fires. A very interesting excursion also may be made to the hot baths of Abano, four or five miles from Padua; and to Petrarch's villa and monument at Arqua.

About

About eight miles from Padua, at Sala, is a fine villa belonging to Signor Filippo Farsetti. He has built a palace, decorated with granite columns and the finest marbles: he has also a magnificent botanic garden, rich in the scarcest plants.

From Padua you may go to Venice, either by the post to Fusina; and from thence in a gondola, which will cost twelve livres: or else leave your carriage at Padua, and hire a *burchiello*, or covered boat; for which you will pay three sequins; and for drink money to the men, putting your baggage on board, &c, about twelve pauls more. In eight hours you will fall down the Brenta, cross the Lagunes, and land in the great canal of Venice.

SECTION

SECTION XII.

Description of Venice.

MOST travellers endeavour to be at Venice on the day of the Ascension, in order to be present at the ceremony of the espousal of the sea by the Doge; or if not, during the Carnival. Venice, however, is at all times one of the finest cities in the world; and certainly the most singular, with respect to its situation: being built on piles, in the midst of shallows, called the *Lagunes*. The great canal, which divides the city into two almost equal parts, is in form of an S, and generally about an hundred paces over. The famous bridge of the Rialto is nearly in the middle: it is of one arch eighty-nine feet wide; and a double row of shops is built upon it. They reckon four hundred canals, forming communications all over the city, and bridges many more in number. The main city is surrounded with a multitude of islands, many of them occupied by convents. The *Giudecca*, pronounced *Zuecca*, has abundance of pleasure houses and gardens, with eight or nine convents. S. Giorgio maggiore. Murano, Torcello, Mazorbo, and Burano, situated to the north-east, are covered with habitations. S. Andrea del Lido. S. Elena. S. Michele. S. Nicolo del Lido. Lazaretto vecchio and nuovo, &c.

The principal curiosities of Venice are the Piazza di S. Marco, and the buildings that surround it, the Mercerie, the bridge of the Rialto, the Arsenal; the churches of S. Giorgio, le Zitelle, S. Maria della carità, il Redentore, all by Palladio; and many Palaces by him, Sansovino, Scamozzi, &c. A view of the whole may be taken from the quadrangular tower of S. Mark, which is 300 feet in height.

The buildings, the pictures, the public entertainments, the riches, the government of Venice, are all interesting objects to a stranger. The singular approach to this fine city

---

* De La Lande says only 100,000. By a survey in 1581 the number was 134,871. Sansovino reckons 180,000: some make them 300,000, but they speak at random. The length, according to De La Lande, is 2000 toises, and the greatest breadth 1500.

R   must

must be always striking, both from its novelty and beauty: perhaps after residing in it some time, the monotony of a watery surface, with the want of meadows, hills, and woods, may tire, or even disgust; unless pleasure is kept alive by constant amusement, or the charms of society; both which the Venetians seem to relish as well as any nation upon earth.

A considerable time is required to see all that is curious in Venice: almost all the Churches and Schools, and many of the Palaces, have something to attract notice. Every body knows the rank which the Venetian schools of Architecture and Painting hold with persons of taste.

The churches most remarkable for picture or good architecture, are—

S. Angelo Raffaelle.

S. Bartolommeo.

La Caritá, by Palladio.

I Carmini.

S. Caterina.

S. Francesca della Vigna, by Sansovino.

Li Frari.

S. Geminiano. An elegant piece of architecture by Sansovino, who is buried here

S. Geremia. A handsome church.

I Gesu

I Gesuiti.

S. Giacomo dell' Orio.

S. Giacomo della Vigna.

S Giorgio maggiore, belonging to a rich convent of Benedictines, on an island facing the Piazza di S. Marco, wholly occupied by their pleasant walks and gardens. The church is by Palladio: and there are two beautiful cloisters, one by him, and the other by Sansovino *.

S. Giovanni e Paolo, belonging to the Dominicans; rich in pictures.

S. Lucia, by Palladio.

Madonna dell' Orto.

S. Marco, the ducal church. The architecture of a mixed kind, mostly gothic, with

* In the church, a fine nativity, by Old Bassan.

The raining of manna, and the last supper; both by Tintoret, &c.

In the refectory the famous marriage of Cana; by Paolo Veronese.

In the Abbot's apartments, a good collection of cabinet pictures, by Zuccarelli, Canaletti, &c.

In their well-chosen library, a manuscript of Dante, with figures in water-colours—of Petrarch, of 1432—of Cicero—in both which are said to be things never printed

many grecian columns of different kinds of marble; the whole crowned with five domes. The front has five brazen gates, with historical bas-reliefs on them*.

S. Maria maggiore.

Gli Mendicanti.

Ognissanti.

Il Redentore · from designs of Palladio.

S. Salute, or S. Maria della Salute, by Michele.

S. Sebastiano †

S. Simeon grande.

---

* No paintings, but many mosaics, and a variety of curious marbles brought from Constantinople. The principal curiosity—the four antique brazen horses, placed aloft on the outside, facing the great square: they are said to be the workmanship of Lysippus, and to have been presented by Tiridates to Nero: they were removed to Constantinople by Constantine, and remained there till the taking of that city by the French and Venetians, in the beginning of the thirteenth century.

† Paolo Veronese painted the cieling, the shutter of the organ, the high altar, &c. and in the refectory Christ at the Pharisee's house. He painted the sacristy when he was twenty-five years of age, and dying in 1588 was buried in this church, where there is his bust.

S. Sofia.

I Tolentini: from designs of Sansovino's; esteemed a fine building; and the portico good.

S. Trovaso, or S. S. Gervaso e Protaso.

S. Zaccaria.

Le Zitelle, by Palladio.

The *Scuole*, belonging to the Confraternities, and answering to the halls of our Companies in London, are decorated with some of the finest paintings in Venice.

Scuola della Carità is full of pictures: one of the presentation in the temple, by Tiziano, is much esteemed.

Scuola de' Mercanti is almost all painted by Domenico Tintoretto and Aliense. In the Albergo is the presentation of Christ, by Palma; the birth of the Virgin, by Benedetto Veronese, brother of Paolo: the virgin with S. Christopher, and the birth of the virgin; both by Jacopo Tintoretto.

Scuola grande della Misericordia. The Albergo by Tintoretto.

Scuola di S. Orsola. Painted by Vittore Carpaccio, with the history of this British Saint, in nine pieces.

Scuola di S. Rocco. The whole painted by Tintoretto. The most capital piece is a large crucifixion, in the Albergo: in the cieling of this room is the trial piece, which gained Tintoretto this work from his competitors. On S. Rocco's day, the Signory goes in procession to that Saint's church: and the painters of the present Venetian school exhibit their performances in the Scuola.

There are other Schools which deserve attention—as, Scuola di S. Fantino, di S. Marco, &c.

The *Palace of S. Mark*, or the Ducal Palace, is very spacious. Besides the apartments of the Doge, there are also halls and chambers for the Senate, and all the different Councils and Tribunals. The principal entrance is by the giant's staircase, so called from the colossal statues of Mars and Neptune placed at the top, and intended to represent the naval and military power of the state; they are of marble, and the work of Sansovino. Under the portico, to which you ascend by this staircase, are the lion's mouths placed to receive letters, informations of treasonable practices, and accusations of magistrates for abuses in office. From the palace is a covered bridge of communication with the state prison, on the other side of the canal. Prisoners pass to and from the courts over

th

this bridge, and hence it is named *ponte del sospiri*. Within the palace is a little Arsenal which communicates with the hall of the great council: here it is said a great number of musquets are kept ready charged, that the nobles may arm themselves, in case of a sudden emergency. This palace is adorned with a profusion of noble pictures by Paolo Veronese, Tintoretto, and the other celebrated masters of the Venetian School*.

The lower gallery, or portico, under the palace, is called the *Broglio*. In this the noble Venetians walk and converse: it is only here and at council, that they have opportunities of meeting; for they seldom visit openly,

---

* A full account of this superb collection is to be seen in Cochin, &c. A commodious portable catalogue is to be had at Venice, entitled, *Descrizione di tutte le publiche Pitture della Città di Venezia di Marco Boschini. Venezia* 1733. There is also a copious and accurate history of the Venetian Painters, and their public works at Venice, by Zanetti, in his book *della Pittura Veneziana.* 1771, octavo.—The pictures suffer from the damp sea air, which is particularly to be lamented, since brilliancy of colouring is the first merit of the Venetian school.

or in a family way, at each other's houses; and secret meetings would give umbrage to the state inquisitors. they choose therefore to transact their business on this public walk. People of inferior rank seldom stay on the Broglio for any length of time, when the nobility are there.

The treasury of S. Mark is very rich in jewels and relics: to have leave to see it, you must apply to one of the Procurators of S. Mark.

The old *Procuratie* is built of black marble; and the new, of the *pietra dura* from Istria. Sansovino and Scamozzi are the architects of the latter. The Library of S. Mark, and the Prisons, are by Sansovino.

The Palaces of the nobility at Venice are in an elegant style of architecture. the fronts are enriched with columns to each story; the orders consequently are small, but then each story is supported in a distinct and natural manner. Palazzo Tiepolo and Balbi are by Palladio; palazzo Cornaro and Delfino, are by Sansovino. Pesaro and Rezzonico, by Baltasar Longhena. Palazzo Grimani and Cornaro à S. Paolo are by San Michele. The palaces in general are furnished with velvet and damask, fringed or laced with gold; the
floor

floors are of plaster, coloured in imitation of marble: the doors, architraves, surbases, &c. are elegantly painted with pale tints for the ground, ornamented with various devices, festoons, fruits, &c. They also paint in fresco on the walls with much facility and taste. There are some good pictures in the palaces, but no such collections as we see at Rome and Genoa.

In Palazzo Barbarigo is a room of pictures by Bonifaccio: another of pieces by various masters, of which there is an exact catalogue in the room; a third of pictures by Tiziano, who lived four years in the house: and from him this palace is called *Scuola di Tziano**.

In

---

* The subjects are—

A satyr and nymph.

Prometheus chained to the rock.

Tobit and the Angel.

Christ with the globe.

Venus and Adonis.

The virgin, Christ, and Mary Magdalene.

Christ bearing his cross.

Portrait of Agostino Barbarigo, dated 1486.

There is also a room of portraits, by Tiziano, of persons famous in his time.

In *Palazzo Farsetti* is a great collection of casts from the best antique statues at Rome, Florence, &c. In the gallery are four large pictures by Luca Giordano.—In the apartments. Herodias carrying S. John's head; and portraits of a father, mother, and child, by Tiziano. The virgin, Christ, and Joseph, by Andrea del Sarto.—The satyr with peasants that blow hot and cold, by Jordaens. S. Francis, by Prete Genovese.—An old woman, by Ferabosco. A fine portrait, and the death of Lucretia, by Rembrandt.— A fair, by Giacomo Bassano.

Palazzo Pisani. Christ driving the money changers out of the temple; by Paolo Veronese. Old Palma's portrait; by himself. Pictures over the door of Fame, Force, Peace, &c. by Cav. Liberi. The crucifixion by Tintoretto. King Charles I. and his Queen, full lengths, by Vandyck. The virgin, Christ, and two saints; by Lucas van Leyden—and many indifferent pictures.

In *Palazzo Pisani Moreta* is the famous picture of Alexander, with the family o

The pictures are in bad condition, and much spoiled, they have not however been meddled with or retouched.

Darius

Darius; by Paolo Veronese: and some others mentioned by Cochin.

Palazzo Labbia has some pictures by Luca Giordano and others. *Palazzo Sagredo* has a considerable cabinet, of which the particulars may be found in Cochin: and there are some, but few of distinguished merit, in *Palazzo Morosini*.

One of the singularities of this singular city is its *Conservatorios*, musical schools or academies, for instructing young women in music. of these there are four, the *Ospedale della Pietà*, the *Mendicanti*, the *Incurabili*, and the *Ospidaletto à S. Giovanni e Paolo*. At each of these, Oratorios, and other pieces of sacred music, are performed, every saturday and sunday evening, and on other festivals. All the parts, both vocal and instrumental, are supported by the young women, in a superior style.

The *Piazza di S. Marco* is the only open area in Venice large enough for a considerable number of people to assemble in, and walk about at their ease. At the opening next the lagunes stand two lofty granite pillars, between which criminals condemned to suffer death publicly, are executed. A few paces from the church of S. Mark are three tall poles, on which flags are displayed, on days of public rejoicing: these are in memory of the three kingdoms of Cyprus, Candia, and Negropont, which once belonged to the Republic; and the three crowns are still kept in the Ducal Palace. At the foot of the tower of S. Mark is a small neat building, called the *Loggietta*, where the Procurators of S. Mark constantly attend to do business.

This being the only place of public resort, there is a great variety of objects assembled in it. In the evening it is crouded with all sorts of people, and in fine weather numbers pass the greatest part of the night there. When the square is illuminated, and the shops in the adjacent streets are lighted up, the whole has a brilliant effect; and as it is the custom for the ladies as well as the gentlemen to frequent the caffinos and coffeehouses, S. Mark's place answers all the purposes of Ranelagh and Vauxhall to the inhabitants.

The nobles and wealthy people sometimes prefer little apartments of their own, neatly fitted up, but without magnificence, where they

they may receive a few friends in a more easy manner than they could do at their palaces. These are their *Caſſinos*; where, inſtead of going home to a formal ſupper, and returning to this place of general reſort, they order refreſhments, and amuſe themſelves with cards. That theſe Caſſinos may be occaſionally uſed for the purpoſes of intrigue, is not improbable; but that this is the general purpoſe for which they are frequented, is certainly falſe.

There are no leſs than ſeven *Theatres* at Venice, one for the ſerious opera, two for comic operas, and four play-houſes; but they are all open only during the Carnival, which begins on S. Stephen, and continues till Lent; and then they are all full every night. In autumn the houſes are open for the comic opera and plays: and at the Aſcenſion there is a ſerious opera. A trifle is paid at the door for admittance; this entitles a perſon to go into the pit, where he may look about, and determine what part of the houſe he will ſit in. There are rows of chairs towards the front, the ſeats of which fold back, and are locked, they who chooſe to take them, pay a little more to the doorkeeper for unlocking the

the feat*. Very decent people occupy these chairs; but the back part of the pit is filled with servants and gondoliers. The nobility and better sort of citizens hire boxes by the year; and there is always a sufficient number for strangers. The price varies according to the season and the run of the piece.

It is the custom to go masked during the carnival, in autumn, and at the Ascension: with a mask, and a silk cloak, a man is then sufficiently dressed for any assembly in Venice. Masks in character are used only three or four weeks before Lent.

The ARSENAL is on an island, about three miles in compass. Here are docks for the gallies and men of war, and repositories for all sorts of military and naval stores. Here also they build their men of war under cover, cast cannon: make cables, sails, anchors, &c. The arms are arranged in the armories, as in other arsenals.

---

* In the playhouses ten soldi at going in, and five more for a seat.

At the comic opera forty or fifty soldi, and twenty more for a seat.

At the serious opera eighty soldi at entrance, and as much more for a seat.

The *Bucentoro*, or state galley of the republic is laid up here. It never goes out, but when it carries the Doge to the espousals of the Adriatic. It is loaded with ornaments, gilding, and sculpture; and is a heavy broad-bottomed vessel, that draws little water, and might easily overset in a gale of wind. Of this however there is little danger; for not only the patriarch pours some holy water into the sea, as soon as the vessel is afloat; but the admiral has a discretionary power of postponing the marriage ceremony, when the sea shows any signs of being boisterous.

When the weather however is favourable, the ceremony of the espousals is performed on Ascension day. The solemnity is announced in the morning by the ringing of bells, and the firing of cannon. About noon the Doge, with the Pope's nuncio and the Patriarch on each side of him, and attended by a numerous party of the Senate and Clergy, goes on board; the vessel is rowed a little way into the sea, accompanied by the splendid yachts of the foreign ambassadors, the gondolis of the Venetian nobility, and an incredible number of small vessels of every kind, many of them covered with canopies of silk or rich stuffs, with the gondoliers in sumptuous

tuous liveries. A band of music plays, while the Bucentoro, and its train, slowly move towards the Lido. The Doge drops a ring into the sea, pronouncing these words—*desponsamus te mare in signum veri perpetuique dominii.* He then returns in the same state, inviting those who accompany him in the galley to dinner. The day following, the Fair begins at S. Mark's place, which lasts ten days.

One of the great singularities of Venice is its *Gondolas*, or long narrow boats, which have a room in the middle, six feet by four, covered with black cloth; and with sliding windows. Two persons sit very commodiously at the end, and two others may sit on each side. They are rowed either by one or two gondoliers standing. These gondolas are the only carriages at Venice; and there are stands of them every where, as there are of hackney-coaches at London, and *fiacres* at Paris. The gondoliers are robust, good-humoured, and lively; pique themselves upon the quickness of their repartees, and are esteemed for their fidelity and attachment.

In fine weather, they frequently challenge one another to a contest: they put up a little flag or a bough for a prize, which they
display

display the greatest ardour to obtain. If any person of consequence, or a stranger, show any desire to see the contest, arrangements are made for a more orderly course, and the city is amused with a *Regata*.

But on particular occasions, a grand *Regata* is sometimes exhibited, under the direction, and at the expence of government. On these public occasions, the competitors are chosen from families of the first reputation among the gondoliers. When the day arrives, their relations encourage them, by calling to mind the triumphs of their families; the women present the oar; and religion has its share in the preparations. The course is about four miles, along the great canal, and back again. The prizes are four, marked by flags of different colours. The great canal, upon these occasions, is covered with barges, boats, and gondolas; and on each side are placed bands of music*.

* A regata of this kind was given in honour of the Grand Duke of Russia, and in 1784 there were two, one for the King of Sweden, and a second for the Archduke Ferdinand of Austria and his Consort. The Countess of Rosenberg has given an elegant account of this spectacle more at large.

One

One of the principal *Manufactories* at Venice, is that of glass, on the island of Murano. They blow large mirrors, and make abundance of trinkets *(margaritine)*, and flowers to decorate lustres, and for nosegays to adorn the churches. They export little now but to the Levant.

Printing also still makes one of the chief branches of trade. Few countries make better velvets or silk stockings. The wax brought from Dalmatia, Greece, and all the Levant, employs several manufactories. Jewellery forms a considerable branch of foreign commerce. Drugs are imported from the Levant, and are esteemed excellent: their Theriaca is in great reputation. Their marasquin, or cherry water, and their liqueurs are famous. Though they have nothing within themselves, yet no city is better furnished with the necessaries and luxuries of life from the Paduan and Polesin.

SECTION

SECTION XIII.

Journey to Vicenza, Verona, Mantua, Brescia, and Bergamo.

IF you did not take the route of Venice from Milan, you will now go to Vicenza; in order to which you will either cross the Lagunes to Fusina, and take the post; or hire a Burchiello to return up the Brenta to Padua. From thence to Vicenza is a journey of eighteen italian miles, or about four hours. The road is indifferent, the country flat, and well cultivated; the crops, corn, mayz, and grass. The wine of the Vicentine is good.

VICENZA is charmingly situated between two mountains on a large plain: though but four miles round, it contains between thirty and forty thousand souls. It is the native place of Palladio; and the best works of this celebrated architect make the great ornament of the city.

Teatro Olympico is one of the finest specimens of modern architecture: it was begun early in 1588, the very year that Palladio died.

died. The house in which the architect himself lived was built by him, and is no less modest than elegant. *Palazzo della ragione*, or the town-hall, is by the same great hand in the *sala di consiglio*, over the door, is a picture of the virgin, with the infant Jesus, S. Joseph, two magistrates, Gio. Moro, and Silvan Cappello, on their knees, and other figures, a strange composition, but good picture, by Giacomo Bassano. 1572.

Palazzo Prefettizio—De' Conti Chiericati—Barbarano—Orazio Porto—Conti Tiene—Conti Valmarana—Sig. Girolamo Franceschini; are all certainly by Palladio.

In the environs, Marchese Capra's famous *rotonda*, copied by Lord Burlington at Chiswick, is by Palladio. In the gardens of Conte Valmarana, which are much admired, there is a pretty *loggia*, which passes for Palladio's: and the staircase of *la Madonna del Monte*, with the triumphal arch before it, are said to be by the same architect.

The east front of *Palazzo Pretorio* is by Scamozzi: as is also the Nievi palace, and that of the Conti Trissini on the Corso.

Vicenza, though of no extraordinary extent, has above sixty churches, convents and hospitals. In the church of *la Corona*, is
the

the adoration of the Magi, by Paolo Veronese: S. Antonio giving alms, by Leandro Bassano: and the baptism of Christ, by Giov. Bellino.

In the refectory of *la Madonna del monte*, S. Gregory, with Christ at supper as a pilgrim, and other figures; a large picture, by Paolo Veronese.

S. Bartolommeo. Dead, Christ, the virgin, S. John, and Magdalene; by Buonconsiglio. Adoration of the Magi, &c.; by Marcello Fogolino.

S. Biagio. Flagellation of Christ; by Guercino.

Corpus Domini. The taking down from the cross; by Gio. Battista Zilotti.

S. Croce. The same subject; by Giacomo Bassano.—In the Sacristy; Christ dead in the arms of the Father, &c.; by Paolo Veronese.

S. Michele. S. Augustine in the air, and several persons healed by him of the plague, below; by Tintoretto.

S. Rocco. S. Roch healing the plague; by Giacomo Bassano. Pool of Bethesda; by Antonio Fasolo*.

* See Descrizione delle Architetture, Pitture e Scolture di Vicenza. 1779, 8vo with plates of the buildings.

A natu-

A naturalist will visit the *Grotta de' Cavoli*; the mineral waters of *Recoaro*; the tepid waters of *S. Pancrazio di Barbarano*; the hills of *Bretto*; and the mountains to the north of the city, in which are abundance of shells, petrifactions, &c.

In the volcanic mountains near Vicenza, are nodules of chalcedony, from the size of a pea, to the diameter of an inch, bedded in the lava: they are commonly hollow; and that hollow sometimes has water in it; they are then called *enhydri*.

Dr. Antonio Turra, a physician of Vicenza, is an able naturalist. He has a fine collection of fossils found in the Vicentine calcareous mountains; a good cabinet of insects; and a considerable *hortus siccus*. He is perpetual secretary of the *Academia d' Agricoltura*, and has almost completed a *Flora Italica*.

From Vicenza to Verona the road is good; the country pleasant; the crops — corn, mayz, clover, lucerne, grass, hemp. On the right hand, at some distance, are the Alps, which separate Italy from Germany, or the Vicentine and Veronese hills: on the left, a flat, rich, cultivated country, extending to the Apennines beyond Bologna.

These Vicentine and Veronese hills are calcareous, furnishing fine red, yellow, and variegated marbles; and have been shattered by violent volcanos.

Among the volcanic curiosities in the Veronese, *Bolca* and *Ronca* are most worthy of notice. *Bolca* is a miserable village, which would never be visited, were it not for the famous mountain that produces the petrified fish and plants. The fish are found in a calcareous shivery stone, and are well preserved; their bones, and frequently their scales, being entire: there are also crabs, large oyster shells, bones of exotic animals; leaves of fern, and other foreign plants. There are few spots more romantic than *Ronca*; and the whole bears evident marks of a volcano: it is singular in having a quantity of marine shells mixed with the lava.

There is nothing more remarkable in the Veronese than the apparent barrenness of the country, and the astonishing number of mulberries it produces. They grow rice in the vallies that are unfit for pasturage or corn.

VERONA is pleasantly situated, and the neighbourhood of the mountains constantly refreshes it in summer with a cool evening breeze. The society is good, and they have a taste

taste for literature. The women are well shaped, and have a fresh complexion.

The river Adige divides the city almost equally; and the two sides are connected by four good stone bridges. The best street is, as usual, called the *Corso*; and the largest area is *la Piazza d' Arm*, where the two fairs are held, in spring and autumn. The number of inhabitants is supposed to be forty-nine or fifty thousand.

The principal churches of Verona are—

Il Duomo, the Cathedral; a gothic building, wherein is a picture of the Assumption, by Tiziano. Over the door of the choir, a crucifix in bronze, by Michele di San Michele. In the chapel of S. Nicola, a crucifixion, by Bellino.

S. Anastasia. The Saint with several angels; and below, S. Peter Martyr; by Torelli Veronese. Christ in the garden, by Francesco Bernardi. The flagellation of Christ; by Claudio Ridolfi. There are pictures also in the Sacristy and Refectory.

S. Bernardino. The Pellegrini chapel, by Michele di San Michele.

I Capuccini. A dead Christ, by Alessandro Turchi, surnamed Orbetto.

I Carmelitani Scalzi. The annunciation

by Antonio Baleſtra. The high altar, and others, are adorned with fine marbles.

S. Elena. The Virgin; and below, the croſs, S. Elena, Conſtantine, &c. by Felice Bruſaforzi.

S Eufemia. David with his harp. Moſes with the tables of the law; by Bruſaforzi. S. Paul cured of his blindneſs; by Battiſta del Moro.

S. Giorgio, a church of Auguſtine nuns, moſt beautiful architecture; the body by Sanſovino, and the cupola by San Michele. Two pictures by Paolo Cagliari, ſurnamed Veroneſe from this his native place: one at the high altar, repreſenting the martyrdom of S. George, with many figures large as life. The other of S. Barnabas curing the blind. Chriſt feeding the five thouſand; by Paolo Farinati. The Iſraelites gathering manna, by Bruſaforzi. Over the church door, the baptiſm of Chriſt; by Tintoretto.

S. Giovanni in Fonte. The baptiſm of Chriſt, by Farinati.

Maria della Vittoria. Deſcent from the croſs, by Paolo Veroneſe; in the ſacriſty.

Maria in organis. S. Bernard beaten by devils; Luca Giordano. The guardian angel, by Guercino. In the ſacriſty, S.

Francis, with other Franciscans; by Orbetto.

La Misericordia, an Hospital. Descent from the cross; by Orbetto.

S. Paolo. Virgin and Christ, S. John, and three other saints; by Paolo Veronese

Several of the Palaces are in a good taste by Michele*, and the gate called *porta Stupa*, or *del Pallio*, is by him.

In the *Gerardini* and *Bevilaqua* palaces are a few tolerable pictures: and in the latter some good busts of the Emperors, with a fine antique figure of Endymion.

Palazzo di Consiglio, the Town-hall, is by Sansovino.

The Mausolea of the Scaligers are curious old monuments, in a bad taste.

From the gardens of Conte Giusti there is a good view of the city, and of the neighbouring country.

The great glory of Verona is its ancient *Amphitheatre*, the arena and inside of which are perfect. The outer circumference 1331 feet; the longer axis 464, and the less 367 feet; the greater axis of the arena 2

---

* Canossa, Terzi, Bevilacqua, Pompri, Pelegrini.

the shorter 136 feet. It has 46 rows of seats, and is calculated to hold 23,484 persons conveniently. I was told, that when the Emperor was at Verona there were no less than 40,000 people crouded into it. In this amphitheatre there are plays during summer.

A modern *Theatre* is erected near this, which is used only in the month of november, for the serious Opera, before the carnival begins in the other principal cities of Italy. It has five rows of boxes, 27 in each row. The entrance is through a noble portico, decorated by Marchese Maffei with Etruscan marbles and inscriptions: the bust of this celebrated antiquary is placed upon the portico

The Museum, or collection of antiquities, belonging to the Academy, and the *lapidario* built in 1719, compose a part of this edifice. One of the apartments serves as a rendezvous of good company of both sexes every evening; it is called *camera della Conversazione*, and is furnished at the public expence.

Marchese Canossa has a cabinet of Fossils, very rich in fish from monte Bolca.

Abundance of silk is made and manufactured here and at Vicenza. The other commodities that the Veronese trade in are olives, oil, wine, and some linens and woollens: their olives, and some of their wines, are reckoned very good. There is a variety of fine marbles here, and in the Vicentine a *Judio* consists of about 136 pieces, for which they ask 24 or 25 sequins.

If you have not already seen MANTUA, you have now an opportunity of making an excursion to it. It is surrounded by a morass formed by the overflowing of the Mincio, and can be approached only by long bridges or causeways. It is about four miles in circumference; some of the streets are wide and straight, with a few good houses, but they are generally unequal, and mostly indifferent. The population is estimated at 20,000.

There are eighteen parish churches in Mantua, and fourteen convents. The *Cathedral* is spacious, and has five ailes, Giulio Romano was the architect, and also painted the tribuna with a part of the cieling. In the upper sacristy is a night piece of the temptation of S. Antony, by Paolo Veronese.

S. *Andrè* is an old church, in a simple good taste, with some fifty fine chapels, in one of them on the left hand, is a statue of Andrea Mantegna, over the altar, is a painting by him, of the death of S. John Baptist. In chapel on the right hand are two great frescos, in the style of Giulio Romano. In the transept, are two large pieces of the stoning of S. Stephen, &c. fine, but much injured.

Giulio Romano lies in the church of *S. Barnabas*, where Carlo Cignani has painted the marriage of Cana. Near this church, is the house where Giulio lived: it is distinguished by a statue of Mercury over the entrance.

In the church of the *Theatins*, about the high altar, hang seven large pictures by Guercino: to the right, is an Annunciation, said to be by Annibale Carracci: and in the next chapel is a martyr kneeling before the executioner, by Lodovico, who painted a duplicate of it for the cathedral; it stands between two pictures by Maffari, a disciple of Carracci. Opposite are some good pieces, much blackened.

In the Castle or Ducal Palace are some cielings by Giulio Romano: some pictures by Palma, Annibale Carracci, &c. and one of the twelve Cæsars by Tiziano. In Palazzo di Thè, so called from its being built in form of the letter T, are some fine frescos by Giulio Romano, who gave the plan and elevation of the palace: the most admired pieces

are

are the fall of Phaeton, and Jupiter's victory over the giants.

In going from Verona to Brescia, you will coast the *Lago di Garda* for several miles. It is about thirty-five miles in length, and twelve in breadth though not the largest, it is by far the noblest lake in Italy. The eastern side is romantically magnificent; whilst the western has the softest and most delicious views. The *Riviera di Salò* is on this side. *Salò*, the principal town, is well built, and has about 5000 inhabitants. The whole country for at least twenty miles is one continued garden. Though Salò is but twelve miles out of the direct road, it is seldom visited by travellers.

Monte Baldo, which hangs over this beautiful lake, and was once as famous for timber as for its medicinal and rare plants, is now naked, and exhibits the most dreary prospect imaginable.

BRESCIA is a handsome, large, and populous city, on the river Garza; the number of inhabitants are said to be 100,000: the figure of it is almost square, with the castle at one corner. Between the city and the foot of the Alps is a fine rich plain; with an extensive one on the other side, at the extremity

Brescia.

of which appears Cremona thirty miles distant.

Brescia is remarkable for its iron works; and the fire-arms that are made here are famous through all Italy.

The *Cathedral* has been lately built: it is large, and in a great style; the ornaments within are in a good taste. Some of the other churches, as S. Affra, S. Nazaro, I Carmini, &c. have paintings of the Venetian school.

Palazzo della Giustizia is a mixture of gothic and greek architecture. There are many pictures in it, some of which are said to be good.

Casa Avogadri has some good pieces by Tiziano, Paolo Veronese, &c.

The *Theatre* is splendid; the boxes much ornamented with glasses, painting, front-cloth of velvet or silk fringed; the seats in the pit are roomy; every row of this, and every box, is numbered.

The *Brescian*, though not naturally fertile, has been converted into a garden, by force of industry, by a judicious choice of manures, and by a skilful distribution of water.

From Brescia to Bérgamo you coast the Alps

Alps at the distance of two or three miles. This province is very populous and fertile; and the inhabitants are very industrious.

Bergamo is situated on a mountain, overlooking a plain, covered with trees as far as the eye can reach. As you approach it, the appearance of the suburbs, with the city rising above, and the mountain crowned with the citadel, is fine. It is not near so populous as Brescia, many of the inhabitants quitting the town to seek a livelihood at Milan, Genoa, and other places. Bergamo is the native country of Harlequin; and the people have a sort of humorous repartee, and an arch manner, which, with their peculiar jargon, give them an air different from that of other Italians.

The church of *S. Maria maggiore* is handsome. In the cieling of the sanctuary are four ovals by one of the Bassans.—Christ and his apostles, by Giulio Romano, who painted the Deluge, in the right transept. Moses striking the rock, by Cav. Liberi. In the nave—Pharaoh, &c. drowned in the Red Sea, by Luca Giordano. Cielings by Malinconico. The cupola of a chapel adjoining is by Tiepoletto.

S. Alessandro is also a handsome church. Leandro

Leandro Baſſano painted the nativity, and laſt ſupper.

The plain of Bergamo is divided into three parts by the river; and that part which lies between the Bremba and the Adda, called the *Iſola*, is not naturally ſo fertile as the other two; but the produce is much more conſiderable. It has twelve communities or pariſhes, that vie with one another in carrying cultivation to its utmoſt extent. They do every thing with the ſpade, and reckon four acres a maintenance for five perſons: the whole exhibits a ſight more truly pleaſing than all the pompous pageantry of churches and palaces.

SECTION XIV.

Return to England, by the Tyrol, Germany, and the Low Countries.

RETURNING to Verona, you will now think of going to England by the TYROL; in which you will find clean inns, good roads, and a romantic country. The ascent of the Alps is trifling all the way, till you come to Colman. The approach to INSPRUCK, the capital, is fine; a handsome triumphal arch marks the entrance, it is well built, and stands on the river *Inn*. In the Emperor's palace is a suite of ten handsome rooms, with portraits of the Austrian family. Between *Nazareit* and *Lermes*, a lake of a bright green colour, roaring torrents, and a wild, romantic country, high enough to produce rhododendron, cacalia, and other true alpine plants. Between *Lermes* and *Reita* a narrow valley, and a fortification, where the guard examine travellers: and between *Reita* and *Fueßen*, before you quit the Tyrol for Suabia, is another fortification in a narrow pass.

AUGS

AUGSBOURG, a free Imperial city, is well built, and has good wide streets: the inhabitants are half catholic, half lutheran. The town-hall has a decent front, and a handsome large room.

ULM, another free Imperial city, on the Danube; the government wholly, and the inhabitants chiefly Lutheran. It is old and ill built of brick and timber, with the upper stories projecting. The Cathedral is an ancient, large, *sombre*, Gothic building.

STUTGARD is in a bottom, surrounded by hills, covered with vines: it is an irregular town, by no means handsome, or well built. The inhabitants are Lutherans, and their sovereign, the Duke of Wirtemberg, a Catholic. The military Academy is on an excellent footing. There is an Opera house; and in the neighbourhood a palace of the Duke's, called the Solitude, with a garden of sixty acres, and a forest for hunting.

MANHEIM is a beautiful little city, which has in a manner grown up during this century. It is well fortified, and well built, with all the streets at right angles. The Electoral palace is very spacious: it has handsome apartments, an opera house by Bibiena, a considerable, well-chosen library, a cabinet of natural history; and a collection of pictures in a suite of nine rooms. The Llector has also casts in plaster from all the famous antique statues and busts. The Observatory is a good building, well furnished with instruments. There is a bridge of boats here across the Rhine.

WORMS is a forlorn and desolate city.

MENTZ is built chiefly of red sandstone: the pavement is of lava. Here it will be much more pleasant to embark on the Rhine, than to go post to Cologne. A large commodious covered boat, with three rooms in it, may be had for eight louis d'ors and an half; and you may repose at Coblentz and Bonn.

In going to Coblentz the shores are frequently covered with vines to the water's edge; sometimes they are bolder, with castles and villages. The narrow pass of *Bingenlock*, the Mouse Tower, *Baccarach*, and mountains of black slate.

COBLENTZ belongs to the Archbishop of Triers, who has built a new palace. The pavement is chiefly lava.

From Coblentz the shores are flat. *Andernach*, one of Drusus' forts. Hills on both sides with vines. Pass *Unkell*, and high volcanic

canic hills. Flat shores with vines and pastures to Bonn.

Bonn is in a good situation, and well built. The Electoral palace has a very long front to the gardens, which are pleasant. The pavement of the town is lava, and there are many basaltine columns, used as posts. The shores of the Rhine are flat from Bonn on both sides.

Cologne is an old-fashioned, ugly town, built of brick, with narrow winding streets, ill paved with lava, and posts of basalt every where. In the Cathedral is the rich tomb of the three kings. Here is also a good picture, of St. Peter crucified with his head downwards, by Rubens.

Hence you might go by the river to Holland, were it not that the king of Prussia will insist upon your taking the post through his dominions.

Here, quitting the river, you will enter on a straight paved road, planted with elms; and go by *Juliers* to Aix-la-Chapelle, a free imperial town, famous for its hot baths. In the cathedral are the *regalia* of Charlemagne, used at the coronation of the Emperors.

Hence

Hence by SPA, LIEGE, LOUVAIN, and BRUSSELS: by GHENT and BRUGES to OSTEND*: and so across the Channel to MARGATE; where you will perhaps not be sorry once more to set foot on old ENGLAND.

* See the Itinerary.

THE END.

INDEX

OF THE

NAMES OF PLACES,

&c.

A.

	Page
Abano	358
Acquapendente	303
Aiguebelle	4
Aix-la-chapelle	382
Albano	241
Albenga	15
Albifola	*ibid.*
Aleffandria	51
Ancona	117
Antibes	13
Arezzo	317

Arqua

INDEX.

	Page
Arqua	358
Ascension at Venice	375
Asti	50
Augsbourg	395

B.

Baiæ	278
Baldo mountain	390
Bauli	278
Bergamo	392
Bocchetta	52
Bolca mountain	383
Bologna	101
——— to Rome	109
——— to Venice	352
Bolsena	301
Bonn	397
Borromean islands	88
Bosco, Abbey del	51
Brescia	390
Brunetta	12

C.

Calais to Dijon and Geneva	3
——— to Nice	23
Camoccia	316
Campo Marone	52, 53

Capri

INDEX.

	Page
Capri	294
Capua	297
Carrara	68
Case nuove	122
Caserta	293
Cashnos, what	373
Castel Gandolfo	241
Castiglione	316
Catacombs at Rome	173
Cattolica	117
Cenis, Mount, passage of it	6—11
Cento	352
Cesena	109, 110
Chambery	2, 3
Chartreux near Pavia	70
Chiandola	16
Civita Castellana	127
Coblentz	396
Col du Tende	16
Cologne	397
Como, Lake of	89
Con	16
Core	245
Correggio	99
Cortona	316
Cremona	91
Cuma	274

Euganean

INDEX.

E.
	Page
Euganean mountains	358
Enhydri, what	382

F.
Faenza	109, 110
Fano	116
Ferrara	353
Finale	15
Florence	318
——— to Bologna	352
Foligno	122
Fondi	247
Forli	109, 110
Frefcati	240

G.
Gaeta	248
Garda, Lake of	390
Gavi	52
Geneva to Turin	3, 4
Genoa	53—67
——— to Leghorn	67
——— to Milan	68
Genfano	242
Graffe	23
Grotta Ferrata	241
Guelfo, Caftle	97

Hercu-

INDEX.

H.
	Page
Herculaneum	286

I.
Imola	109
Inspruck	379
Ivri	247

L.
Lago di Garda	390
—— Maggiore	88
Lannebourg	6
Lariccia, or Riccia	241, 242, 245
Leghorn	351
Lerici	68
—— to Pisa	68
Limoni	16
Lodesan	90
Lodi	90
Lorenzo delle grotte	302
Loretto	118
Lucca	346
Lyon to Genoa	13—16
—— to Turin	2

M.
Macerata	122
Manheim	395
Mantua	

INDEX.

	Page
Mantua	388
Massa	68
Mentz	396
Milan	72—89
—— to Bologna	9?
Medena	99
Mola di Gaeta	248
Monaco	1?
Monte Cassino	296
Montefiascone	301
Montmelian	4
Mosaics	163

N.

Naples	249
—— to Rome	29?
Narni	1?
Nemi Lake	24
Nice	17—2?
—— to Turin or Genoa	1?
Noli	1
Novaleze	6, 8, 10, ?
Novi	15, 5?

O.

Oneglia	1
Orvieto	3?
Otric?	

INDEX.

	Page
Otricoli	127
Otteggio	52

P.

Padua	354
Pæstum	292
Palo	122
Parma	94
Pavia	69
Pausilipo	268
Perugia	312
Pesaro	115
Pesto	292
Piacenza	92—94
Piedmont	48—50
Pietra	352
Pignole, what	114
Piperno	246, 298
Pisa	348
Pistoia	346
Po	17
Pompeii	288
Pontine marshes	246, 208
Pont Beauvoisin	2
Porto	281
Pozzuoli	271

Radicofani

R.

	Page
Radicofani	303
Ramasser, what	11
Ravenna	111
Recoaro	382
Regata at Venice	377
Reggio	98
Riccia	241, 242, 245
Rimini	110
Riviera of Genoa	15
Rivoli	12
Romagna	110
Rome	128, &c
——— to Florence	299
——— to Naples	245
Ronca, mountain	383
Ronciglione	300
Rubicon, river	109

S

Sabina	127
S. Agata	248
S. Bernard, Passage of	24
S. Gothard, Passage of	25
S. Jean de Maurienne	5
S. Remo	14
Sala	359
Salò	390

INDEX.

	Page
San Marino	114
San Quirico	303
Saorgio	16
Savona	15
Savoy	2
Secchia rapita	100
Seravezza	68
Sermoneta	245, 298
Serravalle	122
Sestri	15, 68
Sezze	246
Siena	304
Sinigaglia	117
Spoleto	123
Stabia	292
Stutgard	395
Suze	11, 12

T.

Tende	16
Terni	124
Terracina	246, 298
Thrasymene	316
Tivoli	243
Tolentino	122
Torricella	315
Tremenzina	89
Turin	27

Turin

INDEX.

	Page
Turin to Genoa	50—53
—— to Milan	89
Tyrol	394

V.

Valais	24
Valcimarra	122
Varese	89
Veletri	246
Venice	360
Ventimiglia	1.
Vercelli	89
Verona	38.
Vesuvius, Mount	270
Vicenza	370
Vico, Lake of	300
Viterbo	ib.
Ulm	38
Voltaggio	5
Volterra	31
Voltri	1
Urbino, Dutchy	11

W

Worms	39

Z.

Zendado, what	10